# WOMEN'S ROLES AND POPULATION TRENDS IN THE THIRD WORLD

The World Employment Programme (WEP) was launched by the
International Labour Organisation in 1969, as the ILO's main
contribution to the International Development Strategy for the Second
United Nations Development Decade.

The means of action adopted by the WEP have included the following:
— short-term high-level advisory missions;
— longer-term national or regional employment teams; and
— a wide-ranging research programme.

Through these activities the ILO has been able to help national
decision-makers to reshape their policies and plans with the aim of
eradicating mass poverty and unemployment.

A landmark in the development of the WEP was the World
Employment Conference of 1976, which proclaimed *inter alia* that
'strategies and national development plans should include as a priority
objective the promotion of employment and the satisfaction of the
basic needs of each country's population'. The Declaration of Principles
and Programme of Action adopted by the Conference have become the
cornerstone of WEP technical assistance and research activities during
the closing years of the Second Development Decade.

This publication is the outcome of a WEP project.

# Women's Roles and Population Trends in the Third World

EDITED BY RICHARD ANKER, MAYRA BUVINIC AND
NADIA H. YOUSSEF

A study prepared for the International Labour Office within
the framework of the World Employment Programme with
the financial support of the United Nations Fund for
Population Activities

CROOM HELM
London & Canberra

© 1982 International Labour Organisation
Croom Helm Ltd, Provident House, Burrell Row,
Beckenham, Kent BR3 1AT
Reprinted 1983

British Library Cataloguing in Publication Data

Women's roles and population trends in the Third World.
1. Women — Underdeveloped areas — Social conditions
2. Demography
I. Anker, Richard  II. Buvinic, Mayra
III. Youssef, Nadia H.  IV. World Employment Programme
V. United Nations Fund for Population Activities
305.4'2'091724    HQ1154

ISBN 0-7099-0508-4

Typeset by Leaper & Gard Ltd, 108 Church Road, Redfield, Bristol
Printed and bound in Great Britain by Professional Books Ltd.
Abingdon, Oxon

# CONTENTS

# PREFACE

In 1978 the International Labour Office (ILO) began an ambitious research programme on the relationship between 'Women's Roles and Demographic Change' with funding from the United Nations Fund for Population Activities (UNFPA). From the outset, it was realised that this research needed to be wide-ranging in its scope and interdisciplinary in its methodology if the programme was to have an effect on government and nongovernment policy as well as on future research. With this in mind, the ILO held an informal gathering of leading researchers from various disciplines. Thus, anthropologists, economists, sociologists and demographers were invited; and even within these disciplines, different points of view were represented, for example those of structuralist and neoclassical economists.

For this informal gathering the ILO commissioned a number of background papers on the major issues of its research programme. The ILO and the International Center for Research on Women (ICRW), who did much of the editing, felt that the papers presented were a unique and practically-oriented collection, offering fresh interdisciplinary perspectives for researchers interested in women's studies and population dynamics. Hence the origin of this volume. A number of case studies are being carried out by researchers in developing countries under the ILO research programme. In keeping with the interdisciplinary nature of the ILO project these studies employ a variety of methodologies; there are in-depth, anthropological case studies, using the life history approach, as well as studies using household, individual, employer and community questionnaires. These ongoing studies are concerned with issues related to women's integration in development, interrelationships between women's economic activities and demographic variables, and sex discrimination in the marketplace. Particularly interesting from a methodological point of view are the research field instruments developed by the ILO for survey questionnaires and in-depth case studies.

The editors of this volume hope that others will find these papers as interesting and useful as they have. We would like especially to thank the following for their helpful comments in preparing this volume: Martha Anker, Valentina Bodrova, Martha Loutfi, Isabel Nieves, Christine Oppong, Gerry Rodgers, Ilsa Schumacher and Rolph van der Hoeven. Judith Johnson's editorial skills added clarity and simplicity to the volume; we are particularly grateful to her for her assistance.

# PART ONE: OVERVIEW

# 1 INTRODUCTION

What are the economic contributions of Third World women, and what are the two-way linkages between changes in women's productive roles and changes in fertility, mortality and migratory behaviour? The interdisciplinary collection of chapters contained in this volume offer new, interdisciplinary perspectives to understanding the dynamics of population change and women's roles. They include realistic and comprehensive attempts to assess women's economic productivity, critical appraisals of the ability of existing theoretical models to capture the reality of women's behaviour in the Third World, and an awareness that several models and methods are essential to tackle the complex issues involved in the interpretation of the interrelationship between women's roles and demographic change.

This introduction begins with brief summaries of the chapters contained in this volume to give the reader a feeling for their content as well as to show how they complement one another. Then, some of the new perspectives to the study of the interrelationship between women's roles and demographic change provided by these chapters are singled out for further discussion. Finally, the main conclusions of the contributors are presented.

Chapter 2 discusses the objectives of the ILO research project on 'Women's Roles and Demographic Change', as well as the methodologies which were to be used on this project. It also provides a broad outline within which the chapters in this volume can be seen to fit. To accomplish the project objectives, an interdisciplinary approach is recommended. Interrelationships between women's productive economic contributions and demographic phenomena, such as fertility, mortality and family structure, are stressed, since family obligations and child-care continue to be mainly the responsibility of women around the world, and thus greatly affect and are affected by women's economic activities. To study these issues, Richard Anker suggests three broad types of research approaches: first, anthropological, indepth case studies in order to obtain accurate, detailed information on the cultural milieu and class structure, and on factors related to intra-family relationships and family structure; second, to obtain information on the behaviour of household members using household sample surveys, in which information is collected for a fairly large number of households; and, third, urban labour market studies which use an institutional approach, and are concerned with the functioning of urban labour markets in order to obtain a more complete picture of the forces affecting female economic activity, sex segregation and sex discrimination.

In Chapter 3 in the second part of this volume, Eva Mueller reviews the present state of knowledge on how women allocate their time, based on survey data of developing and developed countries. She relates this to education, sex-role norms, age of youngest child, number of children and rigidities of social structures. Mueller also gives considerable attention to the trade-off between child-care, work and leisure, as well as the degree of compatibility between child-care and work. She argues that a simple dichotomy of activities between work and non-work is not sufficiently detailed for analyzing the relationship between work and fertility; one also needs time-use information on all other household members (especially children) who may watch the young children, on whether or not the presence of children at the mother's place of work affects the mother's efficiency in performing her work; and on how much leisure time the woman has, since substitution may not be between child-care and work but between child-care and leisure. In short, Mueller makes the point that, if we are to understand the complex linkages between work and fertility, we need information on household members' allocation of time.

Mueller also points out that activity and time-use data can serve a number of purposes; they can provide a comprehensive picture of women's multiple roles in the society, in the family and in the economy; they can provide the means by which the labour force participation of women can be better measured and conceptualized; and they can improve our understanding of the linkage between fertility/child-care and work, and the potential effects of role conflict and role strain.

Looking at the relationship between production and reproduction in a broad sense (so as to include socialization as well as fertility) from a structuralist Marxist perspective, the chapter by Carmen Diane Deere, Jane Humphries and Magdalena León de Leal concentrates on macro-level factors and how these constrain and help determine the behaviour of individual women. As the authors convincingly argue, since the range of options available to individuals is relatively limited, one will be unable to understand the behaviour of individuals and the dynamics of the situation unless one also understands these macro factors. This underlying premise leads them into well-known Marxist discussions on interactions between the various tiers of development (international, national, regional, class and household), the overriding importance of class structure, the need of some classes to extract surplus value from other classes and the crucial role of women in reducing the cost to employers of reproducing the labour force. Drawing on their previous fieldwork in Peru and Colombia, the authors then go on to provide an outline for prospective field studies. They suggest the importance of doing three complementary types of analysis: (i) analysis of the process of historical development at the national level; (ii) area case studies of development processes; (iii) household-level studies which concentrate on measuring the sexual division of labour. In this last respect, then, both Chapters 3 and 4 stress the need for more accurate and more comprehensive data on women's economic activities as well as the need to collect these data at the micro level.

The three chapters in Part Three are concerned with social and cultural dimensions in the interaction between women's roles and demographic change. Chapter 5 examines female power; how power relates to, yet differs from, female status as well as how female power relates to fertility. In developing her model, Constantina Safilios-Rothschild distinguishes between two main types of power – power which is derived from men (which only allows women to have control over other women, over children or over young men, but not over their own lives or over adult men) and power which is derived independently of men (and which may result in autonomy). She then outlines the various ways in which married women are able to obtain power, for example from fathers' or mothers' social status or wealth, from husbands' social status or wealth, from their own economic activities (if they control this income), from women's collectives and from the bearing of children. The author also lists several indicators of female power at the macro, societal level (e.g., male-female ratios in the 30 to 39 and 40 to 49 age groups, ratio of men to women completing primary school, existence of women's associations, discrepancy between men's and women's wages, and membership in economic and social collectives) as well as at the micro household or individual level. Both sets of indicators are said to be important in studies of female power in diverse societies, since individual women may (or may not) have power in societies where female power at the societal level is weak (or strong). Safilios-Rothschild also indicates how fertility fits into her framework, hypothesizing that reproductive power becomes less important for women the more they have other secure power bases. Thus, as women 'feel socially, economically and psychologically

secure in economically productive activities they may become motivated to use birth control in order to have as many children as they
enjoy rather than as many as they need' (p. 128).

The main aim of Chapter 6 is to bring to the attention of economists
and other social scientists anthropological data and insights relevant to
the study of domestic organization and women's roles in culturally
contrasting contexts. Christine Oppong focuses on the domestic group,
which constitutes an important unit for study in the guise of the household, because it is within the domestic domain that it is possible to find
links between aspects of women's status, productive activities and
demographic phenomena such as fertility, mortality and morbidity. In
so doing, the point is made that various activities which are usually
assumed to be carried out within the domestic domain such as eating,
sleeping, reproduction and economic production are not necessarily
performed by the same sets of people. As a result, the costs and
benefits associated with children may be shared by many more people
than the mother and father or even those said to be co-residential. To
illustrate her argument Oppong presents data on socialization and child-
care in different cultures, and shows that such functions are often
carried out by kin other than parents. Finally, Oppong outlines a simple
framework for the analysis of domestic behaviour and familial rights
and duties that avoids the pitfalls of the culture-bound assumptions
found in analyses based on theories such as the New Household
Economics.

Chapter 7 raises several important issues with regard to the contribution the social anthropological approach can make to a study of
women's roles and demographic change, both regarding conceptual
frameworks and methodology. T. Scarlett Epstein begins by noting some
major hallmarks of anthropology — its holistic approach, its use of
participant observation for data collection, its comparative nature and
its focus upon institutionalized social relationships. Although the kinds
of data anthropologists typically gather (which are not randomly
selected and are often very few in number) are different from those
familiar to many sociologists and economists, Epstein persuasively
argues that social-anthropological studies make up for their lack of
breadth by producing detailed, highly reliable data. Thus, Epstein
stresses the need for complementarity between large-scale sample surveys, where respondents are randomly selected, and socio-anthropological micro studies. Another important issue to which Epstein calls
attention is the usefulness of participant observation for studying
sensitive areas of human life or areas in which simple questioning may

lead to inaccurate data, as in the case of labour force participation. Finally, Epstein calls for studying the roles and status of women according to their different stages of the life cycle.

In Part Four, Chapters 8 and 9 explore how women's economic roles affect fertility and mortality rates respectively. After reviewing previous studies on the relationship between female labour force participation and fertility, Nadia H. Youssef concludes that the evidence to date on this relationship is inconclusive (the relationship is found to be sometimes positive, sometimes negative and sometimes neutral). She also stresses the need for more detailed data on female activities than the simple labour force/non-labour force dichotomy, as do many of the chapters in this volume. Then, instead of continuing in the tradition of investigating the fertility-work relationship using theories based on opportunity costs, work satisfaction or incompatibility of work and child-care, Youssef relates fertility to the sexual division of labour. She points out that the more economically active women are, the greater their resource base is likely to be. Economic activities become a necessary but not a sufficient condition for female autonomy and power relative to men (see also Chapter 5). Youssef then goes on to discuss how the sexual division of labour is likely to change with economic development, and how these changes affect class structure and the level of agricultural complexity, which in turn help determine the demand for labour and, thus, the economic opportunities available to women. Throughout these discussions Youssef persuasively argues that if researchers are to understand the linkage between work, status and fertility, they need to consider class differences in behaviour, values and available work options.

Chapter 9 begins with the irrefutable proposition that an important indicator of women's relative status in society is the ratio of male to female survival rates. T. Paul Schultz argues that an infant's probability of surviving childhood depends on biological and economic factors as well as the care and nutrition a child receives. Since evidence from many countries around the world indicates that females generally have higher survival probabilities than males, deviations from this pattern, he argues, must be due to differential care for sons and daughters. To test this hypothesis, Schultz constructs and tests a simultaneous equations model with male labour force participation, female labour force participation and the ratio of male to female survival rates as dependent variables – an underlying assumption in his model being that the economic contribution of men and women to the family is a primary determinant of their status in society and therefore of their allocation of household resources, including food and medical care. In addition, Schultz makes an important methodological contribution by developing unbiased measures of the relative male-female survival rate for use in multivariate analysis. Using two data sets from India — a country known for having a much higher male than female survival rate — macro district-level data from the 1961 Population Census and micro household-level data from a 1969-71 national survey, he finds that in areas and in households where women are more active economically (based on their reported participation in the labour force), women also have higher survival probabilities relative to those of men. Although Schultz's conclusions are only tentative — not least of all because they are based on data from traditional labour force surveys — they tend to confirm his hypothesis that 'in this formative period children are accorded family resources that influence their health and survival prospects according to their relative expected productivity as adults' (p. 229).

Finally, in Part Five, Chapters 10 and 11 focus on the economic activities of urban women, the importance of macro labour market conditions (which help determine the range of choice, or lack of it, open to individual women) and the high degree of discrimination with which women in urban areas of the Third World must cope. Both chapters also stress the importance of using a broad definition of labour force participation and the need to include economic activities which occur outside of the formal job market.

In Chapter 10, Elizabeth Jelin points out that there is no abstract, universal type of woman, but various groups of women immersed in systems of class relations. She argues that not only are there class differences which greatly affect women's values, behaviour and opportunities, but there are also four distinct types of women in relation to domestic responsibilities. These are: (i) women with few or no domestic responsibilities; (ii) women with domestic responsibilities who can afford to hire others to perform these activities for them; (iii) women who have only their own domestic responsibilities; and (iv) women with domestic responsibilities who must also earn money. Jelin believes that the need to combine market work and domestic work affects the type of market work which women are able to accept only in the last group of women (often in female-headed households). Jelin also stresses the usefulness of concentrating on the household and wider networks of interpersonal relations (as do other contributors, such as Anker, Oppong and Epstein) when studying the interaction between women's economic activities and domestic responsibilities, because these networks play such a significant role in determining the independence or dependence of women.

T.S. Papola, in Chapter 11, draws on data sets from previous surveys he carried out in two of India's largest cities in order to illustrate how extensive sex segregation and sex discrimination are in urban areas of India. Since these surveys are confined to the so-called informal sector where there is easy entry, low wages and low capital intensity, Papola's findings are all the more striking because these are the types of occupations in which women are overrepresented. Within the informal sector women are found to be disadvantaged in two ways. First, women are concentrated in the lowest paying occupations; second, their pay is about one-half that of men when they are employed in the same occupation. However, when Papola compares the earnings of self-employed male and female workers, he finds that earnings of men and women are approximately the same, leading to the conclusion that discrimination 'is not based on differences in men's and women's productivity and performance' (p. 274). Papola goes on to propose a number of hypotheses worthy of study on the interplay between supply-side factors (and the constraints placed on women due to their domestic responsibilities) and demand-side factors (and reasons for the sex discrimination as practised by employers).

The remainder of this introduction concerns itself with some of the common themes of the contributed chapters.

## The Demand for and Supply of Female Labour

The type of work women do and the sexual division of labour within the household result from an interplay of demand and supply factors. According to both neoclassical and structuralist economists, the sexual division of labour is the outcome of individual choice — choice, however, which is constrained by outside factors such as job market opportunities. There is a difference of opinion, however, on how much emphasis should be placed on the demand side compared to the supply side; in other words, the extent to which there is freedom of choice.

Several contributors focus on sexual dualism in the labour market from the demand or employer side. Anker reviews various theories which have been put forward to explain sex segregation in urban labour markets (such as the human capital model, the overcrowding model and the institutional model), and emphasizes the need to study the institutional mechanisms causing sex discrimination and sex segregation if we are to distinguish fact from fiction. Jelin and Papola concentrate on the demand side as it interacts with the supply side within the context of urban Third World labour markets, while Deere *et al.* show that the demand side is also important for rural women. Most contributors show the extent to which female labour force behaviour in terms of occupation and income is determined by social and economic forces outside of the control of women. Jelin takes these arguments one step further by dividing women into several groups according to whether or not they are constrained in their market work by domestic and child-care responsibilities. Furthermore, Epstein makes the often neglected yet obvious point that the activities of women and their control over events are very much related to the stage of the life cycle in which they find themselves.

A common assumption of researchers is that the domestic responsibilities which are placed on women restrict the type of work they are able and willing to do. Thus, women are said to require work activities which are compatible with their domestic responsibilities — for example, work near to home, work where children can be present and work which can be suspended temporarily after the birth of a child. (See Shields, 1977 and Standing, 1978 for good reviews of this research.) While there is considerable truth in this argument and domestic responsibilities do place a major burden on women, too strict an acceptance of this relationship is unwarranted for much of the world. The availability of inexpensive domestics (Chapters 2, 6 and 10), and the fact that child-care is frequently done outside the co-residential unit (Chapter 6) or by older (often female) siblings of the young children (Chapter 3), implies that domestic and child-care responsibilities do not necessarily constrain women in the type of work they are able to do.

## Beyond Accepted Theories of Fertility and Mortality

The literature on the determinants of fertility has been dominated by economists and sociologists. The economic model of fertility is usually traced to Becker (1960), even though he was preceded by Leibenstein (1957), and many important extensions and improvements have since been made (Easterlin, 1969, 1975; Leibenstein, 1974). According to early and somewhat doctrinal versions of the economic model of fertility, children are viewed as if they are consumer durables, costing money and time, and providing non-monetary, psychic returns. The household is said to decide on the optimal number of children (and other goods) given these costs, the household's income level, and the household's relative preferences for children and other goods. In Becker's economic model of fertility, then, the effect of female employment on fertility is negative due to the income which must be foregone when a woman withdraws from the labour force in order to care for her children. A clear and concise description of this theory is provided in Chapter 3 by Mueller — including some of the weaknesses in early versions of the theory when it is applied to developing countries.

The sociologists' model of fertility perceives employment of women outside the home as entailing alternative satisfactions to children (e.g., companionship, recreation, stimulation and creative activity) or as providing the monetary means to such satisfactions. Employment is seen as introducing into women's lives the subjective awareness of opportunity costs in having children. Foregoing employment is thus seen as a cost of having children (Blake, 1965; Hass, 1972; Beckman, 1977).

The chapters in this volume either challenge or attempt to clarify several of the premisses of these accepted fertility models by presenting evidence of discrepancies between these conceptual frameworks and the reality in the Third World. Anker, Youssef and Safilios-Rothschild point out that the household is not a homogeneous unit where men and women necessarily have the same interests regarding family size. Thus, they reject the assumption that there is one utility function or preference map for the household; instead they emphasize the need to look within the household at differences in family-size desires among individual household members,.especially between men and women.

Some contributors, particularly Safilios-Rothschild and Youssef, place great stress on female power in discussing male-female differentials in family-size desires. They see female power as the link to explaining the extent to which women are successful in achieving their desired family size. In particular, Youssef makes the point that class differences and macro-level economic factors are important determinants of female power — thereby showing the link between micro, individual-level power for women (which affects fertility) and macro, society-level factors. Youssef also emphasizes the need to bring class differences into fertility theory. This concern is consistent with recent work by Leibenstein (1974), Hull (1977) and Young (1977).

Eva Mueller stresses the need to move away from the simple dichotomy between work and child-care which is found in some fertility models. She goes on to suggest a trichotomy of work, child-care and leisure, and the possibility that important trade-offs may occur between work and leisure, so that as a result there may be no relationship between work and child-care (and therefore fertility). Although Mueller's trichotomy is an improvement, it is still obviously a great oversimplification; in addition, the categorization of various activities into broad categories such as work, leisure and child-care is extremely difficult where so many activities are done simultaneously (e.g., people may sit around talking while processing food and watching children). Not withstanding the difficulties involved in time-use data, their detail should provide researchers with more appropriate information for understanding some of the trade-offs between economic activities and fertility. Hopefully, as more detailed data on activities and family structure become available, researchers will be able to ascertain for which activities and under which settings work and child-care are incompatible, and thus constrain fertility rates.

As noted in the previous section, many contributors make the point that work and child-care are not necessarily incompatible, and that the degree to which there is incompatibility depends on the activity involved, the family structure, the cost of domestics and the presence in the family of surrogate mothers, such as other siblings and other adults. Indeed, Oppong and Mueller indicate that it is the exception rather than the rule for Third World mothers to do most of the child-care unaided. The lesson to be drawn is that it is dangerous to transfer to developing countries a theory which was developed for industrialized countries, where mothers frequently withdraw from the labour force in order to care for their children. It is the cause of little surprise that in reviewing the evidence to date for Third World countries, Youssef and Mueller conclude that the negative relationship between work and fertility is found almost exclusively in urban, industrialized settings.

Contrary to the enormous effort which has gone into research on the socio-economic determinants of fertility, research on the socio-economic determinants of mortality is a relatively understudied topic, particularly mortality differentials between males and females. Researchers and policy-makers alike generally assume that mortality rates are determined mainly by medical care and public health programmes, and that male-female differentials in mortality are either unimportant or are determined by biological/genetic factors. However, as this volume reveals, these assumptions are not correct (Chapters 2 and 9). There are important differences in the ratio of male-female mortality rates across the world (Chapter 2); and sex differentials in mortality are useful indicators of female status in society (Chapters 5 and 9).

Chapter 9 provides a detailed empirical treatment of sex differentials in mortality rates in India — a country where female mortality rates exceed male mortality rates. An interesting aspect of Schultz's model is how he relates sex differentials in mortality to men's and women's economic productivity (as measured by the degree to which men and women are economically active) — thereby linking economic production, social status and survival. We hope that in the future more attention will be given to the socio-economic determinants of mortality.

## The Methodology Debate

The various chapters in this volume raise five important methodological issues, all of which address the question of what is the most appropriate tool available in the social sciences to 'understand' in a meaningful way the socio-economic context in which women function and the forces that shape their behaviour. The first of these issues relates to the unit of analysis; the second, to the 'measurement' of women's economic activities; the third to dynamic perspectives and class differences; the fourth to female power; and the fifth to interdisciplinary research.

### Unit of Analysis

Some authors in this volume emphasize the household as the conceptual and methodological unit of analysis on the basis that it is the study of decision-making within or by the unit that is necessary to understand behaviour (Mueller); and/or because the household is the mediating structure in women's position in the labour market (Jelin). This approach is consistent with the so-called New Household Economics as well as with recent trends in the social sciences which focus on the household.

There are some limitations to this approach, however, as pointed out by other contributors. Using the household as the unit of analysis and treating households as homogeneous units implicitly assumes that the behaviour of the household, the aggregate unit, is equal to the behaviour of the members, or individual units. Furthermore, the use of households in the Western sense of the word assumes that the various familial functions, such as economic production, biological reproduction, socialization and maintenance are all performed within the same bounded unit — i.e., the household. While this assumption may hold true in some developed countries (although even here there are many important exceptions), in developing countries the assumption of congruence of functions is inaccurate and misleading, since there is so much variety in the world in the composition and organization of domestic groups as well as in the systems of kinships and marriage. Discussion on these points is particularly well presented by Christine Oppong in Chapter 6.

Once the assumption of the so-called household as a single bounded unit is questioned, one must also question the assumption that the 'household' has one preference map or that it is reasonable to assume that one household member (usually assumed to be male) acts as a 'benevolent dictator'. As John Kenneth Galbraith has said, 'the household in established economics is essentially a guise for the exercise of male authority' (1973). Following this reasoning, most contributors stress that there may be a difference of interests (and resources) among family members, and that this divergence of interests (and resources) is crucial to understanding what women do, what power they have (Safilios-Rothschild), how many children they bear (Mueller, Youssef, Anker, Oppong and Safilios-Rothschild), and even whether or not male or female members are the most likely to survive (Schultz and Anker).

Indeed, several authors (in particular, Oppong, Safilios-Rothschild and Youssef) explicitly call for the unit of analysis to be the individual woman and not the household. This approach is supported by recent evidence regarding differential interests between family members, more particularly spouses, regarding family-size desires. Some authors are aware of the usefulness of supplementary information on the activities and characteristics of other family members, including spouse and children, even when the unit of analysis is the individual woman.

If the individual woman is taken as the unit of analysis, one would expect her roles and status to influence fertility behaviour from two directions: first, by affecting the overall level of the household's well-being (which is stressed in the literature of socio-economic determinants of fertility) and, second, through the degree to which her individual interests diverge from those of her husband's with respect to the number of children they wish to have.

## Measuring Women's Economic Contribution

An underlying theme in all Chapters — in some more explicit than in others — is the need for more accurate and meaningful data on women's economically productive roles in the marketplace and in the household. Yet a perennial problem in the literature is the inadequacy — if not actual unavailability — of reliable data on this subject. Unfortunately, as pointed out in most chapters, traditional demographic, sociological, economic and labour force surveys tend to provide crude and often inaccurate information on the economic work of women. The inadequacy of labour force data is due partly to the simple assumption that people are either in or out of the labour force. However, in addition to their crudeness, labour force surveys face other major problems; respondents frequently misinterpret what is meant by phrases such as 'job', 'work' and 'economic activity', particularly when the women are asked to report their 'principal activity' (as occurred on the last population census of India). Additionally, in many societies there is a reluctance on the part of both interviewers and respondents to admit that women are engaged in 'work'. In societies where the male ideal is linked to men's roles as providers, women and men generally recognize only women's supporting roles.

Finally, many of the productive activities done by women are frequently not considered to be economic activities. Thus, women are known to work long hours, for example, carrying water, gathering sticks, processing food and sewing — activities which definitely increase the family's economic well-being. But since these activities do not enter the marketplace or get included in national income accounts, they are usually not considered to be labour force activities.

An alternative procedure for collecting meaningful and accurate data on economic activities proposed by some of the contributors is time-use surveys. In these surveys a detailed accounting is obtained of what people do. Cultural biases which cause an underreporting of work done by women are supposedly avoided in time-use data, which in addition do not contain built-in assumptions about what is and is not an economic activity. In short, time-use data can provide useful information on the economic activities of women and on the sexual division of labour within the household. These data can help one understand how child-bearing and child-care might conflict with various type of economic activities, and how the sexual division of labour is determined.

Time-use data are not, however, problem-free and it is for this reason that many researchers — including those at the workshop — were cautious regarding its use. Deere *et al.* stress some of the measurement problems involved, such as recall error, especially in rural areas where there is seasonal variation in activity patterns; Jelin points out that time is defined in a physical sense only and therefore ignores questions of intensity of effort; Mueller indicates that the theories presently available to estimate empirically the determinants of the sexual division of labour within the household are not nearly as sophisticated as the data. There are other problems as well, such as the large time input required to gather these data, the reluctance of respondents to report socially deviant activities or activities which occur infrequently, activities which are done at the same time (i.e., dual activities), and errors are introduced if one person is asked to report for another person.

In spite of the admitted problems involved with time-use surveys, the inadequacy of traditional labour force data for the study of women's economic roles implies the need to obtain more extensive information on women's activities. The question is not so much whether more detailed data on women's activities are required (because all contributors agree that they are), but how detailed these data need to be and what supplementary information is required. Differences of opinion on this point will continue to exist until researchers are more precise in defining their data needs and until more work is completed in this area of research and data collection. Similarly, differences of opinion will continue to exist regarding the most appropriate methods for collecting time-use type data — whether they should be collected using participant observation as suggested by Deere *et al.* and Epstein, by using survey questionnaires as suggested by Mueller, or by using both techniques as suggested by Anker.

## Dynamic Perspectives and Class Differences

A 'time' perspective is essential to any policy-oriented study since the main interest is change. Anker, Deere *et al.* and Youssef pay particular attention to dynamic considerations. Deere *et al.* stress the usefulness of analyzing historical trends. They further stress the need to understand the historical and class context before attempting to analyze household- or individual-level behaviour. Anker suggests that some of the underlying dynamic trends believed to be occurring in developing countries can be assessed through fieldwork at one point in time by sampling households stratified according to certain criteria (as well as by collecting community-level data). Thus, comparisons of rural and urban households can help in evaluating the effect on women's roles of rural-urban migration; in rural areas, interviewing landless, small, medium and large landowning households can yield information on the effect increasing fragmentation of land and increasing landlessness has on women's roles, migration, fertility and mortality; sampling households in poor, middle-income and wealthy areas can indicate important class differences as well as how upward economic mobility (to the extent that it exists) can affect women's roles.

Throughout discussions at the workshop, as well as in this volume, emphasis was placed on the wide variation among Third World women in terms of values, work opportunities and behaviour. Women from upper social classes usually do not work (except in white-collar occupations such as teaching); women from lower social classes, on the other hand, usually earn a significant portion of family income. The fact is that for poorer women involvement in work activities is usually not a choice, a search for 'alternative' satisfaction: poorer women are usually pushed into the labour force by economic need (Papola and Jelin). Thus, there was general agreement that it is impossible to understand behaviour without explicitly addressing class differences, and, perhaps worse, researchers might inappropriately generalize from results based on distinct groups of women.

## Female Power

Utilizing different levels of analysis and theoretical frameworks, three chapters deal explicitly with women's conditions, particularly as this relates to 'power'. Deere *et al.* use a structuralist model, emphasizing women's power in relation to infrastructural conditions; Youssef draws upon an institutional framework, locating determinants of female power through women's overall position in society; Safilios-Rothschild offers a provoking discussion of the determinants of female power (ability to influence and control events at the interpersonal level), stressing the interaction between the status of women at the macro level and the power of women at the micro level. These three levels of analysis are complementary; if read separately, each conveys different 'realities' of the world in which women function. On the one hand, there are the overriding constraints of the modes of production which shape the choices available to women; on the other hand, there are individual circumstances which interact with women's expected sex-role behaviour and help define and narrow the viable alternatives for women. There is also the understanding stated most clearly by Safilios-Rothschild — that work and a relatively significant economic contribution by women does not necessarily get translated into independence or power. It is interesting to note that the workshop participants implicitly (or explicitly) recognize that if women's economic roles are to affect fertility or status, then they must also have some effect on women's power.

## Interdisciplinary Research

There was general agreement among workshop participants that in order to understand the complex set of interrelationships between women's activities and demographic variables, studies need to be interdisciplinary — both in terms of theoretical considerations and data collection techniques. For example, while structured survey questionnaires can provide reasonably accurate data for relatively large and representative groups of people, questionnaires are not well suited for for collecting data on sensitive subject areas about which respondents may be reluctant to speak, and recall error on survey questionnaires becomes more troublesome the further back in time questions refer. In contrast, the strength of anthropology is its holistic approach and its use of participant observation for small numbers of people. Epstein presents a thorough discussion of the advantages of anthropological studies and Oppong stresses an added advantage of anthropological studies — their tendency not to be culture-bound. Jelin also recommends the use of collecting data on life histories.

The attributes of in-depth case studies and sample surveys complement each other. One yields extensive statistical data which can be generalized, while the other helps provide in-depth understanding as well as accurate information for a few respondents.

## A Common Framework

By the end of the ILO workshop, the contributors to this volume generally agreed on the following points with respect to research on interrelationships between women's roles and demographic change:
(i) This research should focus primarily on observed and reported behaviour.
(ii) All work women do, not only particular types of women's work (e.g., work away from home and/or work for pay), should be considered; thus, the difficult issues related to measurement of work need to be addressed.
(iii) Since households and the organization of domestic groups are so different around the world, cross-cultural research should take into consideration variation in kinship systems; in particular, the relationship between the woman and her husband or 'partner' needs to be stressed.
(iv) Researchers should go beyond the accepted theories explaining fertility, mortality and female labour force participation which are too simplistic, since, for example, cultural factors, family structures and class differences need to be taken into account.
(v) Differences in behaviour between social classes should be emphasized, since societies are heterogeneous.
(vi) Interaction between macro and micro factors should be considered.

(vii) Work opportunities and demand factors which constrain individual behaviour should be stressed.

(viii) Dynamic/change considerations need to be at the centre of this type of research if the research is to be useful to policy-makers.

(ix) In studying demographic variables and female labour force participation, an important intervening factor is the power and autonomy of women.

(x) This research should be interdisciplinary.

(xi) Various data collection techniques should be used such as participant observation, survey questionnaires and community-level questionnaires.

By focusing on a 'missing link' in economic development – women and their economic behaviour – researchers should be in a better position to advise policy-makers interested in equity, poverty, development, employment, women and population issues. The chapters in this volume should be seen as a step in this direction.

# References

Anker, R. (1980). 'Research on women's roles and demographic change: survey questionnaires for households, women, men and communities – with background explanation,' working document for restricted circulation, Geneva, ILO

Becker, G. (1960). 'An economic analysis of fertility', *Demographic and economic change in developed countries*, Universities National Bureau Conference Series, no. 11, Princeton, Princeton University Press

Beckman, L.J. (1978). 'The relative rewards and costs of parenthood and employment for employed women', *Psychology of Women Quarterly*, 2, 215-34

Blake, J. (1965). 'Demographic science and the redistribution of population policy', *Journal of Chronic Diseases, 18*

Easterlin, R. (1969). 'Towards a socio-economic theory of fertility' in S.J. Behrman, L. Corsa and R. Freedman (eds.), *Fertility and family planning: a world view*, Ann Arbor, University of Michigan Press

—— (1975). 'An economic framework for fertility analysis', *Studies in Family Planning, 6*, 3

Galbraith, J.K. (1973). *Economics and the public purpose*, New York, Signet

Hass, P. (1972). 'Maternal role in compatibility and fertility – urban Latin America', *Journal of Social Issues, 28*, no. 2

Hull, V. (1977). 'Fertility, women's work and economic class: a case study from Southeast Asia' in S. Kupinsky (ed.), *The fertility of working women: a synthesis of international work*, New York, Praeger Publishers

Leibenstein, H. (1957). *Economic backwardness and economic growth: studies in the theory of economic development*, New York, John Wiley and Sons

—— (1974). 'An interpretation of the economic theory of fertility', *Journal of Economic Literature, 12*, 2 (June)

Oppong, C. (forthcoming). *The seven roles and status of women*, Geneva, ILO

Shields, N. (1977). 'Female labour force participation and fertility: review of empirical evidence from L.D.C.s', Washington, Population and Human Resources, World Bank

Standing, G. (1978). *Labour force participation and development*, Geneva, ILO

Young, K. (1977). 'Modes of appropriation and the sexual division of labour: a case study of Oaxaca, Mexico', paper presented at the Latin American Studies Association Meetings, Houston, Texas

# 2 DEMOGRAPHIC CHANGE AND THE ROLE OF WOMEN: A RESEARCH PROGRAMME IN DEVELOPING COUNTRIES

Richard Anker

## Introduction

In the past several decades enormous changes have taken place in the developing world. Not least of these have been those related to women's roles and demographic levels. In most developing countries population growth rates (and thus family sizes) have risen due to decreasing mortality rates and more or less constant birth rates (although fertility rates have now begun to fall in many developing countries); there has been a large movement of people away from rural areas and towards urban areas; there has been a tendency for women to marry at later ages; and the structure of the family is changing. Women's roles have also been changing. In addition to the significant effect the movement of women from rural to urban areas and rising education levels have had on women's roles, there have also been important changes within rural and urban areas due to nondemographic factors. In rural areas, for example, the introduction of new crops and new technology, the increasing monetarization of agriculture, increasing landlessness and parcellization of land have all greatly affected women's roles; in urban areas factors such as decreasing job opportunities in modern or formal sector employment and changing industrial structure have also had large effects on women's roles. It is now widely recognized that social, political and economic changes have differential effects on men and women, and that a conscious effort should be made to improve the relative position of women in the economy and in the society. But what do we really know about what women are doing, how this has been changing over time, the factors that are responsible for these changes and what important feedbacks are associated with changing women's roles?

Under the ILO Labour and Population Programme, a global research programme was recently begun to study the 'Role of Women and Demographic Change'. As implied in the project's title, the research programme will focus on the interaction between changes in women's roles and changes in demographic behaviour, such as fertility and mortality. What, for example, are the economic roles in which women are engaged; do these have an effect on demographic factors such as fertility and mortality; how in turn, do family size and family structure affect women's roles? Preliminary thinking on the methodologies to be used and questions to be addressed in this research programme are contained in the present chapter.

In order to study questions related to women's roles and demographic change, the research programme will employ an interdisciplinary approach, and the research will be set in a broad social, economic and cultural frame which takes account of dynamic change over time using three broad types of studies: (i) collection and analyses of socio-anthropological data; (ii) collection and analyses of household survey data; and (iii) analyses of urban labour markets. In addition, the in-depth country case studies may be supplemented by small studies describing the success and failure of specific policies undertaken around the world which are directed towards improving the role and status of women.

The first two types of studies are quite complementary, and it is hoped that they will be undertaken in one country in each of the four major regions of the developing world — sub-Saharan Africa, Latin America, Asia and the Middle East, as well as in the Asian region of the Soviet Union, thereby forming 'representative' in-depth country case studies for each of these distinctive regions.[1] The third type of study will be treated somewhat independently of the other two, although wherever feasible it will also be done in a country where the others are being done. The research programme is then designed to be cross-cultural, and the country case studies, particularly the in-depth case studies, will be drawn together to provide insights into the major differences and similarities across the world in regard to the interaction between women's roles and demographic change.

## Cultural Factors, Family Structure, Socio-anthropological Studies and Women's Roles

All of humankind make decisions and behave in a manner which is greatly affected by their culture and their social class.[2] Indeed, it is common to find behaviour which is considered acceptable in one culture or class and unacceptable in another culture or class. As a result, global generalizations on the role and status of women are easy to make but difficult to defend. Indeed, there are already a number of articles criticizing previous generalizations.[3]

It is important to know the family structure as well as the rights, duties and obligations that men and women assume, since these factors are particularly important in determining behaviour in developing countries where extended family relationships are usually quite strong. However, since these relationships vary so greatly in different settings, it is necessary to obtain an in-depth understanding of these relationships in each of the cultures, classes and households to be studied. For example, what ties do women maintain with their parents, brothers, sisters, etc? What are the duties and obligations within the household between various household members, particularly between husband and wife, wife and mother-in-law, wife and sister-in-law? To what degree are families extended and to what degree are they nuclear? Do women have explicit economic responsibilities towards their children, such as paying for school fees or providing food? Who cares for children if the parents divorce or separate? How stable are marriages? How would one define 'household' and, consequently, on what basis should individuals be included in, or excluded from, the household?

Using answers to these questions, some of the following questions could be addressed. Are women's roles related to the degree of economic independence afforded them by the ties they maintain with their siblings and their parents? Are women's roles related to their position in the household relative to other household members, such as the husband, mother-in-law and sister-in-law, perhaps as this position relates to measurable factors such as the woman's age, number (and sexes) of children, education, age at joining the present household and distance to her parents' house? Are women's roles affected by the presence of other adult household members who may help care for their children. There are also similar questions regarding the determinants of fertility which can be asked using this information. For example, is fertility related to the separate obligations of men and women towards their children, to marriage stability and to who supports the children if the father and mother become separated?

It is also important to know the degree of substitutability in various tasks between men, women and children in each country. In most countries and population subgroups it is generally believed that women are *supposed* to do certain tasks and *not supposed* to do other tasks. Where deviation from the societal norm entails high social and psychic costs (as it does in most developing countries), there should be a low degree of substitutability between the sexes in the work they do, thereby reinforcing the tendency for behaviour to emulate these norms. *A priori*, one would expect behaviour to be less traditional where economic circumstances make it necessary, such as in low-income and female-headed households, where family members have been exposed to new ideas and new ways of life, such as occurs as a result of migration and formal education, and where the social structure is less cohesive, such as in urban areas.[4]

There are important methodological questions regarding the best way to obtain this information on societal norms and family structure. A three-pronged research approach is suggested below. First, it is proposed that researchers, with relevant field experience in the areas where household sample surveys are to be carried out, could be asked to write background papers describing the cultural milieu, class structure, family structure, norms and women's roles in these regions. They would draw upon secondary sources and their own field experience. Second, these researchers could be asked to answer a series of specific questions. In a sense, they would self-adminster questionnaires composed of open-ended and close-ended questions.[5] The key question regarding the above two exercises is whether present knowledge in these areas is sufficiently accurate (i.e., not comprised of myths) or whether new fieldwork is required. Third, concurrent with the collection of the household survey data discussed in the next section, it is proposed that anthropologists spend extended periods of time in at least some of the sample areas. In this way, it will be possible to check the accuracy of the survey data and, more importantly, to provide an in-depth understanding of sample areas and sample households that cannot be obtained using household surveys and structured questionnaires.

## Allocation of Time, Economic Productivity, Household Sample Surveys and Women's Roles

Women play an important economic role in all countries — in addition to their non-wage earning household and family activities. In most parts of the world this contribution to the family's well-being is non-monetized, and it frequently goes unrecognized and unrecorded by governments and social scientists. Thus, women often help gather sticks for firewood, help care for domestic animals, such as cows, goats and chickens, walk long distances for water and arduously prepare food — as well as work on the family farm. These tasks contribute greatly to the family's economic well-being, and many of them would need to be purchased (or foregone) if they were not provided by the woman.

To help answer questions related to the economic contributions of women, it is necessary to have fairly detailed and accurate information on the activities of a sufficient number of women and other household members. For this purpose it would be useful to have the type of information found in time-use surveys. Typical labour force surveys are not sufficiently detailed, since people are usually categorized only as in or out of the labour force; more detailed labour force surveys, which divide the labour force into several categories, while better, still will not be able to answer the questions of concern to the programme described here. In addition to their crudeness, typical labour force surveys face other major problems; respondents frequently 'misinterpret' what is meant by phrases such as 'job', 'work' and 'economic activity',[6] and in some societies there is a reluctance to admit that women are engaged in 'work'.[7] For these reasons, it seems appropriate to collect data by asking respondents what they do during the day. In this way, respondents should be less reluctant to report their actual activities without having to decide what is or is not economic activity.

Time-use and activity surveys are not without their own problems, however, and there are a number of methodological issues in these surveys that have not been resolved. For example, how much detail should there be in the time-use schedule — should a day be divided into fifteen-minute blocks, hour blocks or longer blocks? How far back in the past should respondents be asked to recall — yesterday only, last week, last season, the entire year? How many times should respondents be visited — once, each month, each season? How detailed should be the categorization of activities? Should dual activities be recorded? Is it also possible to gather information on the intensity of work? How does one obtain information on activities which tend to occur sporadically or infrequently?

Unfortunately, there are no easy answers to the above questions — partly because there has been only limited experience using these instruments in developing countries, but largely because the choices one makes depend on the purpose of the study being undertaken.[8]

Given the key economic role played by women, especially in the rural economy, an important focus for the present study is how various demographic changes affect the woman's economic contribution. (For how this in turn affects fertility and mortality see pp. 37-41.) For example, how do women cope with the increasing burden placed on them as a result of rising survival rates for their children? Do women spend less time in economic activities, thereby reducing the average family's income; do women work longer hours or more intensively to compensate for these additional burdens; do women spend less time with their children, thereby reducing the investment in the human capital development of their children; or do other family members, particularly children, assume greater responsibility? Conversely, what do women tend to do when the demands on their time sharply decrease as a result of falling fertility rates or as a result of exogenous changes, such as the building of a well or a grain mill near their house? Another question of great importance is determining when men begin to share more equally in the household responsibilities and women begin to attain a more influential position in the family. Do the various relations differ depending on the family structure and the presence of certain family members such as the mother-in-law?

This discussion on women's roles has been based largely on a static schema being mainly concerned with differences between households at *one* point in time, and with questions related to family size and family structure at *one* point in time. It is necessary, however, to broaden this scope by introducing time (i.e., dynamic considerations) into the study, for unless dynamic considerations are introduced one may draw misleading conclusions about likely future changes.

A 'time' perspective could be brought into the present study in three ways. First, available background material could be gathered on historical trends (particularly in women's roles), changing economic structure, social institutions and laws, and written up into an introductory paper. Second, the sample of households could be stratified on criteria that can be easily generalized and in such a way as to provide a glimpse of some of the underlying dynamic trends believed to be occurring in developing countries; in addition, macro or community-level data could be collected for each sample sub-location in order to help provide a picture of the broad structural context within which sample households find themselves. Thus, rural and urban households could be interviewed to observe the effect on women's roles of rural-urban migration. In rural areas, landless, small, medium and large landowning households could be interviewed to observe the effect on women's roles of increasing rates of parcellization and landlessness which are believed to be occurring in developing countries, as well as the effects a land redistribution programme might have on women's roles.

Figure 2.1 presents diagrammatically the major sampling strata, outlined above, which are believed to both operational and relevant for this research programme. These strata are by no means exclusive and there are many other important divisions which have not been included such as: sex of household head, type of household (e.g., nuclear,

**Figure 2.1: Schematic Diagram of Suggested Sampling Stratification for Household Sample Survey**

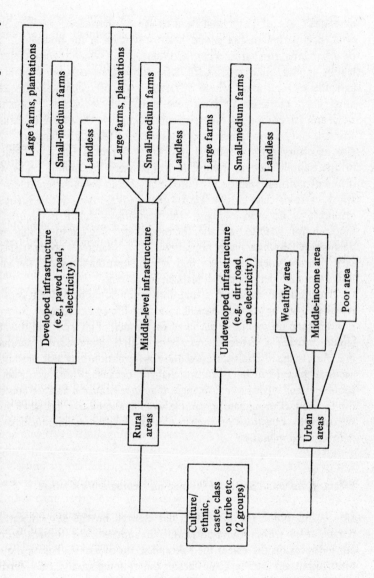

extended), age of household head or age of married women in household, occupation of household head or women in the household, size
of urban area, rural areas where crops are grown which require different
labour inputs, rural areas with different degrees of monetization of
agriculture, rural areas where different levels of technology are used,
areas where there are different government policies, women's organizations and /or co-operatives attempting to improve the role and status of
women, and pastoral areas as well as areas of sedentary farming.[9] It is
also necessary to take cultural and class differences into consideration
in the sample design. Hence it is necessary to sample areas with
different cultural traditions and/or households from different ethnic,
tribal, caste or class groups. Unfortunately there may not be sufficient
resources to do even as many stratifications as shown in Figure 2.1.
Since choices need to be made, the crucial sampling questions that must
be answered are how many households in each sample stratum are necessary for analytical purposes and which stratifications are the most
important and can be operationalized fairly easily?

The third way in which a time dimension could be brought into the
research is via an explicit consideration of life-cycle changes. Information on time use could be gathered for women of all ages, and thus this
would provide a cross-section, point-in-time glimpse of a woman's
life. As discussed above, cross-section information may not present an
accurate picture of likely future changes, because of important social,
economic and institutional changes that have occurred and are continuing to occur. Consequently, sample women should also be asked some
retrospective questions on such topics as education, economic activity,
marriage and migration.

### Effect of Role and Status of Women on Demographic Change

Up to this point the discussion has centred on the determinants of
female roles within the household. In contrast, the present section
concentrates on the effect the role and status of women has on the two
most important demographic factors determining family size — fertility
and mortality. The exclusion of other demographic factors, such as
migration, from the discussion in this section does not imply that these
other factors do not have important effects on women's roles. Rather
this is done so as to focus the research programme's efforts in investigating the effect of women's roles on the determinants of demographic
variables.

*Fertility*

The literature on women's issues and family planning generally stress (implicitly or explicitly) the divergence between the interests of the wife and other family members, especially her husband, and especially with respect to child-bearing and child-rearing. Wives in developing countries are often said to suffer from frequent and closely spaced births and to be exploited by the male members of the household. This has been the motivation for women's groups and family planning agencies to stress the need for a woman to have control over her body and the reproductive process.

The extensive literature on fertility differentials, on the other hand, particularly the economic literature, has largely ignored these issues.[10] Economists have developed a theory of household decision-making which concerns itself with the family or the household as if it were a homogeneous unit.[11] While differences between household members (especially husband and wife) are stressed in this literature, it is only in so far as they affect the household's overall utility. Thus, higher educational attainment by the wife is hypothesized to have a negative effect on fertility since it increases the opportunity cost to the household of the woman not working and higher educational attainment by the husband is hypothesized to have a positive effect on fertility since it increases family income. Similarly, employment of the husband is hypothesized not to have an effect on fertility and employment of the wife is hypothesized to have a negative effect on fertility.[12]

There would seem to be two major issues regarding the direct effect on fertility of economic activity of the woman. First, under what conditions does work away from home by the woman have its greatest effect on fertility? Is its effect greatest in low-income households where the opportunity cost of foregoing current income is highest, in female-headed households where a 'man' is not present, or in households where kin ties are weak and thus there is greater reliance on the earnings of the woman, in nuclear households where alternative child-care by adults is not necessarily available and free, where jobs are far from the house and where there are no maternity benefits?

Second, while most previous analyses of fertility differentials have not found a relationship between work in or around the home by the woman and her fertility, these results may be due to measurement error and to the 'aggregate' nature of the variable measuring work in or around the home. With the detailed activity data to be collected in the course of the present research programme, measurement error should be minimized and it should be possible to subdivide work which is done in or around home into separate categories. Thus, it may be that certain types of work in or around home have an effect on fertility, particularly among poorer households and households where the wife does physically taxing work. For example, do certain of these economic activities affect fecundity and the ability to carry to term? Do some of the economic activities cause women to reduce the period of time they breast-feed their children, thereby decreasing the period of post-partum amenorrhea and shortening the birth interval? Are there some of these activities which cause the wife to wean her children sooner, thereby increasing the infant and child mortality rate and the need for more births to achieve the same desired family size?

The above discussion notwithstanding, there is conspicuously missing in the socio-economic theories of fertility a recognition that the household is not a homogeneous unit — that family members have different interests and that family members do not derive the same benefit (or cost) from all actions.[13] In particular, husbands and wives *should* have different family-size desires since the number of children a couple has *inter alia* has a greater effect on the wife than it does on her husband. But whose family-size desire is more likely to be acted upon?[14]

Thus the role and status of women can be expected to affect fertility from two directions. First, it can affect fertility by affecting the overall level of the household's well-being (which is stressed in the literature on socio-economic determinants of fertility); second, it can affect fertility through the degree to which the interests of husbands and wives diverge and the relative ability of each spouse in determining the number of children they should have.

There are numerous Knowledge, Attitude and Practice of family planning surveys (KAP) and World Fertility Surveys (WFS) presently available or soon to be available. These surveys usually include information on fertility and family-size desires and in many cases this information is provided separately for husband and wife. Thus, using these surveys, as well as the prospective surveys to be carried out in this research programme, it would be possible to study family-size desires of the spouses as well as fertility levels to answer some of the following questions.

(i) To what are family-size desires of the husband and wife related?[15]

(ia) In particular, how do the factors related to the family-size desires of the husband and wife differ?

(ii) Is actual family size more likely to be closer, on average, to the wife's or to the husband's family-size desires?

(iia) What are the factors which help to determine the relative ability of the wife and husband to determine actual family size? Are husband-wife communication and family planning awareness, which are stressed by population education programmes, important determinants of the relative ability of the wife to determine actual fertility? Are the wife's age, education, height and economic contributions to the family *relative* to the husband's age, education, height and economic contribution important factors in determining actual fertility? Do the ties the wife maintains with her siblings and her parents affect the wife's position versus her husband; similarly, is the wife's position affected by the presence (and age) of her mother-in-law, her sister-in-laws and her children?

(iii) Is fertility related to women's economic activity?

(iiia) Are there different types of economic activities for women which have an effect on fertility? In addition to the usual distinction made between work away from home and work in and around home, are there divisions within the work in or around home category which have different effects on fertility?

(iv) How do the hypothesized relationships mentioned above interact with factors such as class, income level, family structure and presence of other adults in the household?

*Mortality and Morbidity*

It is argued here that child-care and nurture during the late prenatal and early postnatal period is not completely determined by cultural norms, and that the health of the child in this period is partly a function of the mother's other roles in life.[16] Thus, it is hypothesized that when a mother's other roles are not compatible with care for her child, she will tend to reduce her 'input' to the child, and that this conflict is particularly important for 'working' women and for women in low-income households.

In urban areas it is usually not possible to breast-feed one's child during working hours and, as a result, 'recent' mothers who are working away from home usually bottle-feed their children. In most developing countries this implies a reduction in the child's health and survivorship probabilities because bottle-feeding is less hygienic and thus more likely to 'introduce' disease organisms, which may lead, in particular, to diarrhoeal diseases — among the most important causes of death in developing countries. In addition, the child loses the natural disease immunities contained in mother's milk.

In rural areas the conflict between the mother's economic activity and the health of the child is also important even though it is not quite so obvious as it is in urban areas. Where women contribute to the economic well-being of the household in physical activities, such as in agriculture, the child's health is affected both directly by the extent to which this physical activity affects the mother's health and indirectly through the extent to which the mother spends less time with her child (e.g., breast-feed for a shorter period and wean earlier).[17] Thus, a child born to an undernourished, unhealthy mother is more likely to be underweight at birth and less likely to survive. In addition, after birth, because of the need (especially among poorer women) for the 'income' generated by the woman's work activities, the woman may spend less time with her child.

Up to this point, the discussion on mortality has been couched in general terms. It is necessary to complicate matters somewhat, because in rural areas work activities are seasonal. Since it is often difficult and expensive to hire labour during peak seasons, in most societies all household members generally work during the peak season. Indeed, where farms are small and family incomes are low it may be disastrous if any member of the family is unable to work. In these circumstances, in order to maintain family income, it seems likely that mothers would tend to spend less time with a child who is born in or around the peak season than with a child born in the slack season — causing this child to suffer from his or her untimely arrival.[18]

A number of hypotheses can be presented: (i) in rural areas fertility rates and infant mortality rates are seasonal in nature, with fertility rates highest in the slack season and mortality rates highest in the peak season; (ii) role incompatibility of working mothers causes economically active mothers to breast-feed for a shorter period of time and to wean sooner, and this has important implications for the health of the children; (iii) children born to economically active mothers, especially in rural areas when the child is born in or around the peak agricultural season, are, on average, less healthy and less likely to survive the first year of life than other children.[19]

These hypotheses, if true, have important implications for social welfare, economic development and women's issues. First, they imply that for the poorest families there is a vicious cycle of poverty in the current generation and poor health in future generations. In contrast, there is no such cycle among more well-to-do families who can afford to forego current income in order to build up the physical and mental stock of their newly born. Second, they imply that, in rural areas, family planning programmes should address their attention towards attempting to space births so that they tend to occur in slack seasons. Third, institutional arrangements for the breast-feeding of children for working urban women would have a positive effect on the health of those children.

To test the above hypotheses it would be necessary to gather the following survey data from a detailed pregnancy history: miscarriages, year of each birth (to control for secular decrease in mortality rates), sex of each birth (to control for male-female differences in mortality), age at death (to control for differences in age patterns of mortality), cause of death (to observe differences by cause of death) and season of birth (to control for seasonality in mortality). In addition, it would be necessary to collect information on at least the following: health practices, sanitary facilities, weaning and breast-feeding practices, climate, education and income. It is obvious that recall error for the mortality data will increase the further back in time a child is born, and this should be particularly a problem with regard to information on season of birth and cause of death. Partly for this reason (i.e., measurement problems) and partly to improve our understanding of the processes involved, detailed anthropological information should also be collected. This would be particularly useful in any investigation of differentials in mortality rates of sons and daughters, to which attention is now turned.

One other point should be raised: sex differentials in mortality. Surprisingly little is known of the reasons for the large differentials in mortality rates by sex found in developing countries. For most of the developing world, it is believed that girls have a greater chance of reaching adulthood than do boys, but these differentials are by no means uniform around the world and in some areas (most notably South Asia) boys have higher survival rates than girls.[20] In a cross-cultural study such as the one proposed here, it should be possible to throw light on some of the reasons for male-female differentials in mortality rates by asking some of the following questions. Are sex differentials in mortality related to the relative position of women in the society and in the economy, as measured by factors such as size of dowries or bride prices, economic contribution of male and female children, who children live with when they marry, ownership of land, etc?[21] Are sex differentials in mortality related to the parity of the birth and the number of siblings of each sex already in the family?[22] Are they related to the sex preference for children? Are they related to the mother's educational level and the family's economic position? How have sex differentials in mortality been changing over time and how are they expected to change in the future?

## The Functioning of Urban Labour Markets and its Effect on Female Roles

The present section focuses mainly on macro job market conditions and institutional mechanisms (which are exogenous to each woman), and how they affect women's roles. Thus, a concern of the present programme will be to focus on the factors related to 'sex segregation' in employment, whereby employed women become concentrated in occupations that usually require less skill and that have lower wages than male-dominated occupations. Unless sufficient attention is given to these demand-oriented factors, an important element will be missing in what determines the economic activities of urban women.

It is important to note that while attention in the remainder of this section is directed towards the formal sector, this does not imply a lack of concern with the so-called informal sector where many women work because of the flexibility of this work and the easy entry into it; indeed, in many countries more women work in the informal sector (e.g., domestics, prostitutes, traders) than work in the formal sector. Consequently, wherever appropriate and wherever possible, informal sector establishments will also be studied.

A number of general models have been developed to explain the way in which job markets function.[23] Probably the most widely researched is the human capital model which attempts to explain pay differentials by differentials in the workers' productivity.[24] Thus, female workers are said to be paid less than male workers because they are said to be less productive than male workers. These differences in productivity are said to be explained by factors such as differentials in physical strength, differentials in labour turnover and absenteeism caused by the additional household responsibilities women bear, and by lower levels of human capital which are accumulated by women because they tend to have less relevant and fewer standards of formal education, less on-the-job training and higher discontinuation rates.

Recently a good deal of attention has been given to the so-called 'overcrowding' model.[25] As with the human capital model, wage differentials result from the functioning of the market place given some exogenous constraints. According to the overcrowding model, women are restricted, or crowded, into particular occupations for cultural and/or conspiratorial reasons. Being thus locked into these occupations, women must compete among themselves for the relatively few positions available, pushing down their wages.

Since job segregation is undoubtedly due to some extent to cultural factors, or at least to factors which are outside the confines of a strictly economic model concerned with marginalism, it is not surprising that a third model — the so-called segmentation or institutional model — has an increasing number of advocates. According to one variant of this model, there are said to be two types of jobs.[26] One type of job is said to be 'static' in nature: the skill level required to do this work is low, as is the degree of skill acquired while working at this job. High rates of discontinuity in work and labour turnover tend to occur in these jobs, but this does not greatly concern either the worker or the employer since the worker does not build up important skills which would deteriorate if employment were discontinued. 'Progressive' jobs, on the other hand, are said to be dynamic in nature; there is considerable on-the-job acquisition of skills as well as the possibility to move up to better jobs. In such 'progressive' jobs, discontinuity in work and labour turnover are undesirable to both employees and employers. Employees do not want their 'human capital stock' to deteriorate and employers do not want their investment in training to be lost by discontinuity in employment.

For economic and cultural reasons women are supposedly pushed into the 'static'-type jobs, according to this model (thus its under-lying assumption is similar to that in the overcrowding model), because, for example, employers believe women are more likely to leave the job due to family responsibilities or because women are less well trained to begin with.

All three models offer some insight into the job market problems faced by women. Part of the male-female differential in pay and occupational distribution is undoubtedly due to the fact that women generally build up less human capital than men — beginning with formal education; women are usually 'crowded' into particular occupations and these occupations do tend to be relatively 'static' in nature. None the less, these models do not provide very useful insights as to how to reduce the degree of sex segregation in employment — other than the obvious, such as raising female educational levels, directing female education towards more 'practical courses' of study, requiring that a certain percentage of jobs be reserved for females, eliminating legal barriers to female employment, providing child-care services and maternity leave benefits, and making work more flexible (including part-time work). While these actions should be stressed, and the effec-tiveness of such policies should be studied, it is not necessary to under-take research to garner support for these policies in the abstract.

However, to be able to conclude which of the above policies would be most effective, as well as to come up with less obvious policies to reduce sex segregation in employment, one must understand the way in which job markets operate in developing countries. Unfortunately, at the present time very little is known about this. Indeed, there is not even much information by sex on important factors which help determine labour productivity (e.g., labour turnover rates, absenteeism rates, tardism rates); instead it is usually assumed that women are less 'committed' to the labour force than men and that women are more frequently late and absent. Yet there is not much evidence to support these conclusions in developing countries. For example, women may have similar turnover and absenteeism rates as men, and women may be at least as committed to the labour force as men.[27]

The most fruitful approach to studying labour markets would seem to be an 'institutional' approach which looks at the points in the job process (hiring, training and promoting, firing) and the types of jobs (e.g., part-time, night work, physical) where women may be discriminated against. In this way it should be possible to devise policies which enhance the position of women and which are likely to be effective, since these policies would use the labour market mechanisms in the country. The following strategy is proposed:

(i) Establish the levels (and trends, if possible) in the distribution of employment, pay, hours of work and security of employment by sex. This analysis could be relatively simple – basically providing background material for further work as well as a possible sampling frame for the survey work described below. Using this information, for example, it would also be possible to estimate how much of the change in the average female employment rate is due to changing employment patterns, and how much is due to changes in the proportion of women employed in various industries and occupations.

(ii) Establish the levels and trends in the education of males and females. Again, this type of information would provide useful background material, since educational attainment is an important element in determining an individual's job market prospects.

(iii) Establish the extent to which there is legal discrimination against women in areas such as employment, pay, working conditions and fringe benefits.

(iv) Interview employers, employees and union officials.

*Employer's Interview*

These interviews should obtain information on how employers behave with regard to hiring, promotion and training, and firing, in addition to information on turnover rates, absenteeism rates, and the occupational distribution of employment by sex. Although practical considerations will limit the sample of employers, it would be useful to interview nongovernment firms and government agencies, foreign-owned firms and domestic-owned firms, large and small firms, unionized and non-unionized firms, as well as firms in different industries.[28] Within each firm, information could be gathered separately for different types of jobs with particular reference made towards problems faced by women.[29]

It would also be necessary to collect data on employees in sample firms, e.g., their sex, age, occupation, education, pay, absenteeism, breaks in employment and length of service. This information would be useful in choosing a sample of employees to be interviewed since it would allow the sample to be stratified so that women in all types of occupation could be interviewed — women in 'static' and 'progressive' occupations as well as women in male-dominated, female-dominated and sexually mixed occupations; in addition, employers could be asked questions specifically directed towards different types of jobs. With this information, it would also be possible to observe the degree to which particular occupations are dominated by men or women; whether women tend to have higher absenteeism rates, more breaks in employment and shorter periods of employment than men; whether women tend to receive lower pay in similar jobs; and whether women with equivalent qualifications tend to be in lower paying jobs than men.

## Employee's Interview

It would be useful to supplement the employer interviews, discussed above, with interviews administered to female and male employees as well as union officials.[30] It is possible, for example, that occupational segregation by sex is only partly the result of the actions of employers (e.g., who possibly screen applicants on the basis of their sex), and that employees self-discriminate by not making themselves available for particular jobs or that male workers refuse to work with female workers.

The employee's interview should collect information on work experience, fertility and marriage, with particular reference to the effect fertility and marital status have on employment status. In addition, employees should be asked about their jobs: how they found their jobs, why they believe they got the job, why they believe they were promoted, fired or left, and what were the major problems with the job. These questions should be asked sequentially in conjunction with questions on fertility and marriage, so that periods of unemployment, withdrawal from the labour force and unpaid family work can be captured with particular reference to fertility and other life cycle considerations.

In addition to this occupation-fertility-marital history, background information should be collected on age, religion, education and place of birth, as well as information on the household — its size, its structure, and the income and occupation of its members. Last, there should be questions concerning the woman's feelings about work and family — the main reasons she works, the problems with her job and the effects of work on her children. Thus, are there certain types of jobs as well as certain working conditions which women find unacceptable? Is the flexibility of a job important; in particular, how does this relate to marital status, family size and family structure?

The interviews with union officials should be somewhat parallel to the employer's interview. Background factual data should be collected wherever possible on union members by sex, occupation and firm, and on union officials by sex and position. Interviews with union officials should also determine the role played by unions and their relative bargaining power in the process of hiring, promotion and firing of workers; the selection criteria they feel should apply; the degree to which unions have a bias against women workers for particular occupations; what unions feel are the major problems faced by male and female workers; how unions feel these problems can be solved and what they themselves are doing to improve the situation. Thus, do unions contribute to, or reduce, job segregation by sex? If so, how? To what extent are unions dominated by men? Does increased unionization provide an avenue through which sex segregation of employment can be reduced?

### Small Studies on Policies Aimed at Improving the Role and Status of Women

Many countries are actively attempting to improve the position of women. For example, rural extension services are now approaching women as well as men; co-operative schemes are attempting to increase the income which women are able to earn; literacy courses and health education courses are attempting to improve educational and health levels. These policy measures are, in a sense, the prescription of government and nongovernment agencies for improving the situation of women. What are these programmes and how effective have they been?

It would be worthwhile to undertake small, investigative studies of these various policies and by so doing build up a menu of possible actions.[31] To accomplish this task researchers would at least need to address themselves to the following questions. What are these policies? How well have these policies succeeded in their objectives? What are the reasons for their success or failure? Do these policies appear to be transferable to other countries and other cultures? Thus, as part of the present research programme, it is envisaged that a number of small studies on specific policy prescriptions will be undertaken to help answer some of the above questions.

The research programme described here is quite ambitious − in terms of the range of issues it plans to study, the broad frame within which it plans to study these issues, its global coverage and the inter-disciplinary approach it plans to use. Despite inherent difficulties in such encompassing approaches, it is strongly felt that questions related to women's roles and demographic change should be studied from such a broad perspective.

## Notes

1. See Boserup's (1970) classical work for a discussion of the broad cultural groupings in the world with regard to women. Obviously, even the broad cultural groupings listed here are not completely homogeneous.

2. In most countries there are distinct groups of people (based on factors such as religion, race, tribe, class and caste) with different behaviour patterns, *ceteris paribus*, due to varying customs and norms.

3. For example, see Palmer (1977); Standing (1977).

4. In a cross-cultural study such as this one, it would also be useful to know (at least roughly) the social ordering of the status attached to various economic activities, for without such information one might unwittingly draw inappropriate conclusions concerning the implications for the observed patterns of female economic activities found in different countries.

5. A similar procedure has been followed in a successful study by Molnos (1972) in East Africa, in which researchers were asked to write short essays addressed to a series of questions put forward by Molnos. The procedure proposed here differs from Molnos's method in two ways. First, researchers would be asked to provide factual answers to a series of specific close-ended questions; and, second, the open-ended questions, to which short essays are directed, would be relatively few in number, and researchers will have no choice as to which questions to answer.

6. In a recent study in Kenya, estimates of the adult female economic activity rate based on questions from a household survey were very sensitive to the word used to elicit responses. Estimates varied from about 20% when the word 'job' was used to about 90% when the word 'work' was used. See Anker and Knowles (1978).

7. The reluctance to admit that women in the household 'work' is

particularly prevalent in Muslim countries and at least partly helps to explain the extremely low economic activity rates recorded for women in these countries.

8. An excellent discussion (along with suggestions and alternative survey instruments) of methodological issues associated with time-use surveys appears in a recent paper by Mueller (1978).

9. There is a good deal of overlap in these divisions. Thus, for example, the type of crop grown is related to the level of technology used, and the sex of the household head is related to the age of the household head. None the less, if stratification is to be used in the sample design, it must be based on certain criteria.

10. For thoughtful exceptions in the economic literature, see Birdsall (1976); Cochrane and Bean (1976). For more frequent examples in the sociological and anthropological literature, see Hawthorn (1970) and Oppong (1978).

11. The head of household is implicitly assumed to be more or less a benevolent dictator.

12. According to this theory, the effect of education or labour force participation of the wife has an indeterminant effect on fertility, since there is a positive income effect and a negative substitution effect. The text stresses the negative effect since it seems to dominate in most societies.

13. The discussion in this section does not imply that societies are completely individualistic where each person always acts in his or her own best interest. Indeed, such a society does not exist. All societies have sanctions and constraints which make completely selfish behaviour unlikely, and these sanctions and constraints are especially strong within the household. None of this negates the fact, however, that there is some degree of self-interest in actions taken by individuals.

14. This analogy can, of course, be extended to household members other than the husband and the wife. For example, in societies where the extended family is still strong, the grandparents may have a major effect on fertility.

15. Desired family size could be defined as the number of children which is considered ideal or as the present number of children plus the additional number of children which are desired.

16. For nine months before a child is born and for approximately one year after a child is born the mother is indispensable to the child's health and survival (e.g., in the first year of life when breast-feeding is better than other forms of feeding). Although it may also be true that the mother's inputs to her children are superior to those provided by others during all of childhood, there are three reasons for emphasizing the effect of the woman's role on the child's health in the prenatal and postnatal period. First, the degree of substitutability of other forms of care for the mother is more limited in this period than in other periods. Second, the effect on the child's health of changes in the mother's inputs is more direct than in other periods. Third, some of the changes in this period are measurable (e.g., birth weight and prenatal role; breastfeeding, weaning and postnatal role).

17. Nerlove (1974) found in a cross-cultural analysis of 83 societies that women begin supplementary feeding of their infants earlier in societies where women participate to a relatively large extent in subsistence economic activities.

18. If the mother does not work or works less diligently because of a 'recent' child, the rest of the family would suffer more than the child because of the reduced level of farm output which has been generated. Another possibility is that the mother would work just as hard as before, in addition to caring for the child; in this case the mother (and child) would bear the greatest burden within the family.

19. Other factors, such as the prevalence of disease (which is associated with

the weather) and the availability of food, are also seasonal in nature. Thus, in tropical countries one would expect mortality rates to be higher in the peak seasons because of the weather, and lower in the peak season because of the greater availability of food. Factors such as these (which affect mortality rates and which are seasonal) make it difficult to estimate the independent effect on the probability of a child surviving to a particular age associated with the mother's economic activity. It is none the less possible to estimate this effect if the sample includes various groups of women – for example women who do and do not engage in particular economic activities, women from high and low-income households and women from different climatic zones. Thus, for similar women engaged in the same economic activity, one would expect the seasonal variation in mortality rates to be heightened in areas where diseases which attack infants and children are seasonal, and to be dampened among low-income households where the availability of food is quite seasonal. Additionally, it should be possible to study how weaning and breast-feeding practices vary according to the season for women engaged in different economic activities.

20. See El Badry (1969).

21. The relatively high mortality rate of females compared with males in South Asia is frequently attributed to the low status of women and poorer care females receive (see Singh, Gordon and Wyon, 1962). Yet, there is no evidence from Arab countries, where women also have low status, of a similar relationship (see Hammond, 1977).

22. In a study in Bangkok, 'girls born into families where girls are in the majority are significantly more likely to die before age five than girls born into families with more boys than girls' (Ben-Porath and Welch, 1976).

23. For good reviews of various labour market theories, see Blau and Jusenius (1976); Standing (1978).

24. Although the possibility of outright sex discrimination is allowed for and is explored in the human capital model, its effect is often found to be relatively small. For example, see Polachek (1975).

25. Although the overcrowding approach has received much attention recently, it is far from new. Its origin stretches back to Edgeworth (1922).

26. See Standing (1978).

27. In Jamaica, industrial employers are said to *prefer* female workers because they are more stable employees than men (see Standing, 1977). In a Pakistani factory turnover rates were low for both men and women, although slightly higher for women (Hafeez, forthcoming). Similarly, in a Ghanaian factory absenteeism rates were only slightly higher for men (see Date-Bah, 1976).

28. For a study of the way in which an urban labour market in India functions, based on survey questionnaires, see Papola (1977). A possibility would be to collect less detailed information for a fairly wide sample of firms and detailed information for a sub-sample of firms.

29. In developed countries, for example, employers are said to 'screen' applicants on the basis of identifiable characteristics such as age, sex, education and race, and only from a list of already screened job candidates (i.e., those having only the 'good' characteristics) are people hired. Such a procedure is relatively efficient for the employer, but it causes applicants without the 'good' characteristics to find it difficult to get a job. In a sense this model provides an explanation for why women tend to be crowded into particular occupations or 'types' of jobs. In loose labour markets, such as in developing countries, there would be a sufficient number of applicants with the good characteristics so that those without these characteristics would not get any jobs. Thus, even though the unacceptable group (often women) may be less acceptable only on

average (perhaps by only a small percentage), those in the unacceptable group will not receive any jobs. This bias has come to be called statistical discrimination.

30. It is necessary to interview a sample of male employees in addition to a larger sample of female employees because a certain number of job-related problems are faced by both male and female employees.

31. A similar series of small studies on migration policies is being carried out by the ILO's Population and Labour Policies Research Programme on migration.

# References

Anker, R. and J.C. Knowles (1978) 'A micro analysis of female labour force participation in Africa' in G. Standing and G. Sheehan (eds.), *Labor force participation in low-income countries*, Geneva, ILO

Ben-Porath, Y. and F. Welch (1976) 'Do sex preferences really matter?', *Quarterly Journal of Economics, 3*, 2 (May), 297

Birdsall, N. (1976) 'Women and population studies', *Signs, 1*, 3, part 1, 713-20

Blau, F. and C. Jusenius (1976) 'Economists approaches to sex segregation in the labour market: an appraisal' in M. Blaxall and B.B. Reagan (eds.), *Women and the Workforce*, supplement to *Signs, 1*, 3, part 2

Boserup, E. (1970) *Women's roles in economic development*, London, George Allen and Unwin

Cochrane, S.H. and F.D. Bean (1976) 'Husband-wife differences in the demand for children', *Journal of Marriage and the Family* (May), pp. 297-307

Date-Bah, E. (1976) 'Ghanaian women in factory employment: a case study', mimeo., Geneva, International Institute of Labour Studies

Edgeworth, F.Y. (1922) 'Equal pay to men and women for equal work', *Economic Journal, 32* (September), 431-57

El Badry, M.A. (1969) 'Higher female than male mortality in some countries of South Asia: a digest', *Journal of the American Statistical Association* (December)

Hafeez, S. (1978) *Women factory workers: explored insights*, mimeo., Karachi, Pakistan

Hammond, E. (1977) 'Sex differences in mortality: an enquiry with reference to the Arab countries and others', *World Health Statistics Report, 30*, 3

Hawthorn, G.P. (1970) *The sociology of fertility*, London, Collier-Macmillan

Molnos, A. (1972) *Cultural source materials for population planning in East Africa, 1-3*, Nairobi, East African Publishing House

Mueller, E. (1978) 'Employment surveys for developing countries', mimeo., Ann Arbor, Michigan University Press, September

Nerlove, S. (1974) 'Women's workload and infant feeding practices: a relationship with demographic implications', *Ethnology, 13*, 2, 207-14

Oppong, C. (1978) 'Modernization and aspects of family change in Ghana' paper for Aspen Institute/Iran workshop, Gajereh, Iran, 17 May-2 June

Palmer, I. (1977) 'Rural women and the basic needs approach to development', *International Labour Review, 115*, 1 (January-February), Geneva, ILO

Papola, T.S. (1977) 'Mobility and wage structure in an urban labour market: a study in Ahmadabad, India' in Subbiah Kannapar (ed.), *Studies in urban labour market behaviour in developing areas*, Geneva, International Institute of Labour Studies

Polachek, S. (1975) 'Discontinuous labour force participation and its effect on women's market earnings' in Cynthia Lloyd (ed.), *Sex discrimination and the division of labour*, New York, Columbia University Press

Singh, S., J.E. Gordon and J.B. Wyon (1962) 'Medical care in fatal illnesses of a rural Punjab population: some social, biological and cultural factors and their implications', *Indian Journal of Medical Research, 50,* 6
Standing, G. (1977) *Labour force participation in historical perspective: proletarianisation in Jamaica*, mimeo., World Employment Programme Research working paper, restricted, Geneva, ILO
——— (1978) *Labour force participation and development*, Geneva, ILO

# PART TWO: CONCEPTUALIZING AND MEASURING WOMEN'S ROLES

# 3 THE ALLOCATION OF WOMEN'S TIME AND ITS RELATION TO FERTILITY

Eva Mueller

## Introduction

The particular aspect of women's roles on which this paper focuses is the use which women make of their time. Time use is of interest here because it may influence and be influenced by demographic characteristics of the population, particularly fertility. The available statistical evidence will be examined to see what light it throws on theories of fertility in which time and the value of time play an important part. The paper concludes by suggesting a number of hypotheses about the relationship between time use and fertility which should be tested in further research.

The idea that time may affect fertility is not new. However, previous research — because there were no comprehensive time-use data — has been narrowly focused on women's labour force participation. The results have been somewhat inadequate, since available labour force and employment statistics do not reflect all the various facets of women's working lives. Traditional labour force surveys determine whether a woman is or is not in the labour force and, if she is in the labour force, whether she is employed or unemployed; sometimes a distinction is made between full-time and part-time work; and the reference period is usually too short to be really meaningful (one week is common). Time-use surveys, on the other hand, can provide estimates of hours worked during a longer reference period, thus giving a measure of degree of involvement in market work.[1] Time-use studies are also more likely to give an adequate estimate of time spent on unpaid family work, which often is either underreported or omitted altogether in conventional labour force surveys; they can systematically record activities on the borderline between market work and housework, which may not be classified consistently in labour force or employment surveys. Examples of such borderline activities are tending a vegetable garden, raising chickens, taking in laundry, and processing food which may be sold or consumed in the home.

A further important advantage of time-budget studies is that they also measure time devoted to child-care, housework, and leisure pursuits

– the activities which compete with market work for a woman's time. It is hoped that studies of how women allocate their time among these activities will lead to a better understanding of the women's choices and the consequences of their choices.

Finally, a comprehensive picture of women's time use is one way of defining their role in the family and in society. Different perceptions of women's roles, associated with different time uses, may help to explain demographic behaviour.

Time-use studies have been concerned primarily with how time is allocated among activities. But there are other dimensions of time use which are of interest for demographic analysis: time can be analyzed according to the location of an activity – at home, near home or away from home; an adult's time can be divided according to the presence or absence of children; or time periods can be defined by type of social interaction – time spent alone, with household members, with relatives, with people outside the household. All these categories can be subdivided even further.

This chapter is concerned primarily with activities, since this is the aspect of time use most relevant for fertility studies and is also the aspect on which most of the existing time-use studies have concentrated. For demographic analysis, the locational dimension and the categorization of time by presence of children are also valuable, since such data help to show the compatibility between child-care and other activities.

**Figure 3.1: Interactions Between Time Use and Economic, Demographic and Education Factors**

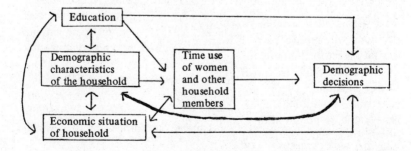

The interrelationships with which this paper is concerned are depicted in Figure 3.1, where the central variable is women's time use. It is intuitively obvious that the time uses of women and those of other family members are interdependent. We shall look at the time allocation of other family members where relevant, but for the sake of brevity, time use of other family members is treated only peripherally.

Three major sets of determinants of time use are considered: education, demographic and economic factors, although others could be added. The most relevant demographic factors for this review are those which relate to household composition: number and ages of children in the household, ages of husband and wife, and presence of 'other relatives' and servants. Education, demographic and economic factors influence each other, they influence time use, and they influence demographic decisions — especially fertility decisions — directly as well as indirectly (via time use). Demographic decisions, in turn, may modify the demographic characteristics and economic situation of the household. This system of interrelationships has not been subjected to comprehensive statistical analysis, as most time-use research to date has focused on the left-hand side of Figure 3.1 — the determinants of time use. Earlier studies on women's labour force participation may help us to formulate some hypotheses regarding the right-hand side — the consequences of time use for fertility decisions. However, while the chapter takes a rather careful look at the available large-scale time-use studies, there will only be a few references to the many studies of female labour force participation and fertility that have appeared since the early 1960s. Excellent systematic reviews of this literature have been published recently by McGreevy and Birdsall (1974), Dixon (1975), and Standing (1978).

The theoretical framework for this chapter is the New Household Economics or more specifically, the Economic Theory of Fertility. This means that economic determinants of time use and fertility decisions will receive particular attention. The Economic Theory of Fertility is set forth briefly on pp. 58-61.

The causal relationships in Figure 3.1, as well as those postulated by the Economic Theory of Fertility, operate in a particular cultural, economic, institutional and historical setting, which conditions behavioural responses. For example, studies of the effect of female labour force participation on fertility have shown that this relationship may be positive or negative, depending on various intervening variables. Similarly, the impact of education, income or family size on time use is modified by intervening variables. The nature of these intervening variables is discussed on pp. 61-2. The following section (pp. 63-5) calls attention to inertia in time use, lags in the adjustment of time use to changing circumstances and the problem of drawing causal inferences from time-use data. The subsequent three sections deal with the three major sets of determinants of time use — education, demographic characteristics of the household and its economic situation. These sections will review empirical findings that have emerged from time-use studies, particularly those conducted in developing countries. It should be noted, however, that the number of completed large-scale time-use studies that are relevant to the subject at hand is small, and some of the most recent and potentially most useful studies are still at an early stage of analysis. The aim of this review of empirical evidence will be to suggest hypotheses to be tested in future research, rather than to put forth conclusions.

## The Economic Theory of Fertility[2]

Essentially, the Economic Theory of Fertility attempts to explain in economic terms the household demand for children. Originally the theory was formulated with reference to urban, Western, industrialized economies. However, proponents of the theory have suggested that it is also applicable to developing economies, in so far as parents are willing and able to exercise some choice over the number of children they have.

In simplified terms, the theory views the household as a decision-making unit which maximizes its utility subject to certain constraints. The household derives satisfaction from 'commodities' $(S)$, children $(N)$ and child quality $(Q)$. Commodities are created by a combination of market purchases, housework and leisure. These inputs produce the satisfactions which the household seeks to maximize — for example, eating a meal, obtaining good nutrition, seeing a play, being comfortably housed or maintaining good health. Thus the family utility function may be written as

$$U = U(S, N, Q).$$

It is assumed that each commodity is produced according to a household production function with inputs of market goods $(X_i)$ and time $(t_i)$ of the various family members. Thus child services $(C)$ are produced by inputs of market goods $(X_c)$ — such as food for children, clothing, etc. – and the inputs of household members' time $(t_c)$ needed to raise the child and to achieve the desired child quality. This function may be written as

$$C = NQ = f(X_c, t_c).$$

Likewise, all other commodities $(S)$ are produced by inputs of market goods and household time, so that

$$S = g(X_s, t_s).$$

Under these assumptions, the family's demand for $S$ and $C$ services is limited by two constraints: its total income and its total time available for consumption and production activities. When income rises, families can afford more of both $C$ and $S$ services. This is called the 'income effect'. Economists recognize that some goods are demanded primarily because they are cheap, so that demand for them declines as income rises (potatoes are sometimes cited as an example). These goods are called 'inferior goods'. The demand for all other goods is expected to increase to some degree with rising income (or at least remain constant). Since children are hardly 'inferior goods', the demand for children should be positively related to income.

The relative costs of the various time and goods inputs are presumed to affect the relative costs of children as compared with other commodities, and quantities demanded are believed to be affected by relative prices. For example, if inputs into child services become more costly relative to inputs into other commodities, there may be a marginal shift in demand from children to these other commodities. This is called the 'price' or 'substitution' effect. Thus there should be a negative relationship between the cost of the time and goods needed to raise children and the quantity and quality of child services demanded.

The proponents of the Economic Theory of Fertility view children as 'time-intensive'. That is, compared with other 'commodities', required inputs of household time are large. This is particularly true if children are to be well cared for, well trained and well educated (i.e. to be of high quality). Therefore the cost of time inputs has an important influence on desired family size. Child-rearing time is assumed to be provided largely by mothers, so that the cost of the mother's time takes on central importance for these theorists. The more children a mother has to care for, the more time she must take from other activities.

The Economic Theory of Fertility has paid little attention to the subdivision of women's non-market time. Gronau (1973) has proposed a threefold classification of women's time; market work (which may include production of market commodities or income in kind in the home), housework (which includes child-care) and leisure. Becker (1965) himself stresses the homogeneity of all the time of a given person, since it can be put to various uses and has the same opportunity cost in all uses. Hence there is a presumption in this literature that there is a trade-off with respect to a household's time allocation between mother's market time and child-rearing time. Little attention is paid to the possibility that other housework and leisure may be curtailed to make room for child-care in the time budget. There further seems to be an expectation that, if a woman devoted less time to child-care, she could readily find more market work. A related assumption is that time uses are quite flexible, so that small units of time are readily transferable from non-market to market work, or vice versa.

Given these assumptions, the value of the mother's time is determined by the amount she could earn if she were to engage in income-earning activities. The value of the mother's time can be determined readily if she works for a market wage. It is more difficult to determine if she works in a family enterprise (such as a farm) with other family members, or if she spends all her time in the household. The opportunity cost of a woman's time has most often been estimated on the basis of her education, supplemented by years of labour market experience; sometimes occupation, location or other variables have also been taken into account.

In brief, the key influences on the demand for children are income effects and price effects, particularly the cost of the mother's time. Education affects the demand for children primarily by its effects on (i) the opportunity cost of the mother's time, (ii) the father's and mother's income, and (iii) the modernization and aspirations of the family.

Numerous empirical tests of the theory have related income and cost variables to fertility, bypassing detailed information on time allocation, which is in a sense an intermediate variable. It is characteristic of this group of economists that they judge the validity of a theory in terms of behavioural manifestations rather than in terms of evidence that the postulated steps of the decision-making process correspond to reality. To be sure, in this particular case, the unavailability of time-use data dictated this approach. The recent interest in time-use data stems, in part at least, from a desire to examine time allocation in relation to the decision-making process just described.

## Intervening Variables

Proponents of the Economic Theory of Fertility do not expect that time-use or fertility decisions can be fully explained by economic factors alone, or even by economic and demographic variables and education jointly. They merely postulate that, *ceteris paribus*, economic factors have some bearing on these decisions. Cultural factors, tastes and other environmental conditions do not explicitly enter into the model, but are subsumed under the *ceteris paribus* assumption. If the intervening variables have an important influence or a wide range of variation when compared with the economic variables, the predictions from the economic model may be weak and uncertain. Empirical studies of fertility decisions have indeed found that women's labour force participation does not have a simple and uniform relation to reproductive behaviour. Replacing data on labour force status with time-use data is one step towards clarifying this relationship. Paying more attention to the intervening variables may be another step.

There could be many variables that might intervene (i) between economic and demographic variables and time use, and (ii) between time-use and fertility decisions; in this discussion they are divided into three categories. First, there is the set of attitudes and expectations regarding women's roles that prevails in a society or subgroups of a society; the society's emphasis on familial and non-familial roles for women; the values placed on women's segregation, seclusion and dependence; and women's tastes, goals and aspirations. These attitudes affect women's responses to opportunities in the labour market and their preferences for alternative uses of their time.

Attitudes towards women's roles have their origin in culture, religion and socio-economic background. Usually they are acquired in childhood and hence have considerable persistence. Nevertheless, later experiences, group pressures and exposure to mass media may modify childhood attitudes over time. Time use itself may influence women's perceptions of their role; it may, for instance, determine the extent to which women are exposed to new currents of thought or the extent of their economic dependence.

If there is some interdependence between time use and attitudes, an analytical model that ignores attitudes might be misspecified — that is, it might attribute to certain time-use patterns behavioural consequences that in fact depend on intervening attitudes that are not rigidly related to time use. As a result, policy implications drawn from the model might be misleading. It has been shown repeatedly that 'modern' attitudes have an important bearing on demographic decisions, and modern attitudes may also affect time use. It is desirable to separate out attitudinal influences in an analysis of the influence of time-use on demographic decisions.

A second set of intervening variables relates to the structure of the labour market. Most of the work available to women may be work that is home-based or in the informal sector and, therefore, is compatible with child-care. Alternatively, it may consist of office, factory or service jobs, which are much less compatible. Child-bearing is more costly if foregone work experience affects the woman's lifetime earnings profile. If the labour market is one in which labour supply is very large relative to demand, not only will wages be depressed, but women may be able to find only very unpleasant or very low-status work. The disutility of the available work may tilt the choice between market work and having more children strongly towards children, even among the more educated women.

A third important set of intervening variables are those that may be called 'tastes'. Of particular relevance is the question of quantity versus quality of children, which is stressed by the Economic Theory of Fertility. The relative value that parents place on children as compared to a higher standard of living is also an important determinant of time-use decisions; it should also affect women's disposition to combine market work and child-care. A further aspect of tastes − one which has been neglected in the literature − is the preference for market work as compared with domestic activities. Economists tend to assume that the only utility that women derive from market work is the financial reward; whereas, in fact, market work may be inherently more or less satisfying than domestic activities. Finally, the uses to which people put their leisure time may affect the pleasure they derive from a large family.

Such intervening variables may account for much of the observed variance in time use and in reproductive behaviour. As long as these variables are not measured and are not included in an analysis, the causal links among (i) economic and demographic factors, (ii) time use, and (iii) fertility will not emerge clearly and consistently from statistical studies.

## The Time-use Decision: Adjustments in Time Use Over Short and Long Periods

The Economic Theory of Fertility assumes that people have a good deal of discretion in how they allocate their time, and that time use responds fairly readily to changes in economic and demographic circumstances. While the empirical evidence gives some support to this assumption, it also suggests that rigidities and inertia characterize time-use patterns. That is to say, there is considerable similarity in time-use data among countries representing different cultures, political systems and stages of development, and among subgroups of these populations, as well as among stages of development in one country.

This observation is based, in part at least, on the Multinational Time Budget Project (to be referred to henceforth as the Multinational study), conducted in 1964-5 in 15 locations (mostly towns and small cities) spread over 12 countries.[3] This study will be referred to repeatedly, not only because of its scope and excellence of design, but also because it is the only large-scale study that permits comparison of time use under different cultural and economic conditions. It should be noted, however, that only one of the survey sites included (Lima, Peru) is in a developing country; the rest range from Eastern Europe to the United States. The similarities in time use among survey sites that emerges from the Multinational study[4] is all the more remarkable, since the 15 sites cover a fairly wide spectrum of economic development. For example, at the time of the survey, 66 per cent of households in Kragujevac (Yugoslavia) had no running water and only 6 per cent had telephones. More generally, technology in the home and at work was considerably more advanced in the highly developed cities of West Germany and the United States than in some of the provincial towns of Eastern Europe. The disparity in education levels was also wide. True, the similarity in time use holds only for broad activity categories (such as housework, market work and leisure) rather than for highly specific activity codes (such as water-carrying or telephoning); for many purposes, however, the broader activity categories are of greater interest than the narrow ones.

The social scientists who analyzed the Multinational study found, somewhat to their surprise, that vast differences among survey sites in the availability of labour-saving household amenities had little impact on time spent on housekeeping tasks. It appears that as housework becomes less onerous, women opt for a higher quality of household services — more elaborate and diversified meals, washing clothes more often, cleaning larger houses, etc. As transportation becomes more efficient, people cover larger distances in connection with their everyday activities. As technology increases productivity on the job, people reduce their working hours in favour of more leisure time, but they also translate part of the increased productivity into a higher standard of living. These responses may be attractive partly because they leave accustomed patterns of time use more or less intact.

The most important factor differentiating time use among study sites in the Multinational study is the variation in the proportion of women who are employed and those who are full-time housewives. In the mid-1960s Eastern European women devoted considerably more time to market work than did Western European or American women. When intercountry comparisons are made separately for men, employed women and housewives, the similarities in time use are even more pronounced.

Some broad limits on time use are set by biological factors. All people need a certain amount of sleep and recreation, they require similar amounts of time to eat, and they seldom work more than 50 hours per week over a period of time. Another element of uniformity in time use derives from the fact that many jobs require a full-time or at least half-time commitment. Another apparent uniformity in time use arises from the fact that work may be paced to fill the available time. No matter what the occupation − farmer, housewife, vendor, cobbler − variations in workload are sometimes accommodated by adjusting the intensity of work.

Norms regarding time use may be reinforced by the fact that people become used to routines in their daily lives which they are reluctant to disrupt. It is convenient to have a time schedule similar to one's friends and neighbours. Rational decision-making involves a careful weighing of alternatives and a responsiveness to changes in the environment; that is, it requires thought and effort. Therefore, people may respond only to fairly large or continuing changes, and their response may be delayed. Economists have observed lags in the adjustment of consumer expenditures to changing income, and a similar phenomenon may affect the response of time use to changing economic incentives or technology.

In the very short run, say one to three days, people are prepared to make adjustments in time use that are not feasible in the longer run. For example, when a crop has to be harvested, much of the housework that normally occupies a woman may be postponed. When relatives come to visit from a distance, a man may put off his agricultural work for a few days. Time-use data relating to a single day, or to a very small number of days, may reflect very temporary adjustments in time use to an undesirable extent. This problem may be bothersome when micro-level analysis is used to investigate trade-offs in time use.

In the intermediate run, a family may accommodate itself gradually to changes in economic incentives, in technology, or in its own demographic characteristics. This is the time span during which the lags and rigidities discussed earlier may be operative.

In the long run, some of the factors that are exogenous in the short run become endogenous. This is particularly true of the demographic factors that the household may affect through contraceptive use, migration, age of marriage of children, the amount of care given infants and pregnant mothers, the decision to form a nuclear or extended family, etc. As we shall see, the number of babies a mother needs to care for over her reproductive life has a large impact on her time use, and this number is of course amenable to some control. Family size also has an important influence on income relative to needs, which is one of the determinants of female labour force participation. In the short run, the income-earning capacity of the husband and other family members is a given; in the long run, it may be modified via decisions to save and invest, to adopt innovations, to start a new business, to take advantage of new training opportunities or to migrate.

These demographic and economic changes may be made in part in order to achieve a more satisfactory allocation of time. It is hardly plausible that families in developing countries make long-range plans that determine their allocation of time, family size and consumption for the rest of their lives. To assume such long-term planning horizons would be unrealistic, given the uncertainties and the degree of social and economic change that characterize developing countries. However, it appears plausible that when couples consider whether to have an additional child, the time-use and economic implications of that decision will be considered jointly. Thus, in the long run, time allocation, demographic and economic decisions may be viewed as being simultaneously determined, and as being subject to certain common exogenous influences.

To the best of my knowledge, the available large-scale time-use studies have not dealt with problems of causality. The data have been analyzed as if demographic and economic factors were exogenously determined and time use was the dependent variable. As research findings from these studies are examined in the next three sections, it must be kept in mind that associations between time use and other variables do not imply causality.

## Education as a Determinant of Time Use

The intra-household allocation of time may be viewed as the outcome of two decisions: (i) the decision as to how total household time should be divided among market work, household tasks, child-care and leisure, and also among subcategories of these major time uses; and (ii) the decision as to how members of the family should allocate the planned work and leisure among themselves. While the actual planning of time use may involve these two decisions, they are not entirely distinct. The capabilities and preferences of individual family members may affect total time allocation by the household; conversely, the family's overall goals and needs may modify individual time-use decisions. For purposes of data analysis, however, the two decisions are quite distinct. If time-use data have been collected for every member of the household, time spent on various activities can be added across household members. Household time use can then be treated as the dependent variable and its determinants analyzed. There are only one or two instances in the literature where this has been done. The alternative is to focus on individual time use. In that case, the time allocated by individuals to various time-use categories is the dependent variable, and the characteristics of individuals and the family of which they are part are treated as the determinants of time use. Since this has been the more common approach, it will dominate the discussion that follows.

Most of the available information on the effect of education on time use pertains to Europe and the United States. Parallel data for developing countries are sparse. Moreover, these data often do not show any significant influence of education on time use; or they show relationships that vary from country to country. This section will summarize some of the more consistent findings and discuss their interpretation.

Quite consistently, the amount of time that women devote to housework decreases with education, while leisure time increases. The decrease in housework time with education is evident for most countries included in the Multinational study, in a later United States study (Stafford and Duncan, 1977), and in data for Laguna Province in the Philippines.[5] It holds for most household tasks, except child-care.

Leibowitz (1972) and Hill and Stafford (1974) found that, in the United States, education increases the time women spend with their children. Supporting evidence is also available in a study based on time use in two Polish towns.[6] The Laguna and Malaysia studies, on the other hand, do not reveal a significant relationship between child-care time and education.[7]

The Laguna study shows that leisure time rises with education, as do the Polish and United States studies. The latter distinguish between active and passive leisure pursuits. Active pursuits include reading and other educational activities, cultural activities, active sports, participation in meetings and organizations, social activities outside the home; time spent on these increases with education. Passive pursuits include resting, talking, and watching TV; they occupy less time as education increases. United States data also show that sleeping time declines with education.

Time spent on market work may be positively or negatively related to education, depending on the characteristics of the labour market and on the way in which the data are analyzed. For example, in two Polish towns where almost all women are in the labour force, hours of market work decline slightly with education for both men and women. The reason is that working hours seem to be somewhat shorter in white-collar occupations – in which the more educated workers are engaged – than in blue-collar occupations. By contrast, the market time of United States women rises with education. For one thing, female labour force participation increases with education; for another, the more educated women appear to be motivated to spend somewhat longer hours on the job when they do work than do less educated women. The Laguna study shows that increased education has little or no effect on market time of married women. The Botswana data do not disclose a significant relation between education and market work for men or women.[8]

According to the Economic Theory of Fertility, work time should increase with education, and non-market time should decrease, because the greater productivity and wages of the more educated would lead them to add to work time at the expense of non-market activities (this substitution effect would presumably outweigh the opposite income effect). The weak and inconsistent results regarding the relation between market time and education are due in part to the multivariate analysis employed. When education and wages are regressed on work time in the same equation, the partial effect of education appears small, because wages also reflect education. The education effect is further diminished when other variables related to education are taken into account – for example, whether or not the household is engaged in farming.

A number of explanations have been offered for the decrease in women's housework time with education. The more educated may perform housework more efficiently, or they may have more labour-saving household appliances; they are more likely to have servants; they tend to have a less traditional family organization, which implies that the husband is less reluctant to help with housework; they are more likely to eat in restaurants and use other outside services (for laundry, repairs, etc.). Finally, educated women may be motivated to shorten household tasks in order to have more time for active leisure activities. The less educated, on the other hand, may take some of their more passive leisure time in the form of lower work intensity. That is, they may intersperse their housework with occasional rest breaks, talking, listening to the radio, or watching TV while working. In this case, their reported housework time might be inflated and their leisure time underestimated.

As was noted earlier, the more educated do not shorten their child-care time. Indeed, in some cultures, they spend more time with their children than the less educated. Nevertheless, the motivation to reserve time for active leisure pursuits may lead the more educated to opt for fewer children. That is, having children around may be more compatible with the passive use of leisure time than with the leisure-time patterns of the more educated. A good deal of attention has been paid in the literature to the compatibility between work activities and child-care. It would be worthwhile to explore the hypothesis that fertility is also affected by the compatibility between a woman's (or couple's) leisure-time preferences and child-care. People who like to read, engage in cultural activities, go to movies and restaurants, participate in meetings of organizations, or attend social events outside the home may find child-care more burdensome than those who have other tastes.

## Demographic Determinants of Time Use

### Sex

Each culture, religion and political ideology has some explicit or implicit rules defining activities appropriate for men and those appro-priate for women. In some cultures, women are strictly confined to domestic tasks; in others, a limited economic role is appropriate; and in still others, active participation in the political and economic life of the country is encouraged. Cultures differ not only in the extent to which they assign familial and non-familial roles to women but in the degree of choice a woman has in selecting or combining various roles. The sexual division of labour does not necessarily correspond to differ-ences in physical strength. For example, in India women do very heavy work on construction sites (such as carrying wet cement) and in Nepal they carry heavy loads on their backs over long distances. In rural Africa, crop growing seems to be for the most part the responsibility of women, while animal husbandry is largely the responsibility of men (and boys). The reverse pattern prevails in Guatemala and other Latin American countries.

Alexander Szalai (1975) refers to evidence regarding the sexual division of labour as one of the most striking findings emerging from the Multinational study. Almost everywhere men spend more time on income-earning activities than women, although in Eastern Europe female labour force participation is very high. Men do much less house-work than women, whether their wives are in the labour force or not. Child-rearing is also largely the duty of women. Eastern European men do slightly more housework than men in Western Europe, the United States or Lima, Peru; but the geographic variations are small compared with the sex differences, even if men are compared only with working women. When men do participate in housework, they tend to help with shopping and errands, gardening, outdoor cleaning, occasional repairs, and other fairly diversified activities which do not bind them closely to the house. Men's involvement in child-care revolves largely around the older children. The division of labour by sex is also pronounced in such diverse developing countries as Java, Botswana and Bangladesh.[9]

In developing countries, a division of labour by sex may also be found among children. We know that role perception and attitudes are formed early in life. If little girls help only with housework and child-care, and little boys only with market work, sex-role stereotypes are acquired at an impressionable age. When children find early in life that the kinds of market work boys and girls do are quite different, occupational segregation by sex is bound to be viewed as a normal state of affairs during adulthood.

Descriptive data on time use of children by age and sex is available for the village of Char Gopalpur in Bangladesh, and for Botswana, Java and Nepal. The division of labour by sex among young children is particularly striking in Bangladesh and Botswana. Cain (1977) read to respondents in Bangladesh a long list of household activities and for each activity asked whether it had ever been performed by unmarried sons and daughters aged 4 and older. The only income-earning activity in which daughters participate more often than sons is 'tending fowl'. Two other activities seem to be shared equally: 'harvesting chillies' and 'tending goats'. The remaining 22 income-earning activities are reported very infrequently by girls, although they are commonly reported by boys. For example, only 2 per cent of unmarried daughters ever helped with weeding, paddy transplanting or harvesting, while 31-51 per cent of sons engaged in this work. The activity codes in the Botswana study are broader. It appears that boys under the age of 15 assume a major responsibility for herding animals; girls spend a considerable amount of time assisting with child-care and housework.

The existence of sexual dualism in labour markets is more important than the particular division of labour that prevails in a country. Segmented labour markets make it possible to pay lower wages to women than men (relative to productivity). In most developing countries, women's wages for unskilled labour are 40-70 per cent of men's wages. Also, women tend to be assigned jobs that use relatively little capital equipment, which diminishes their productivity. A low female-to-male wage ratio may be expected to diminish female labour force participation and to reduce the opportunity cost of child-care. Thus the sexual division of labour has a positive effect on fertility.

However, it is an open question how significant this influence is. Low birth rates coexisted in Western and Eastern Europe with a pronounced differentiation in sex roles, as measured by time use in the mid-1960s, when the Multinational study was conducted. The proposition that fertility will decline in developing countries only 'when sex role socialization is no longer clear-cut, unambiguous, and universal',[10] seems too extreme.

## Age of Children

The major, available time-use studies agree in showing that age of the youngest child is one of the most important determinants of women's time allocation. In the countries covered by the Multinational study, child-care time averages 1¼ hours per day for employed women with children and over 2 hours for housewives with children, counting only time in which child-care is a primary activity (Stone, 1972). The time inputs are increased by roughly 50 per cent when account is taken of time spent on child supervision as a secondary activity, occurring as housework is being done. Young children (defined as 3 years of age or less) are much more time-consuming than older children. Across the 15 survey sites a rather strong correlation is reported between the proportion of households with children aged 3 or less and time devoted to child-care. Housewives spend about one-third more time in the presence (not necessarily in active care) of an only child under the age of 3 than in the presence of an only child over the age of 3. The corresponding increase for working women is about one-seventh (Stone,

1972). Fathers make only a very minor contribution to the care of very young children. Time contributions by children in the household were not measured in the Multinational study.

Elizabeth King (1976) studied time use in 99 households in Laguna Province in the Philippines. The time allocation was actually observed; so the accuracy of her data must be high, even though the sample is small. Market time, household time (a combination of housework and child-care) and leisure time are the dependent variables in three parallel regressions that reveal the trade-off between these major time uses for mothers and fathers. She finds that the presence of an infant increases the mother's household time by nearly 3 hours per day. This large amount of time seems to be set aside almost totally at the expense of leisure time, which is reduced by more than 2 hours per day when there is an infant in the household. Children between the ages of 1 and 6 also increase the mother's household time, but by less than an hour per day. Still older children tend to relieve the mother of some household and child-care duties, and permit her to increase her market work correspondingly; but these later effects are not statistically significant.

Bryan Boulier (1976) performs a similar analysis for Laguna Province, based on retrospective time-use data for a larger sample of households (573 cases). His results pertaining to the impact of infants and young children on mother's time use are quite similar to King's. They underline once again the substantial time commitment entailed by the birth of a baby. Unlike King, however, Boulier finds that the mother's market work, not merely her leisure, is reduced by an infant in the household. Children between the ages of 1 and 6 make significantly smaller demands on the mother's time, and this time is provided by cutting down on leisure.

Preliminary findings of the Malaysia study confirm some of the findings of the Multinational and the Laguna studies. DaVanzo and Lee (1978) report that age of children is the most important determinant of child-care time, as well as of total time required for household services. An infant increases total household hours spent on child-care by about 4½ hours per day and other housework by about 25 minutes. Two- to five-year-olds add less than half that much time and 6- to 10-year-olds about a quarter. The general consistency of these findings is more important than the discrepancies between studies in hours added per additional child. These discrepancies probably result in part from different analysis methods and, more importantly, from differences in measurement. Since child-care is often a secondary time use, the data are likely to be sensitive to definitions and methods underlying data collection.

*Number of Children*

These same studies also provide some information on the impact of number of children on parents' time use. In the areas covered by the Multinational study, large families (4 or more children) were rare and hence are represented by a small number of cases. Thus a 'large family' is typically one with 2 or 3 children. The data indicate that in Europe and the United States, women who have several children spend roughly the same total amount of time on child-care activities as women who have only one child over the age of 3, but their husbands record slightly more child-care time. In some study areas, time devoted to housework increases by a small margin in households with 2-3 children over smaller households; in others it decreases slightly. Overall, time spent on housework by mothers and fathers appears to be quite insensitive to family size (Stone, 1972). This finding may be viewed as an indication that there is a quality-quantity trade-off in household tasks, allowing women whose household duties are expanded by growing family size to reduce the quality of household services or to increase their work intensity so as to keep total household time fairly constant. Also, in larger families, children may do some housework, thus supplementing the mother's time input. As mentioned earlier, the Multinational study did not include children in the survey population.

In developing countries, children spend less time in school than children in Europe and the United States. Hence, they are in a better position to relieve possible time pressure on parents created by large family size. For Laguna Province, Boulier (1976) finds that the number of children (holding age of youngest child constant) does not affect the father's time allocation appreciably. As the number of children increases, there is a small increase in market work by mothers and a corresponding decrease in housework and child-care time. Presumably this shift reflects a growing need for family income and the presence of older children who can assume some child-care and other household responsibilities. Boulier also reports that a baby adds considerably more to the mother's child-care time in families with 1 to 3 children than in families with 4 or more children. This finding again suggests that in larger families some help from siblings supplements the mother's child-care time. (Boulier did not analyze the determinants of children's time use.) There may also be economies of scale in caring for children. And there may be a diminishing marginal rate of substitution between child services and leisure or consumer goods.

King (1976) and Quizon and Evenson (1978) report that in Laguna Province leisure time of both mother and father increases with number of children. They attribute this finding to the substitution of older children for parents in market work and in the household. DaVanzo and Lee (1978) obtain somewhat different results for Malaysia. They state that 'although other family members help in large families, and the wife's share of total hours is less in such instances, the number of hours that she devotes to non-market production is generally positively related to family size'.

Although these findings are not consistent, they warrant some tentative inferences. The first is that number of children influences household time requirements less than does age of youngest child. The second is that in developing countries, help from older children alleviates the demands which large family size makes on parent's income-earning and home obligations.

## The Trade-Off Between Home Time, Market Work and Leisure

In addition to analyzing the determinants of each separate component in the household's time budget, it is instructive to analyze substitution patterns among components and among household members. When another baby is born, or when a woman decides to allocate more time to market work, other time uses must be curtailed. There has been a presumption in the recent literature that child-care and market work are the major trade-offs a woman faces. Time-budget data call attention to the fact that a variety of other adjustments are possible. Women who enter the labour force may choose to give up leisure, economize on housework time, or devote less care to older children. And, in addition, the husband and children may change their time uses in order that the household as a whole may achieve an optimal consumption balance (including consumption of leisure and household and child services).

In ordinary consumption analysis, economists postulate that necessities have an inelastic demand, while discretionary consumption is more responsive to changes in prices and income. By parallel reasoning, inflexible time uses may represent essential or minimal demands for income, leisure or household services, while more flexible uses may have lower priority in the time budget. For example, if the addition of an infant reduces leisure among a group of women but has little impact on the mothers' market work, it would appear that, at the margin, the utility of an hour spent on earning income is greater than the utility of another hour of leisure.[11] Identification of such trade-off patterns so far has not been a major focus of attention in the analysis of time-budget data. We shall explore the available evidence, such as it is.

The Multinational study allows comparisons of average time use for women who are employed and those who are full-time housewives. Across the survey sites the demand for leisure and sleep seems to be fairly inelastic. Working women show a reduction in leisure and sleep of only about one hour per day. Most of their market work is carried out at the expense of the housework. They report about half as much housework time as housewives with the same number of children, suggesting that housework has a quality component that allows for considerable flexibility in time inputs. Husbands in Eastern Europe and hired household help in Western Europe make up for some of the housework time foregone by working mothers (Robinson, Converse and Szalai, 1972). (Since the Multinational study did not collect data on time use by children, we cannot tell how far children assume responsibility for household tasks for which employed mothers are too busy.)

Child-care time is also severely curtailed when mothers are employed. In Eastern Europe, working women spend only about 60 to 63 per cent as much time on child-care activities as housewives. In the West, the corresponding figures are 52 per cent for employed mothers with children 3 years of age or under, and 65-70 per cent for employed mothers with older children only. If time spent in the presence of children is compared, rather than child-care time specifically, across all survey sites employed women spent 56 per cent as much time with a single child 3 years old or under as did housewives, 67 per cent as much time with a single child over 3 years old, and 64 per cent as much time with multiple children (Stone, 1972). Thus, the data for Europe and the United States bears out the assumptions of the Economic Theory of Fertility that there is a high rate of substitution between market work and child-care time.

Data for developing countries point to a different pattern, although the evidence is too meagre and inconsistent for firm conclusions. Tentatively, it appears that leisure may be a rather flexible component of mother's time budgets in developing countries, with the result that leisure is reduced very significantly whenever market work or child-care demand a lot of time. Quizon and Evenson (1978) present data for Laguna Province that show amounts of time spent on various activities as mother's market work increases from 0 to more than 6 hours. At least half of the mother's working time is balanced by a reduction in leisure, roughly one-quarter by reduction in housework, and one-quarter by reduction in child-care.

An interesting feature of DaVanzo and Lee's work (1978) is that the mother's hours of market work are introduced as an explanatory variable in the regressions explaining amount of time spend on household tasks and child-care. There is clear evidence of intra-family substitution. Husbands, and to a greater extent children, spend more hours in household activities, the more hours the wife allocates to market activities. The wife's household time is reduced progressively as she extends her market activities, but not sufficiently to protect her leisure time. No analysis of the effect of demographic characteristics of the household on hours of leisure has come out of the Malaysia study so far.

It is also instructive to see how women in developing countries free time for the extra child-care required when there is a baby in the household. Quizon and Evenson (1978) show that the additional three hours mothers with infants devote to child-care impinge on both market work and leisure, leisure being more strongly affected than market work. Boulier's analysis of the Laguna data (1976) also indicates that both market work and leisure time are reduced substantially under these circumstances, with leisure time declining more than market work; housework increases slightly. The decrease in the mother's market work when there is a baby in the household is accompanied by a smaller increase in the father's market work. Since the father probably earns more per hour, income may be maintained at roughly the same level. The increase in the father's work time is achieved at the expense of leisure. Data on time use in rural Botswana show a minimal reduction in working time for women aged 20-39 when the household includes a child aged 0 to 1, while leisure time suffers to a greater extent. Thus, it may be inferred that in developing countries demands for income and household services are inelastic, while leisure is the more elastic element in the time budget. This would not be surprising, since an additional child raises the need for income and household services. However, when child-care time reduces leisure rather than market work, the cost of that time is more difficult to assess, especially where women's employment opportunities are quite limited.

These findings are suggestive, but they relate to only three rural areas in the developing world and cannot be used for general conclusions. It is to be hoped that future research will throw light on two questions: (i) under what conditions is leisure time more elastic than market work, and under what conditions is the reverse situation to be found?; (ii) to what extent is the flexibility of leisure time a short-run phenomenon rather than a long-term adjustment?

## The Compatibility of Child-care and Market Work

The literature on the relationship between female labour force participation and fertility contains evidence that, when market work and
child-care are compatible, employment of the mother need not restrict
fertility or vice versa.[12] Child-rearing and employment may be compatible (i) when market work can be performed at or near home; (ii)
when small children can be taken to work; (iii) when relatives or older
siblings are available to care for preschool children; and (iv) when the
household can afford servants. All of these conditions are much
more likely to be fulfilled in low-income countries than industrialized
countries.

In most of the earlier studies rather indirect measures of compatibility have been used. A frequent assumption has been that work in
agriculture and other jobs in the traditional sector, especially work at
or near home, are compatible with child-care, while modern sector
jobs are not. The implication is that female employment in the traditional sector may not be a constraint on fertility; it may even increase
fertility because it improves the family's ability to support children.

DaVanzo and Lee's work (1978) illustrates the potential of time-use
studies for the measurement of compatibility. Women and men in the
Malaysia study were asked the following questions for each activity in
which they had engaged during the previous 4 months: 'Were any of
your children 10 years old or younger normally with you when you did
—— (activity)? By "normally" I mean half the time or more.' If
'yes', prompt: 'How many under 2 years? How many 2-5 years? How
many 6-10 years?'

These data make it possible to calculate the attractiveness of seven
occupations for women with children aged 10 or younger and women
with older children only. The percentage of women in each occupation whose children aged 10 or younger accompany them to work is also
calculated. Professional, managerial and clerical occupations employ
a much lower proportion of women with young children (i.e., aged
10 or younger) than sales, service, agriculture and production occupations. A somewhat unexpected finding is that agricultural activities
appear to be less compatible with child-care than sales or production
occupations. 'Nearly 50 percent of women who have sales or production occupations and have children aged 10 or less take (some of) these
children with them when they work, as compared to 24 percent of such
women for agricultural activities and 22 percent for service activities.
Very few women engaging in other market occupations take their
children along.' (DaVanzo and Lee, 1978, p. 32).

DaVanzo and Lee also attempt to examine another aspect of compatibility: the impact of the presence of children on the mother's efficiency in performing her work. Women whose children were with them while they performed market work spent less time on market activities than other women with the same number and age distribution of children. On the other hand, women whose children were present while they engaged in household tasks took longer to complete these tasks. DaVanzo and Lee's interpretation of these results is that women are less productive in market work when children have to be watched, with the result that some redistribution of time towards other activities becomes advantageous. In the case of basic household services, they see inelasticity of demand as a decisive factor, so that lesser efficiency leads to a greater allocation of time to these services. These findings suggest that data on the whereabouts of children during the days for which time use is being studied can add an interesting dimension to time-use analysis.

## Servants and Relatives in the Household

A number of studies have found that the presence of servants or non-working relatives in the household reduces the mother's time spent on housework and child-care, and increases her market work. This finding is hardly surprising. In the Multinational study, it is shown that women's housework time (excluding child-care) is reduced by about 20-30 per cent in all but two of the 15 survey sites when house help is employed (Robinson *et al.*, 1972). A number of studies have found a negative relationship between the wage rate of domestic servants and fertility.[13] Presumably cheap household help reduces the cost of children, alleviates the conflict between market work and child-care, and thus raises fertility. DaVanzo and Lee find that, in Malaysia, availability of servants or relatives increases total child-care time substantially, but reduces the mother's share, enabling her to spend more time working away from home. Boulier's analysis (1976) indicates that help by 'others' increases mothers' and fathers' child-care time. This occurs primarily at the expense of housework time, which presumably is shifted to 'others'. Fathers also work a little more and enjoy less leisure, perhaps because they have to support some of the 'others'. However, none of these effects in the Laguna study are statistically significant.

## Time Use by Children

Time use by children is of interest for several reasons. The first is concern with the quality of care given infants and young children. The available data leave little doubt that in developing countries children assume a large part of the child-care responsibilities. Although an adult may be nearby, the baby receives little direct adult attention. Moreover, in some countries, this seems to be regarded as appropriate work for very young children (6-9 year olds). One hears villagers say that children of that age are too immature to start school, yet they provide care for their younger siblings. The data for Botswana and Nepal suggest that children under the age of 10 devote more time to child-care than children aged 10-19. In Java, child supervision seems to be divided about equally between siblings under and over the age of 10 (aside from the time input of adults). Psychologists believe that the rate of mental development is influenced by the amount of time children spend with adults. Health problems may also be poorly handled when a child aged 9 or under watches younger brothers and sisters. This is quite apart from the obvious fact that breast-feeding depends on the presence of the mother.[14]

A second reason to look at children's time use is that it is a logical complement to the analysis of adult's time use. Time substitution between adults and children is clarified when parallel multiple regressions are available for mother, father and children. Aside from some preliminary analysis for rural Botswana, only DaVanzo and Lee (1978) have analyzed children's time use, and that analysis is limited to housework and child-care. The determinants of time spent in school, and the allocation of children's time to market work and leisure are of great interest as well (Clark, 1979). Ruth Dixon (1976) believes that time use by girls, especially their income-earning activities, affects age at marriage and, hence, fertility.

Data on children's time budgets are also of interest because they can throw light on the value of children. Economists believe that the economic value of children has a bearing on fertility, even if the major motives for having children are noneconomic. Contributions by children to market work and child services are a major component of the economic benefit that is derived from children. Without time-use data, estimates of these benefits for children at various ages are quite uncertain (Mueller, 1976).

## Economic Determinants of Time Use

The economic determinants of time use fall into three categories: income effects, price effects and asset effects. As income rises, people can afford more of the amenities of life. These may include, besides consumer goods and services, leisure, household services, children, education and servants. For women who do heavy, menial or tedious market work, an increase in household income (from sources other than their own earnings) should lead to a reduction in income-earning activities and an increase in housework time, child-care time and/or leisure time. On the other hand, as employment conditions for women improve, some women may come to prefer market work to house-work and child-care, especially those who are well-educated. The family may prefer more purchased consumer goods and services to internally produced household services, children or leisure. The increased income may be used to relieve children of market work, so that they may obtain a better education. Increased income may also be used to hire household help, enabling the mother to work without sacrificing leisure. For all these reasons, women may devote more time to income-earning activities as income increases.

A good case can be made for the idea that 'income relative to needs' is a more meaningful determinant of time use than 'total household income'. Income relative to needs may be measured by *per capita* income, or, better still, by income per consumption unit (a measure that recognizes that the support of children requires fewer resources than the support of adults). A number of studies show that female labour force participation increases with number of children.[15] This finding seems to reflect, at least in part, a decline in income relative to need which exerts pressure on mothers to earn income.

Price effects manifest themselves through wage rates (or earnings) per unit of time. The higher a person's wage rate, the more consumer goods and services he or she has to give up in order to gain time for housework, child care or leisure. Assuming utility maximization, we would expect household members' working time to be positively related, and other time uses to be negatively related, to their wages or productivity. We would also expect that the higher the ratio of male-to-female wage rates, the more advantageous it is for males to earn the household income and for women to specialize in housework and child-care. A sharp division of market work by sex, which seg-ments labour markets and lowers women's wages, would thus decrease the inducement for women to do market work.

In empirical work, price and income effects cannot be readily separated. The higher a person's wage rate, the greater should be his or her inducement to work long hours, but the income effect is expected to work in the opposite direction. Thus the net effect is not predictable *a priori* and may be small. A number of papers based on the Laguna study have employed multivariate techniques to examine the effects of mothers' and fathers' wages on time allocation. These papers are based on different samples, relate to different time periods and use different explanatory variables. Thus it is not altogether surprising that results vary from paper to paper. The most consistent finding is that husbands' market work increases as their own wage rates rise. In consequence, time spent on housework and leisure decreases. Since men spend little time on housework and child-care in the first place, leisure is curtailed more than household time. Wives' market wages do not have a significant effect on husbands' time allocation, except perhaps in non-farm households, where a higher wage earned by the wife may reduce husbands' market and household work in favour of leisure (Quizon and Evenson, 1978). A rise in wives' wage rates seems to induce them to shift time from market work to leisure, child-care and household activities. That is, the income effect seems to outweigh the price effect. However, this result does not emerge consistently. There is no evidence of a significant effect of husbands' wages on wives' market time.

DaVanzo and Lee (1978) find that an increase in wives' or husbands' wage rates leads to a transfer of child-care to 'others' (servants and relatives), and a decrease in child-care time by mothers, fathers and siblings. A similar pattern seems to prevail for housework. That is, increased income is used to free the family of some of its child-rearing and household obligations.

The Laguna analysis also includes some measures of asset holdings, distinguishing between productive assets (farm animals, land and equipment) and consumer assets (housing and consumer durables). Access to farm capital should increase the productivity of labour on the farm and thus make it more advantageous to work longer hours. However, assets may also be a measure of permanent income, and the income effect should work in the opposite direction to the productivity effect of assets. Husbands' market time is in fact positively related to productive asset holdings, but wives' market time is not (Boulier, 1976; Quizon and Evenson, 1978). (Her work may utilize the assets to a lesser extent.) Boulier finds that consumer assets increase the mother's time allocation to housework and reduce child-care and leisure time. The New Home Economics would explain this finding by arguing that consumer assets increase the mother's productivity in housework relative to other time uses. Yet the fact that consumer assets include consumer durables, which may be labour saving, throws some doubt on this explanation. An alternative explanation is that ownership of consumer assets reflects a taste for high-quality household services. In any case the influence of both asset variables on time use is too weak to be statistically significant.

In all, the available studies do not as yet yield much insight into the way in which economic factors influence time use. The somewhat disappointing nature of these results may have a number of conceptual and methodological reasons which are worth considering. First, it is clear that the effects of economic factors on time use are quite complex and that these effects may be small, because price and income effects tend to be partially offsetting. The time-use analysis of the Laguna and Malaysia studies has not yet progressed very far. Further analysis may produce more consistent and statistically significant findings. A second problem is that in micro-level studies, differences in earnings rates reflect, among other things, differences in education and ownership of productive assets between families. As noted earlier, when wage rates are used in regressions with these two variables, the influence of wage rates may be diluted. Third, there is a serious question as to how earnings rates should be measured for people who are not wage earners, but who work jointly with other family members in a family enterprise. There is also the question of how wages should be imputed for people who are not in the labour force.[16] Fourth, Quizon and Evenson (1978) suggest that there may be 'leisure sharing' — that is, husbands and wives may strive to have similar amounts of leisure time, presumably for common pursuits — a phenomenon that has not been considered previously in the literature. To the extent that this phenomenon exists, it may prevent changes in husband's wage rate relative to wife's wage rate from having the expected impact on market work. Finally, it is relevant to remind the reader of the earlier discussion of rigidities in time use and possible lags in the adjustment of time use to changing circumstances.

## Some Conclusions and Hypotheses

The Economic Theory of Fertility stresses the trade-off between market work and child-rearing. It assumes that when child-rearing time is increased, market work is likely to be reduced and vice versa. Thus, foregone earnings from market work are viewed as an important cost of having many children. The implication is that higher wages for women, more education for women (if it raises earning capacity) and an improvement in the demand for female labour may be policy instruments for reducing fertility. A review of the research on this subject does not indicate that these ideas are wrong, but it suggests that the explanations are too incomplete to be readily applicable to developing countries.

Our review of time-use research confirms that children are indeed time-consuming (or time-intensive), as the theory postulates. Yet *child-rearing need not interfere with market work*. One reason is that relatives, servants and older children with time to help the mother are more likely to be found in developing countries than in modern industrial countries. Second, many of the traditional jobs in which women in developing countries are engaged are compatible with child care; that is, they allow the mother to watch her children while she works, and sometimes to take breaks to breast-feed a baby or prepare a meal for older children. Additional time-use studies are needed to show which occupations are most compatible with child-care, which are less so, and how working time is affected by the presence of children. If income data were also collected, the effect of the presence of children on earnings could be determined. Earnings may be depressed, both because work that is compatible tends to be less remunerative[17] and because the work pace may be slowed by the presence of children.

The review of time-use studies in this chapter further leads to the hypothesis that women in developing countries often find time to care for babies and small children by cutting down on leisure and housework. The flexibility in leisure and housework time evident in time-use data suggests that, for at least some of these women, time is not a very scarce resource. Thus their market work and earnings may be reduced only to a small extent by the arrival of another child. This observation is based on time-use studies of rural women whose work time is much more divisible than the work time of women who are employed in the modern sector.

Still another reason why women's potential earnings should not necessarily be viewed as a cost of raising children is that there is a pervasive underemployment problem in many developing countries. Where this is the case, women may not perceive more market work as a realistic alternative to more children. To be sure, labour demand varies from country to country, and very poor women may spend long hours doing hard, tedious and low-paying work. However, in households somewhat above the subsistence level, women may be reluctant to do more market work if the only available work is tiring, demeaning and has low productivity. In some countries, it is important for the family's social status that women abstain from market work or that they limit their work to certain socially approved activities. As long as opportunities for women in the labour market are confined to jobs which have a high disutility and low productivity, couples will not perceive market work as an attractive alternative to child-rearing.

Finally, it is necessary to realize that market work is not the only activity that might compete successfully with child-care for women's time. Although this subject has not been investigated specifically, there are some tentative indications in time-use studies conducted in middle-income countries that active leisure-time pursuits are less compatible with child-rearing than passive ones. If women have an opportunity to form organizations of their own, join other formal groups, use their leisure time to enhance their knowledge and skills, or to participate in entertainment and cultural activities outside the home, a desire for time free of child-care responsibilities may emerge.

In brief, while people in all cultures strive to improve their standard of living, they also strive to fill their lives with activities — work and leisure — that are meaningful to them and are appreciated by others. Raising children is such an activity, and women will be reluctant to allocate less time to it unless alternative uses of their time are satisfying. We conclude, therefore, by returning to an emphasis on intervening variables, such as characteristics of the market for female labour, tastes, social attitudes towards women's roles and familial values. These variables determine the meaning for women of labour force participation, and, hence, influence its effect on fertility. Future research should give attention to the measurement of these intervening variables.

## Notes

1. The term 'market work' is used in this chapter synonymously with income-earning activities, regardless of whether people are paid in money or in kind. Market work also includes unpaid family labour.
2. See, for example, Becker (1965); Willis (1973); Gronau (1973); and Schultz (1974).
3. See Szalai, Converse, Feldheim, Scheuch and Stone (1972).
4. These similarities are described in Robinson, Converse and Szalai (1975)
5. The Laguna study is based on interviews with 573 households in Laguna Province, Philippines in 1975-6, and there was a resurvey in 1977. For a description of the survey see Jayme-Ho (1976, pp. 19-34).
6. See Strzeminska (1972).
7. The Malaysia study is based on a sample of 1,262 households interviewed in 1976-7. See Butz, Da Vanzo, Fernandez, Jones and Spoestra (1978).
8. The Botswana study was conducted in 1974 by the Central Statistical Office of the Government of Botswana; the sample includes about 1,060

households.

9. See Bond (1974); Nag, White and Pzet (1978); Kossoudji and Mueller (1979); see also Cain (1977).

10. See Safilios-Rothschild (1978, p. 2).

11. This statement assumes that the marginal utilities of the last unit of time are *not necessarily* equal. That is, it assumes that the choice functions for the allocation of time *may* be discontinuous (as when there are indivisibilities in units of market work time, or when an additional unit of market work would have much lower utility than the previous unit because it requires heavy labour, or a long journey to work, or pays less).

12. See, for example, Jaffe and Azumi (1960); Stycos and Weller (1967).

13. See McCabe and Rosenzweig (1976, p. 345); see also Cain and Weininger (1973); and Wilkinson (1973).

14. See Popkin (1978).

15. See references cited by Standing (1978, pp. 192-205).

16. Boulier (1976) as well as DaVanzo and Lee (1978) set the latter wage rates equal to zero in their 'preliminary' analysis.

17. See Merrick and Schmink (1978).

# References

Becker, G. (1965) 'A theory of the allocation of time', *Economic Journal* (September), pp. 493-517

Bond, C.A. (1974) 'Women's involvement in agriculture in Botswana', mimeo., Gabarone, Botswana

Boulier, B. (1976) 'Children and household economic activity in Laguna, Philippines', discussion paper no. 76-19, Institute of Economic Development and Research, University of the Philippines

Butz, W., J. DaVanzo, D. Fernandez, R. Jones and N. Spoestra (1978) *The Malaysia family life survey: questionnaire and interview instructions*, Santa Monica, The Rand Corporation; WN-10147-AID

Cain, G. and A. Weininger (1973) 'Economic determinants of fertility: results from cross-sectional aggregate data', *Demography* (May), pp. 205-23

Cain, M. (1977) 'The economic activities of children in a village in Bangladesh', *Population and Development Review* (September)

Clark, C. (1979) 'Relation of economic and demographic factors to household decisions regarding education of children in Guatemala', PhD dissertation, University of Michigan

DaVanzo, J. and D. Lee (1978) 'The incompatibility of child care with labor force participation and non-market activities: preliminary evidence from Malaysian time budget data', paper presented at International Center for Research on Women Conference, 'Women in Poverty: What Do We Know?', Belmont, Maryland

Dixon, R.B. (1975) 'Women's rights and fertility', *Reports on population family planning*, New York, The Population Council

—— (1976) 'The roles of rural women: female seclusion, economic production, and reproductive choice' in Ronald G. Ridker (ed.), *Population and development: the search for selective interventions*, Baltimore, Johns Hopkins University Press

Gronau, R. (1973) 'The intra-family allocation of time: the value of the housewife's time', *American Economic Review* (September), pp. 634-51

Hill, C.R. and F.P. Stafford (1974) 'Allocation of time to preschool children and educational opportunity', *Journal of Human Resources, 9,* 3

Jaffe, A.J. and K. Azumi (1960) 'The birthrate and cottage industries in underdeveloped countries', *Economic Development and Cultural Change* (October)

Jayme-Ho, T. (1976) 'Time budgets of married women in rural households: Laguna', discussion paper no. 76-26, Institute of Economic Development and Research, University of the Philippines

King, E.M. (1976) 'Time allocation in Philippine rural households', discussion paper no. 76-20, Institute of Economic Development and Research, University of the Philippines

Kossoudji, S. and E. Mueller (1979) 'The economic status of female-headed households in rural Botswana', mimeo., University of Michigan

Leibowitz, A.S. (1972) 'Women's allocation of time to market and non-market activities: differences by education', PhD dissertation, Columbia University

McCabe, J.L. and M.L. Rosenzweig (1976) 'Female employment creation and family size' in Ronald G. Ridker (ed.), *Population and development: the search for selective interventions,* Baltimore, Johns Hopkins University Press

McGreevey, W.P. and N. Birdsall (1974) *The policy relevance of recent social research on fertility,* occasional monograph series no. 2, Interdisciplinary Communication Program, Washington, DC, The Smithsonian Institution

Merrick, T. and M. Schmink (1978) 'Female headed households and urban poverty in Brazil', paper presented at the International Center for Research on Women Conference, 'Women in Poverty: What Do We Know?', Belmont, Maryland

Mueller, E. (1976) 'The economic value of children in peasant agriculture,' in Ronald G. Ridker (ed.), *Population and development: the search for selective interventions,* Baltimore, Johns Hopkins University Press

Nag, M., B.F. White and R.C. Pzet (1978) 'An anthropological approach to the study of the economic value of children in Java and Nepal', *Current Anthropology* (June), pp. 293-306

Popkin, B. (1978) 'Women, work and child welfare', paper presented at International Center for Research on Women Conference, 'Women in Poverty: What Do We Know?', Belmont, Maryland

Quizon, E.K. and R.E. Evenson (1978) 'Time allocation and home production in Philippine rural households', paper presented at International Center for Research on Women Conference, 'Women in Poverty: What Do We Know?', Belmont, Maryland

Robinson, J.P., P.E. Converse and A. Szalai (1972) 'Everyday life in twelve countries', in A. Szalai, P.E. Converse, P. Feldheim, E.K. Scheuch and P.J. Stone

Safilios-Rothschild, C. (1978) 'The demographic consequences of the changing roles of men and women in the 80's', paper presented at the IUSSP Conference on Economic Demography, Helsinki

Schultz, T.W. (1974) 'Fertility and economic values', in T.W. Schultz (ed.), *Economics of the family*, Chicago, University of Chicago Press, pp. 3-22

Stafford, F. and G. Duncan (1977) 'The use of time and technology by households in the United States', mimeo., Ann Arbor, University of Michigan

Standing, G. (1978) *Labor force participation and development*, Geneva, ILO

Stone, P.J. (1972) 'Childcare in twelve countries' in A. Szalai, P.E. Converse, P. Feldheim, E.K. Scheuch and P.J. Stone

Strzeminska, H. (1972) 'Educational budgets', in A. Szalai, P.E. Converse, P. Feldheim, E.K. Scheuch and P.J. Stone

Stycos, J.M. and R. Weller (1967) 'Female working roles and fertility', *Demography, 4,* 1

Szalai, A. (1975) 'The situation of women in light of contemporary time budget research', paper presented for the World Conference of the International Women's Year, Mexico City, Doc. E/Conf. 66/BP/6
———, P.E. Converse, P. Feldheim, E.K. Scheuch and P.J. Stone (eds.) (1972) *The use of time*, The Hague, Mouton Press
Wilkinson, M. (1973) 'An econometric analysis of fertility in Sweden, 1870-1965', *Econometrica* (July), pp. 633-43
Willis, R.J. (1973) 'A new approach to the economic theory of fertility behavior', *Journal of Political Economy* (March-April), pp. 514-64

# 4 CLASS AND HISTORICAL ANALYSIS FOR THE STUDY OF WOMEN AND ECONOMIC CHANGE

Carmen Diana Deere, Jane Humphries and Magdalena León de Leal

There has been a growing awareness in recent years that Third World women have not only been excluded from development programmes, but also, in many cases, have been adversely affected by the process of capitalist development. A number of studies have argued convincingly that development policy should be responsible to women's needs, as the burdens of poverty and attendant exploitation fall disproportionately upon Third World women. However, the proposition that sexual inequality as well as poverty can be alleviated by reforms which attempt to incorporate women into the development process has not been adequately examined. In our view, analysis of the effects of development policy on women's socio-economic position requires a comprehensive theoretical and analytical framework based largely on the relationship between the sexual division of labour and the overall process of social change. The objective of this chapter is to propose such a comprehensive framework for the study of women in the Third World.

Our analysis begins with the proposition that women's position in society is based upon: (i) human reproduction (in terms of the social relations which regulate the formation of families and the bearing and rearing of children) and (ii) production (in terms of the social relations which govern the production of goods and services). The sexual division of labour emerges as an expression of women's roles in both production and reproduction.

The analysis of women's position within the Third World must also be studied in terms of the particular context of national development. In all societies, capitalist development commences with the process of primitive accumulation, that is, the separation of producers from the means of production. But for today's Third World countries the process of capitalist development is necessarily affected by their place in the international division of labour. Our task is to specify the interaction between the mode of incorporation of less developed countries into the world economy and changes in the socio-economic structure within such nations.

The chapter is organised as follows: in the next section we introduce a theoretical framework for the study of women in less developed countries by relating sexual division of labour to the national and international divisions of labour, and attempt to develop this analysis within a historical context. In the following section (pp. 92-102) we look to the relevant literature in order to develop this particular perspective. Finally, we summarize the research propositions and hypotheses derived from the theoretical framework and review of the literature, and illustrate their investigation in a research design for national-level studies of women and underdevelopment.

## The Household in Uneven Capitalist Development: Tiers of Interaction

In this section our aim is to locate the household in the wider economy in order to identify the processes that link the sexual division of labour in production with that in reproduction (see Figure 4.1).[1]

The particular socio-economic structure of the underdeveloped nation must be studied in the context of the historical development of international capitalism, since peripheral nations have been subjected to the historically specific requirements of more dominant nations in international capital accumulation. At one point in time a specific nation may serve in the world economy either as a supplier of raw materials for export or as a market for centre production. At another historical point, a nation may serve as a source of cheap labour for the production of international wage goods and simultaneously be a recipient of capital exports. These changing forms of incorporation of peripheral economies reflect not only the changing conditions of capital accumulation, but are also partially determined by the specific historical conditions of capitalist development *within* the underdeveloped countries themselves. The historical process of accumulation which generated advanced capitalist development in centre economies, then, has also served to retard development within what are now peripheral economies (Baran, 1957; Frank, 1966).

According to Amin (1976) the pattern of accumulation within peripheral economies can be characterized as one of dependency. The dynamism of the economy has largely been based on the relationship between the growth of the export sector and the capacity to import. Throughout the nineteenth century, most Third World economies focused on the export of raw materials in return for the import of consumption goods largely destined for the upper classes. In the

**Figure 4.1: Tiers of Interaction**

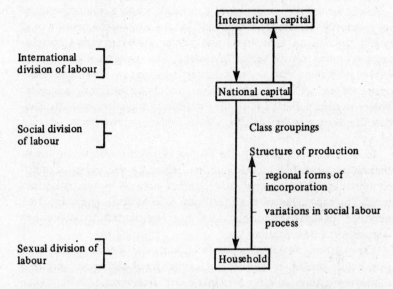

twentieth century, goods that had been imported were produced nationally and imported manufactured goods were largely replaced by the import of capital goods. This process began in Latin America in the period between the two world wars, and proceeded particularly rapidly in the post-World War II period. In many parts of Africa and Asia, however, the process began only with the attainment of national independence in the 1950s and 1960s. The salient feature of capitalist development in the post-World War II period has been the internationalization of capital. Today, foreign capital investment in the Third World is no longer confined to the primary sector, but is increasingly being channelled into manufacturing and industrial development.

The form of incorporation of peripheral economies into the world economy has been important in determining the specific socio-economic structures and class groupings in Third World economies. These, in turn, have affected regional development within nations, and this helps to account for the historical and geographic diversity in the organization of production. It should be stressed that these relationships are interactive: the national structure of production and the related specific class groupings affect the form of incorporation of that economy into the world economy just as the needs of the world economy affect the national structure of production.

The structure of production of dependent economies corresponding to externally oriented development in the nineteenth century was largely focused on agricultural and mining enclaves, with a complementary urban service sector. Internally, the agricultural and mining sectors reflected a diversity of organizational forms — from state enterprises, to capitalist farms and mines, to plantations and haciendas. These, in turn, reflected both the variation in the relations of production that were possible and the uneven degree of development of wage labour.

In the twentieth century, the process of import-substitution industrialization as well as industrialization caused by the influx of multinational capital has dramatically changed national productive structures. The separation of manufacturing from agriculture has involved increased proletarianization, which has contributed to rural-urban migration and urbanization.

Cheap labour, which allows both national and foreign capitalists to earn higher profits, is required for capital accumulation in peripheral economies (Amin, 1976; de Janvry and Garramon, 1977). Cheap labour, at productivity levels equal to those in dominant economies, also results in unequal exchange through trade between countries. And since low wages imply the availability of inexpensive food, de Janvry and Garramon identify one objective condition of underdevelopment as the need for rural areas to provide cheap labour to the export and industrial sectors as well as to the capitalist agricultural sector, and for the latter, along with the petty commodity-producing sector of the peasantry, to provide cheap food for the urban product market.

Import-substitution industrialization, at least in some parts of Latin America, has spurred the development of capitalism in agriculture both directly and indirectly. The development of an industrial goods and fibre processing sector has stimulated the expansion of capitalist agricultural enterprises which produce industrial raw materials (cotton, oil seeds) and high-income food products (rice, milk, beef) for the urban market. The entrance of capital into agriculture has brought about the demise of traditional 'haciendas' as well as their transformation into capitalist farms and has caused massive displacement of the peasantry — either through outright expulsion from haciendas or through the development of a market in land — with the result that the peasantry is concentrated increasingly on marginal land. Lack of access to land, combined with population growth, has stimulated the semi-proletarianization of the peasantry and its migration to urban areas in search of permanent employment. But a specific characteristic of dependent industrialization, reflecting the periphery's insertion into the world capitalist system, is that industrialization has been capital-intensive. One of the principal contradictions of underdevelopment, then, is that while the dynamic development of capitalism in agriculture continually separates the peasantry from access to the means of subsistence production, the pattern of industrialization fails to provide alternative employment opportunities.

In order to understand how peasant households and the sexual division of labour are related to the contradictions of underdevelopment, we must first insert another tier into the analysis: the identification of *regional* differences in the *national* economy. As noted above, the changing historical form of incorporation of national economies into the world market has influenced patterns of regional integration. In different historical periods, regions have been integrated as areas of commodity production or as sources of labour power for other regions. Different modes of incorporation have, in turn, affected the relations of production, and their economic and social institutions. Thus, we find diverse forms of land tenure, as well as varying processes of production, linking households to the national economy.

At any point in time, then, we can identify the various forms of integration of peasant households into capital accumulation by specifying particular relations of production and their relative importance, given different regional forms of incorporation into the national economy. For example, on haciendas, peasants enter into servile relations of production in order to acquire the usufruct of land, thereby producing surplus labour (that is labour in excess of that needed for their own survival) which is appropriated by the landowning class. This surplus labour may be simply consumed in the form of luxury goods, or it may, as an accumulated surplus, generate expanded production. Independent peasant producers, for example, with sufficient land may be integrated into the product market as cheap commodity producers, which may have the effect of lowering the value of labour power within the economy. As peasant households lose access to the means of production, more family members participate in the labour market at low wages, thereby enhancing capital accumulation.

Only by studying the way in which surplus labour is extracted from peasant households can we understand familial strategies of production and reproduction. Only then can we understand the relationship between women's subordination and social change.

**Women, Production and Human Reproduction: Review of the Literature**

The analysis of women's economic position in the Third World requires a comprehensive historical framework from which to view the sexual division of labour, class structure and the requirements of capital accumulation. It is also necessary, as suggested earlier, to theorize the relationship between production and reproduction. As these relationships have long been of interest to Marxist scholars, we begin by reviewing the contributions of Marx, Engels and more recent authors.

Marx and Engels begin with the premiss that 'men must be in a position to live in order to "make history". But life involves before everything else eating and drinking, a habitation, clothing and many other things' (Marx and Engels, 1976, p. 30). Thus historical analysis should begin with a discussion of the way in which the fundamental necessities needed to sustain life are produced. Further '[Another] circumstance which from the very outset enters into historical development, is that men, who daily remake their own life, begin to make other men, to propagate their kind' (Marx and Engels, 1976, p. 31). *Together, the production of basic necessities and the reproduction of the species constitute the material base of the society, an understanding of which is essential to historical analysis.*

This clear location of human reproduction and the social relations of human reproduction (which can be thought of in terms of the family) in the material base of the society recurs in Marx's writings on precapitalist modes of production (Marx, 1964, p. 83) and in Engels's *The Origin of the Family, Private Property and the State* (1972). The latter contains one of the clearest statements locating human reproduction in the material base and therefore assigning to the family a determinant role in the total organization of the society: 'The social organization under which the people of a particular historical epoch and a particular country live is determined by both kinds of production: by the stage of development of labour on the one hand and of the family on the other' (Engels, 1972, p. 72). In the latter kind of production Engels is referring to the physical reproduction of living human beings, but reproduction must further encompass the nurturing and sustenance of the young, as it is adults capable of both labour and procreation who must be reproduced. Historically this process has taken place in the context of the family.[2]

Thus, Engels is insistent that historical analysis must emphasize the interaction between these *two* aspects of the material life, that is between the changing mode of production and the changing form of the family. But in his study (1972) Engels fails to keep human reproduction and material production analytically separate, because in many precapitalist economies kinship relations structure both human reproduction and material production (Meillassoux, 1975). As a result, Engels's historical analysis neglects human reproduction as a relatively autonomous issue and his discussion of the family is subsumed under his discussion of the mode of production. For example, in his famous 'explanation' of the institution of monogamy, Engels described the emergence of transferable wealth in the form of herds as strengthening the man's relative position in the family, and leading to the overthrow of matrilinearity, the hitherto traditional order of inheritance. Given the possibility of bequests, monogamy was then instituted in order to ensure paternity.[3] Here changes in the form of the family are determined by changes in the relations of material production as reflected in changes in property forms. The development of the production capacity of labour, reflected in the growth of herds, 'explains' not only the transition to monogamy, but also the abandonment of matrilinearity which together *symbolize* changes in the structures of both production and reproduction that have had disastrous effects on the social position of women. 'The man took command in the home also; the woman was degraded and reduced to servitude. She became the slave of his lust and a mere instrument for the production of children' (Engels, 1972, pp. 120-1). Monogamy for Engels had nothing to do with love or affection, but was simply a means to protect and to concentrate wealth (Engels, 1972, p. 128).

Women's specialization in the home now increasingly worked against her in other spheres of life. Male control of her sexuality required her withdrawal from social intercourse and the home, once her sphere of power, increasingly became her prison as the dominant male presence pervaded this area as well. The decline of subsistence production and the growth of production centres outside the home even further weakened the woman's position because it undermined her ability to contribute directly to her family's well-being.

As we have seen, Engels attributes the *origin* of the family and the *origin* of male dominance over women to the emergence of private property. Thus, women's oppression is linked to the emergence of socio-economic classes, for with private property came differences in wealth and social standing.

A final insight comes from Engels's treatment of the sexual division of labour. Interestingly, he locates the origins of specialization in human reproduction:

> The first division of labour is that between man and woman for the propagation of children . . . The first class opposition that appears in history coincides with the development of the antagonism between man and woman in monogamous marriage, and the first class oppression coincides with that of the female sex by the male (Engels, 1972, p. 129).

Early forms of specialization in material production were also based on sex, with age as another 'natural' category. Notwithstanding the above quotation, it must be remembered that for Engels division of labour did not necessarily involve hierarchy. Only with the emergence of private property could specialization of function produce class opposition in production and sexual antagonism in human reproduction. Although Engels can be interpreted as founding the school of thought which roots the sexual division of labour characteristic of production in women's reproductive roles (Beneria, 1979), his analysis does not support the contention that a sexual division of labour is inherently disadvantageous to women. Only in a class-structured society does differentation of function by sex carry this implication.

In Marx's writings women's social subordination was theorized in terms of the impact of capitalism traced primarily through the effects on the family of wage labour and private ownership of property. Marx and Engels were unambiguous about their interpretation: in the propertyless working class, there was no material basis for the family, no necessary reason for its continued existence, and it would consequently wither away. In the property-owning class, the material basis of the family in the concentration and inheritance of wealth would become all-engrossing, overpowering any positive aspects of family life (Humphries, 1977a).

These pessimistic conclusions about the future of the family were reinforced by Marx's and Engels's view that direct control of production by families would necessarily decrease. The logic of capitalist development in agriculture dictated the supercession of the family-based farm by large-scale units employing hired labour. In industry, the factory represented the typical production unit of a more advanced stage of economic development.

What were the implications for women? Working-class women, who had previously been integrated into family-based productive activities, found themselves reduced to idleness, a phenomenon widely discussed as a contemporary social problem in early industrial Britain (Pinchbeck, 1969). These women faced three possibilities: (i) to be reduced to complete economic dependence on husband, son or father; (ii) to follow that male relative into the labour market and substitute reliance on wages for a more personal dependence; and (iii) to drift into the informal sector of the economy, where home-based petty commodity production still provided for a marginal existence. Marx and Engels thought the second option would become the predominant one for working-class women; the trend towards increased proletarianization of women and children being further facilitated by the growing use of machinery in production. Interestingly, the mass entry of women and children into wage labour did not materialize in nineteenth-century England.

Why did this tendency fail to emerge? Marx's own analysis was sufficiently flexible to accommodate the existence of countervailing forces as well as the resistance of the working class to the proletarianization of women and children. It remained for neo-Marxists to develop some of these arguments. In the recent literature the emphasis has been on the countervailing forces (Coulson, Magas and Wainwright, 1975). Attention has been drawn to the changing need of developing market economies in terms of the quality and quantity of labour, lack of substitutes for use-values produced in the home, and the association between the continued support of traditional family structures and political stability. Emphasis has been on explanations which suggest that there were restraints on the dissolution of the family, restraints which derived from the latter's functionalism within capitalist accumulation. More recently, working-class defence of the family has been documented and explained with reference to working-class recognition that the family provided some control over the supply of labour and, hence, over the level of wages, and facilitated survival via income pooling (Humphries, 1977a and 1977b).

Despite an eclectic discussion of the interaction between family employment structure and the accumulation of capital (Marx, 1967, p. 395; Humphries, 1977b), Marx's concept of the value of labour power, a cornerstone of the theory of value itself, is based on his assumption that workers exist in families. His treatment of the reproduction of labour power in *Capital* (1967) abstracts from two issues that are crucial to an understanding of women's social subordination.

First, the working-class family constitutes a production unit, which consumes the commodities purchased with family wages and which produces labourers who work for wages. The household itself does not function like the capitalist enterprise and is not governed by the market, but the household is welded to the firm and the market through its provision of current and future generations of labourers. Marx recognised the importance of the household in its reproductive function of supplying workers but did not investigate the process in any detail (Marx, 1967, p. 572).

Second, Marx abstracts from the problem of the domestic production of use-values in the transformation of the wage into renewed labour power by hypothesizing a situation where all workers are engaged in wage labour, so workers consume only capitalistically produced commodities. The wage (which is used to purchase subsistence) is equivalent, then, to the value of labour power. In reality, unpaid domestic labour undermines the unique correspondence between the level of wages and the working-class standard of living, which now depends not only on purchased commodities but also on household activity.

While Marx's failure to deal specifically with the problem of domestic labour is acceptable within the terms of reference of *Capital*, analysis of housework is crucial to an understanding of the relationship between women's social subordination and the organization of production. Not surprisingly, then, many contemporary writers have analyzed the family in terms of its role in the provision of unpaid domestic labour and the reproduction of labour power, through which it contributes to the functional requirements of production for profit. The argument goes as follows: the rate of surplus value or, in price terms, the ratio of profits to wages, can be increased by lowering the value of labour power, either through a reduction in the real wage or through an increase in the intensity of the labour process.[4] In Marx's analysis, the workers' standard of living was determined in the course of a historic struggle between the classes. The struggle focused principally on the level of wages. But in the presence of domestic labour the wage is reduced below that which would have been necessary to maintain the standard of living of the working class if it had been solely dependent on purchased commodities. In this way the household absorbs part of the cost both of maintaining the standard of living and reproducing the working class.

It should be emphasized that the precise conceptualization of these links has been the subject of considerable debate. Some writers argue that the housewife's labour directly contributes to profits; others emphasize the *indirect* effects of a reduction in wages on capital accumulation (Althusser, 1971; Harrison, 1973; Rowbotham, 1973; Gardiner, 1975; Gardiner, Himmelweit and Mackintosh, 1975; see also, Seccombe, 1974 and 1975; and, for a useful review of this literature, see Himmelweit and Mohun, 1977). It does not seem necessary to argue that women directly, or even indirectly, contribute to profits in order to maintain the crucial connection between housework and capitalism (Adamson, Brown, Harrison and Price, 1976; Fee, 1976).

The emphasis on domestic labour raises several important and inter-related issues. First, is it valid to describe the division of labour by sex in advanced economies in terms of women's performance of domestic labour? The existence of sex-segregated labour markets and occupa-tions suggests that there is a need to broaden this focus, as well as to understand the relationship between women's specialization in the home and their concentration in certain areas of paid labour. Second, if domestic labour *does* delineate a fundamental division of labour by sex, is such a situation inherently oppressive? Some authors have argued that the sexual division of labour within the family and/or its counter-part within social production is *sui generis* a situation of dominance and subordination (Hartmann, 1976). Other authors suggest that this is true only in capitalism (Benston, 1969). This theme has been echoed in the suggestion that within advanced economies unpaid work will necessarily be devalued (Rowbotham, 1973). Third, the connection between the sexual division of labour in production and that in repro-duction requires further elaboration. For example, there is an obvious compatibility between women's use-value production in the home and their primary responsibility for child-rearing, and between the social construction of feminine gender identity and the nurturing/assisting occupations in which women are concentrated (Beneria, 1979). But such correspondence need not rule out variation in the sexual division of labour in production or reproduction or both.

We have seen how the implicit assumption in the classical texts that all workers' consumption is exclusively of commodities produced in the market does not take into account woman's labour in the home, and so obscures the connections between housework and production for profit. In a Third World context, where elements of noncapitalist modes of production coexist with the formal market, this assumption is even more misleading Here capitalist expansion has often intensi-fied women's economic participation in the informal sector — parti-cularly in rural areas, where women's work is geared to subsistence agriculture, animal production, petty commodity production and trad-ing. To understand the significance of women's economic participation in the periphery requires a theoretical framework that includes non-capitalist production and builds on the relationship among modes of production within a given society (Deere, 1976).

Numerous empirical studies have shown that women's agricultural participation reflects the conditions that serve to maintain the cheapest source of labour for economic expansion.[5] With the transformation of Latin America, Africa and Asia into the periphery of the world economic system, women's production of subsistence foodstuffs or actual participation in the labour force helped to maintain low wages in these economies. One particularly important variant of the link between family labour and the wages paid in the capitalist sector is that which involves male wage labour and female production of subsistence foodstuffs. Such a division of labour, which is most prevalent in the periphery, demonstrates the interconnection between the maintenance of subsistence production of food and the maintenance of a low prevailing wage in the labour market, and provides a clear example of women's contribution to capital accumulation. The argument is that women's subsistence production in the Third World plays a role analogous to that of unpaid domestic labour in the home in advanced industrial countries. Both have been interpreted as lowering — either directly or indirectly — the cost of labour to capital and therefore raising the ratio of profit to wages.

However, this functional analogy must be qualified (Deere, 1976). The essential difference between the effects of subsistence production and domestic labour on the production and reproduction of labour power is that the domestic unit in advanced economies *stretches* the wage through the transformation of commodities into use-values, thereby maintaining for the worker a standard of living higher than it would otherwise be. The peasant unit in the periphery *produces* the goods and services which are purchased with the wage in the centre.

Second, the household in the centre and the peasant production unit in the periphery have different functions within capital accumulation. In developed economies, labour incomes serve to increase the size of the domestic market. It is not surprising then, that the expansion of market size has been closely related to the increased purchase of the goods and services formerly produced within the household. Women in developed economies are increasingly drawn into wage employment, and the increasing demand for female labour has simultaneously expanded the commodity market for the goods and services formerly produced within the household.

In the periphery, the expansion of the domestic market has been less important as an impetus to national economic development, due to the composition of the export and industrial enclaves. The preservation of noncapitalist elements alongside capitalist development relates to women's role in the reproduction of a future class of wage workers and simultaneous provision of a temporary labour reserve. Women have been relegated to the maintenance and reproduction of the rural, low cost labour reserve.

While the analysis of the relationship between economic development and women's *productive* roles has received considerable attention in the Marxian literature, the interaction between economic change and women's reproductive roles is only beginning to be explored.

Historical studies offer important guideposts to the analysis of the relationships between economic change and familial reproductive strategies. In an article on the process of early industrialization in France, Tilly (1977) describes how peasant families migrating to the cities in search of wage labour tried to maximize the number of wage earners they could acquire by continuing to have large numbers of children. Since women as well as men were incorporated into factory work, their particular incentive to high fertility was that their only respite from wage labour occurred when their children could replace them. Another author, Levine (1977), in writing about the interplay between economic and demographic change in early British industrialization, concludes that the entry of the agricultural labour force into wage labour and their integration into a wider commercial system were the two principal factors which promoted rapid demographic growth. The main effect of the proletarianization of labour in Western Europe was to reduce the age of marriage, but the timing of this decline was crucially influenced by the way in which the larger world impinged upon the demand for labour at the village level. Under conditions of a rising local demand for labour the traditional disincentives to early marriage crumbled.

Similar reproductive strategies have been observed among peasants and working-class people in Third World countries, where to continue to have large numbers of children is seen as a survival strategy (Mamdani, 1972; Gimenez, 1977). In Mexico, the interrelationship between changing modes of production, the division of labour by sex and generational reproduction has been linked to population growth (Young, 1978). Folbre (1977) has also related large family size among poor peasant households to the need for a rural labour reserve. White (1975) has extended this line of enquiry by demonstrating the importance of the economic contribution made by children in Asian peasant households.

The deeper understanding of the relationship between rapidly changing modes of production and family reproduction strategies in our opinion helps explain why fertility levels in Third World countries have not always followed the Western historical patterns as industrialization and urbanization have occurred. In the developed countries, where the demand for unskilled workers has been curtailed and that for skilled workers expanded, it has become rational for working-class families to reduce fertility and take advantage of widening educational opportunities for their children. Thus, changes in the quality as well as in the quantity of labour needed affect the reproductive decisions made by working-class families (Gimenez, 1977). Safa's comparative study (1978) of the reproductive strategies of working-class women in New Jersey, USA, and Sao Paulo, Brazil, confirms the sensitivity of demographic outcomes to the demand for labour in different stages of economic development.

For rural areas of the Third World, we propose that the analysis of the process of social differentiation among direct producers provides the analytical link between changing modes of production and the sexual division of labour, both within the household labour process and human production (Deere, 1978a). The key to the process of social differentiation is whether the peasant household has access to the means of subsistence production. Such access governs the viability of the peasant household as a subsistence unit. On the other hand, effective separation from the means of production leads to the disintegration of the peasantry as it becomes increasingly required to seek wage labour.[6]

Moreover, as the peasant household loses access to the means of production, it becomes less involved in direct production and increasingly geared to the reproduction of labour power for the market. Alternatively, within rich peasant households, as the production process is capitalized, production is gradually divorced from the household, which increasingly specializes in consumption and reproduction. Our analysis of production and reproduction within the household thus takes as its point of entry the household's access to the means of production, and allows us to relate the sexual division of labour, family structure, fertility and migration to the process of capitalist development.

If access to the means of production is highly unequal, there is no reason to suppose that the sexual division of labour is homogeneous.

Rather, if the division of labour by sex in agriculture is responsive to the material conditions of production, we would expect to find heterogeneity in the tasks and activities which men and women of different classes perform. We would expect the sexual division of labour to vary according to: (i) the specific activities undertaken by the household to secure its income; (ii) the stock of labour which the household has at its disposal; and (iii) the varying modes of production in which the household might engage. For example, access to the means of production largely determines the range of income-generating activities available to different households. The range of activities then influences the particular sexual division of labour within the household. On the other hand, separation from the means of production may force the household members into the labour market or into servile relations of production; here, the interests of owners or management − given their control over the means of production − may set the parameters of sexual participation. Such parameters (i.e., male-female wage differentials and sex-specific customary proscriptions on employment) in turn may influence the sexual division of labour in household activities.

Access to sufficient means of production to employ wage labour may also influence the sexual division of labour *within* the household if replacements become available for family labour in the productive process. Here cultural and ideological factors may also interact with the economic structure to define activities considered proper for women and men of different class positions.

Given that the size and composition of the household varies over the family life cycle we would expect the sexual division of labour to vary as the availability of familial labour power changes over time. Here it is important to point out that family size and composition, as reflected in family structure, may also respond to changing economic opportunities. The structure of production and attendant class relationships may mediate the logic of human reproduction.

We view biological reproduction (evidence in fertility and family size) as one component of the reproduction of the household stock of labour resources. Different household structures (nuclear versus extended) must also be explained. Under general conditions of rural poverty, it may be economically rational for all families to reproduce at a biological maximum due to the economic value of children (Mamdani, 1972). But actual family size may vary according to class position, which reflects differences in infant and child mortality rates resulting from variations in household incomes. In addition, the economic value of children may differ according to class position, which is reflected in differing patterns of retention and expulsion of working-age children. As members of the household become proletarianized, there may be a greater tendency for working-class children to leave, and the family will assume a nuclear form. In contrast, among the middle and rich peasant strata, where there is access to sufficient land and the family labour force is the base of agricultural production, working-age children may be retained within the household. Household size will be larger and extended family structure more frequent (Deere, 1978b). In sum, we would not expect human reproduction strategies, family structure and composition or the division of labour by sex to be the same for all peasant households.

If family size is to be maximized, women's work must be compatible with the physical demands of biological reproduction. Certainly, continual pregnancy and lactation place a heavy physical burden on women, but the extent to which women's mobility and productive activities are proscribed by their reproductive work depends also on the social context.

If women's role in reproduction directly determined women's role in production, and all peasant families maximised family size, we might expect all peasant women to engage in the same kinds of activities. While all peasant women do appear to be charged with the daily maintenance activities required for the reproduction of the capacity to work, there are striking differences in the range of other activities that women pursue. As we have argued above, it is access to the means of production within the peasantry that is important in determining the range of activities that women undertake to secure the family's subsistence. In addition, the process of social differentiation of the peasantry has considerable influence on the division of labour by sex. Therefore, it is not possible simply to deduce women's role in reproduction from that in production, or vice versa; the relationship must be viewed as one of *mutual effectivity*.

## The Empirical Analysis of Processes of Socio-economic Change and Third World Women

In this section, building on the theoretical discussion developed above, we outline a research design for a national-level study of women and the processes of socio-economic change in the Third World. The objective is to analyze the interaction between historical processes of socioeconomic change and changes in the sexual division of labour. Within this overall framework, the proposed research project is limited to rural women, and, specifically, to the interrelationship between the process of capitalist development in agriculture and the sexual division of labour within both peasant households and the emerging structure of production.

We first summarize the general theoretical propositions that guide our study of women and underdevelopment, and then illustrate these with specific research hypotheses drawn from the application of this conceptual framework to the study of Andean women (Deere, 1977 and 1978a; Leon de Leal and Deere, 1978a and b). Our objective is not to formulate a set of hypotheses that can be tested cross-culturally but rather to elaborate specific hypotheses that will aid in the formulation of appropriate research propositions for particular socio-economic settings. We then detail a research project design which draws upon our previous experience in carrying out a national-level study on rural women.[7]

## Propositions

### General Propositions Concerning the Sexual Division of Labour

(i) The sexual division of labour in productive activities is neither determined biologically nor socio-culturally, but is determined economically.

(ii) The sexual division of labour is responsive to changing material conditions of production and thus varies over time and space.

(iii) As an economic variable, the rationality of the sexual division of labour is class-specific, and varies according to the social relations of production and reproduction.

(iv) The sexual division of labour appears to respond to the needs of dominant classes to extract surplus labour and particularly to the specific requirements of capital accumulation.

(v) The sexual division of labour within the household or family none the less is neither mechanical nor voluntaristic but is embedded in the dominant value system which interacts in a complex manner with changes in economic parameters.

(vi) Female participation in production is a necessary but not a sufficient condition for the attainment of an equal social status for women *vis-à-vis* men.

(vii) The sexual division of labour which relegates to women the primary responsibility for the activities required for human reproduction is a major factor in the continuing subordination of women to men.

## Hypotheses

### Specific Hypotheses About the Sexual Division of Labour

(i) Among independent agricultural producers the household is the basic unit of production as well as of reproduction. None the less, the sexual division of labour tends to be more flexible in productive activities than in the activities required to reproduce labour power on a daily or generational basis.

(ii) The sexual division of labour in productive activities differs among different strata of the peasantry according to their access to the means of production of subsistence.

(iii) If agricultural work is generally regarded as a male activity, women of the upper strata of the peasantry will seldom participate in field work and the sexual division of labour is consequently more rigid. This task differentiation is related to the household's ability to purchase wage labour for the productive process.

(iv) If agricultural work is generally regarded as a male activity, women will participate in agricultural production as well as in decision-making only when men are absent from the farm, particularly when men migrate to pursue wage employment. If the latter circumstances are widespread, the sexual division of labour will be more flexible.

(v) Women tend to specialize in nonagricultural occupations both as a result of economic necessity (among the poorer strata of the peasantry) and as a consequence of the household's greater access to resources (among the richer strata of the peasantry). However, the specific income-generating activities in which women participate differ and are closely related to the household's access to the means of production.

### Servile Relations of Production on Haciendas

(i) Under servile or semi-feudal relations of production, the basic unit of production as well as of exploitation is the peasant family. A well-defined sexual division of labour on haciendas tends to increase the total surplus labour performed for and appropriated by the landlord class.

(ii) A well-defined division of labour by sex in the productive activities performed for the landlord is reflected in the sexual division of labour within the peasant productive unit, which tends to parallel the given division of tasks.

(iii) Where labour services tend to fall only upon the male, there is a direct relationship between the total time the male must spend performing surplus labour for the landlord and the responsibility women and children take for production of subsistence on their own plots.

(iv) Where the division of labour by sex in the labour services performed for the landlord is well defined, it may be that under conditions of labour scarcity the landlord has to guarantee the reproduction of the labour force, and therefore relegates to women those activities most compatible with biological reproduction and the maintenance of the family.

(v) Patriarchal familial relationships within the peasantry are reinforced through the relations of production which cede to the man the usufruct of land and make him responsible for the provision of rent, although the surplus labour of women and children is also subject to appropriation.

## Capitalist Relations of Production

(i) The entry of rural women into wage labour markets has closely followed the demands of capital accumulation for a rural labour reserve: women are employed as agricultural wage workers when male labour is relatively scarce, which serves to maintain low wages.

(ii) Generally, rural women are employed in capitalist agriculture only on a temporary basis and for the most labour-intensive crops and tasks of agricultural production. The mechanization of agriculture has resulted in few permanent employment opportunities; those that are available are usually filled by males.

(iii) Women employed in capitalist agriculture are often paid on a piecework basis, which both encourages the participation of children alongside the woman and keeps wages low.

(iv) The discrimination against women in the labour market in general is evidenced by unequal wages for equal work as well as by the relegation of women to low productivity jobs.

(v) Capitalist relations of production tend to directly exploit only the individual worker, although unpaid domestic work (which is necessary if capitalist production is to continue) falls on other family members particularly women.

(vi) From the point of view of the supply of labour, female proletarianization is closely related to rural poverty and the family's lack of access to the means of production, both of which tend to break down sociocultural constraints on women's employment outside the home.

(vii) The proletarianization of women in agriculture is related to age and family position as well as to locational opportunity costs.

(viii) The participation of women in the labour market does not affect their responsibility for producing and reproducing the labour force; therefore rural women generally work a 'double' day.

(ix) High fertility rates may limit the participation of women in production. But female participation in paid production as well as in peasant production may also be strongly influenced by the complementarity and substitutability of children and parents in productive activities.

(x) Under generalized conditions of rural poverty, all strata of the peasantry may attempt to maximize the number of children due to the high economic value of children.

(xi) Material conditions may strongly influence infant and child mortality and provide an explanation for differences in the number of live children among different strata of the peasantry.

(xii) Access to the means of production will strongly influence the productive value of children on the farm at different ages. Therefore, the economic value of children will vary among different strata of the peasantry and will be reflected in variations in household size and family structure.

(xiii) For those peasant families whose access to land is sufficient to guarantee their integration into the market, the productive value of children may lie in their contribution to farm work. Family size may be larger due to a higher incidence of extended family structure.

(xiv) For peasant families with insufficient land to produce their subsistence requirements, the economic value of children may depend solely on the prevailing labour market conditions. Material inducements to migration of teenagers may result in smaller household size and nuclear family structure as children leave home at a relatively early age.

## A Project Design for the Study of Rural Women

This research effort is designed as a two-year project with three stages of investigation: the analysis of the national process of historical development; regional case studies of the process of capitalist development in agriculture and changes in the sexual division of labour; and measurement of the sexual division of labour within peasant households. The objectives and the suggested methodology to be employed in each stage of research are detailed below.

*Analysis of the National Process of Historical Development.* The primary objective of this first stage of research is the periodization of the process of development of the particular country under study. The secondary historical and political economy literature should be reviewed in order to identify the major processes of social change that characterize the particular country. In addition, the secondary bibliographic information should allow preliminary identification of the form and magnitude of women's economic participation in different regions during different historical periods.

This preliminary background information should facilitate identification of the key regional patterns of integration into the national economy. Relevant criteria must be designed for the selection of regional field sites based on the information gathered on the specific productive structure of the country and the historical processes which it represents. For example, a region may be integrated into the national economy in one of the following ways: as a producer of export crops; as a producer of foodstuffs for national consumption; or as a supplier of labour power to urban centres or to the export economy.

The role of a region in the national economy will vary over time. Therefore, in order to characterize the agrarian structure at any given moment, it is necessary to describe in more detail the prevailing relations of production and to characterize the level of development of the productive forces as follows: areas with a well-developed rural labour market; areas of haciendas/plantations and tenant farmers; areas of independent peasant producers; or areas of communal, village productive structures.

The manner in which labour, land and capital are combined in the productive process allows regions to be further classified in terms of productivity. Thus, we have: areas of high productivity (mechanized agriculture) or areas of low productivity (traditional peasant agriculture or traditional haciendas).

Quantitative indicators of these processes of regional integration and agrarian structure are needed in order to facilitate the selection of representative field sites. The key quantitative variables to be analyzed include: size distribution of land holdings, forms of land tenancy, economically active population by sex across occupations and sectors, and degree of commercialization of agricultural production.

*Regional Case Studies of the Process of Capitalist Development.* The second stage of the project design focuses on regional case studies of the process of capitalist development and changes in the sexual division of labour. Particular attention is given to the development of the rural labour market and the changes in land tenure systems that have altered productive processes over time.

The second stage of the research has several specific objectives: first, the identification of the prevailing division of labour by sex within both the production process and the daily maintenance activities, and its relation to the family's position in the social hierarchy; second, the identification of changes that have taken place in the sexual division of labour as a result of the development of capitalist relations of production, changes in the land tenure system and the degree of market integration; and third, the analysis of the prevailing sexual division of labour in the labour market, in terms of both industries and specific labour processes, and of the changes that have occurred in this pattern over time. In order to carry out the regional case studies, it will be necessary to train a team of researchers, to devise a specific fieldwork plan and to design specific research instruments.

At least three months should be spent in each region by the team of researchers. The first week or two should be devoted to establishing contact with local and national institutions operating in the area in order to gather data on the history of the local land tenure system, notable economic and political historic events, local agricultural and industrial production, market structure and administrative practice. The primary objective of the orientation period is to obtain the required background information on which to base the selection of specific enterprises and villages in which informal interviews will be carried out.

Study of the local labour market first requires a detailed listing of the sources of employment in the area — enterprises that employ wage labour such as workshops, factories, haciendas and commercial agricultural enterprises. Data should be obtained on the owner and location of each enterprise, and, if possible, on the number of employees and the commercial importance of the enterprise. The sample studies should include enterprises involved in the dominant economic activities but should also reflect the diversity of labour processes in the area.[8] Open-ended interviews should be carried out with the owner or manager of the business and with a representative sample of male and female workers chosen so as to represent different skill levels, work contracts, etc., within the enterprise.

A prerequisite for the study of peasant households is the gathering of information on the distribution of rural settlement, the concentration or dispersion of forms of local land tenancy and crop diversification. Again, the particular villages to be studied should be illustrative of the diversity of the region. Within each village, care should be taken to select for interviews peasant households of diverse economic strength and activities representing different forms of land tenancy.

The objectives of this stage of fieldwork is to construct as broad a picture as possible of the historical development of the particular region, and the implications of the pattern of development for different peasant households and the division of labour by sex. None the less, it may be advisable to structure the open-ended interviews by designing a questionnaire to be filled out during the actual interview. This is particularly important if the research team is inexperienced. Another advantage of a questionnaire is that the information collected is then accessible to other researchers who may not have been involved in the interviews.[9]

This second stage of research should conclude with the compilation of fieldwork reports describing the results of the labour market and peasant household interviews in terms of the historical process of development of the region and the evolution of the sexual division of labour in socialized as well as home production.

*The Measurement of the Sexual Division of Labour.* The quantification of the sexual division of labour in peasant households allows the historical analysis to focus on the difference in men's and women's economic participation, given different socio-economic processes of change and different class positions. It is suggested that a representative sample survey of peasant households is the most appropriate methodology for measuring the sexual division of labour and comparing the effect on it of different forms of integration of peasant households into the wider economy. Once particular historical processes are analyzed, differences in the experience of rural class formation can then be related to differences in the sexual division of labour, fertility, and household structure and composition.

The questionnaire used in the measurement of the sexual division of labour should be developed in relation to the specific research hypotheses which guide the study, as modified by the qualitative stage of fieldwork. It is most important that a sample survey questionnaire be formulated only after the earlier fieldwork has discovered the socio-historical processes and forms of integration of the peasantry into the wider economy. Such knowledge should amend and enrich the hypotheses which guide the measurement effort.

The objective of the questionnaire is to capture the sexual division of labour within the myriad of activities which members of the rural households perform. These activities include the reproduction of labour power on a daily basis (household maintenance, i.e., cooking, cleaning, washing clothes, gathering firewood and water) and on a generational basis (child-care), activities which are directed towards direct production of use or exchange values (agricultural production, processing and transformation, animal raising, artisan production) and income-generating activities which are carried out outside the household (labour market activities, commerce).

Participation can be measured in terms of time actually spent carrying out the activity, in terms of primary and secondary responsibility within the household for the activity, or in terms of the average intensity of participation. The most accurate measurement of participation is one based on the actual time dedicated to the activity over the preceding year. Our experience shows that the only way to measure time allocation accurately is to have an observer actually record on a daily basis the time spent by each family member in each activity. A survey based on family members' recall of the actual time spent in different household activities will not be as useful; at best, its accuracy depends on the skill of the interviewer in culling reasonable responses about the amount of time required by different activities. If interviewers with a minimal amount of experience and training are carrying out the survey, we recommend an alternative 'intensity' measure of participation be utilized whereby each household member is asked if they always, usually or never participate in a given activity.

The theoretical framework requires that the sample be representative of the peasant household's access to the means of production, for access to the means of production most closely captures the economic aspect of class formation among the peasantry. Means of production include the amount of land held in property as well as usufruct, the potential productivity of the land, and the stock of tools, equipment and farm animals. This information is rarely available beforehand, but appears as a product of the survey. Thus, in order to define the universe of the sample, the most easily available data, access to land, must be used as a proxy for the class configuration of the rural area. The sample should then be drawn so as to be representative of the distribution of landholdings in the area.

The qualitative and quantitative data generated through the three research stages described above provide the basis for analysis of regional case studies of the process of capitalist development in agriculture and the changes in the sexual division of labour. Analysis of the different forms of regional incorporation into the national economy will then allow comparative analysis of the particular patterns of socio-economic change in terms of their implications for rural women.

## Notes

1. This section expands the conceptual framework originally proposed in Leon de Leal and Deere (1978a).

2. The family also bears some responsibility for 'socialization', the process by which human beings (the products of human reproduction) are invested with the willingness and capacity to work, bear children and generally support the social relations characteristic of any particular historical conjuncture. The latter responsibility, however, is shared with other institutions, such as the schools, the church, the media, etc., partially or wholly concerned with the reproduction of existing social relations (that is, *social reproduction*). However intertwined in everyday life, the family's ideological functions are theoretically distinguishable from the material practice of human reproduction. In any concrete instance, the *particular* construction of family relations as relations of reproduction, along with the corresponding technical forces and ideological functions of the family, must be seen as a historically specific effect of the interacting social structures.

3. Why herds should be distinguished from older forms of property is not explained. Tools, for example, had been simply bequeathed to members of the tribe of the same sex and, since they do not seem to have been 'owned' in any privatistic sense, appeared undisruptive of the ancient egalitarianism of the gens (Sacks, 1975). Nor is it clear why men controlled the herds when agricultural subsistence production was women's sphere. If when the wealth was produced it was wrested from women's control, men must already have appropriated power (Lane, 1976).

4. Marxian analysis usually proceeds in terms of the labour theory of value, according to which the rate of surplus value is the ratio of surplus labour time to the value of labour power, i.e., socially necessary labour time embodied in the product. In price terms, it can loosely be thought of as the ratio of profits to wages.

5. The following section draws heavily on Deere, 1976. For empirical material supporting the argument, see Boserup (1970); Caulfield (1974); Van Allen (1974).

6. This conceptual approach is fully developed as a model of peasant household economy in Deere and de Janvry (1979).

7. The Colombian Rural Women Research Project, after which the proposed investigation is modelled, was a three-year research project funded by the Ford Foundation and the Rockefeller Foundation, and carried out under the auspices of the Colombian Association of Population Studies (ACEP). The study was carried out under the direction of Magdalena León de Leal and Carmen Diana Deere was a research associate on the project. The actual research design as well as the research will be made known in a volume edited by Magdalena León de Leal (forthcoming).

8. For example, the enterprises should represent both the most advanced and the most backward enterprises technologically; a mixture of permanent versus temporary labour force; in the agricultural case, include both wage labourers and peasants living on the estate, etc. Priority consideration should be given to the selection of at least some enterprises that employ women.

9. During this stage of field research it is also suggested that in-depth interviews on particular topics be carried out with key peasant informants. Topics which particularly lend themselves to in-depth treatment with local experts are historical questions and those dealing with specific aspects of the position of women. The field researchers should be asked to seek out older peasants in each area who are locally known as sources of historical information for conversations on particularly important local events, changes in land tenure, etc. Life histories are also a useful form of collecting a variety of information on local history as well as the peasants' perceptions of how these events affected their lives. The

researchers should also pursue detailed interviews with women on such topics as male-female relations, views on women's participation in the labour force and in agriculture, and their views on marriage, courtship, child-bearing and child-rearing.

# References

Adamson, O., C. Brown, J. Harrison and J. Price (1976) 'Women's oppression under capitalism', *Revolutionary Community, 5*

Althusser, L. (1971) *Lenin and philosophy*, New York, Monthly Review Press

Amin, S. (1976) *Unequal development*, New York, Monthly Review Press

Baran, P. (1957) *The political economy of growth*, New York, Monthly Review Press

Beneria, L. (1979) 'Reproduction, production and the sexual division of labour', *Cambridge Journal of Economics, 3,* 3

Benston, M. (1969) 'The political economy of women's liberation', *Monthly Review, 21,* 4

Boserup, E. (1970) *Woman's role in economic development*, New York, St. Martin's Press

Caulfield, M.D. (1974) 'Imperialism, the family and cultures of resistance', *Socialist Revolution, 20*

Coulson, M., B. Magas and H. Wainwright (1975) 'The housewife and her labour under capitalism', *New Left Review, 89*

Deere, C.D. (1976) 'Rural women's subsistence production in the capitalist periphery', *Review of Radical Political Economics, 8,* 1

—— (1977) 'Changing social relations of production and Peruvian peasant women's work', *Latin American Perspectives*, issues 12 and 13, *4,* 1 and 2

—— (1978a) 'The development of capitalism in agriculture and the division of labor by sex: A study of the Northern Peruvian Sierra', PhD dissertation, University of California, Berkeley

—— (1978b) 'The differentiation of the peasantry and family structure: a Peruvian case study', *Journal of Family History, 3*

—— and A. de Janvry (1979) 'A conceptual framework for the empirical analysis of peasants', *American Journal of Agricultural Economics, 61,* 4

de Janvry, A. and C. Garramon (1977) 'The dynamics of rural poverty in Latin America', *Journal of Peasant Studies, 5*

Engels, F. (1972) *The origin of the family, private property and the state*, New York, International Publishers

Fee, T. (1976) 'Domestic labor: An analysis of housework and its relation to the production process', *Review of Radical Economics, 8*

Folbre, N. (1977) 'Population growth and capitalist development in Zongalica, Veracruz', *Latin American Perspectives, 4,* 4

—— (1978) 'The household mode of production: the family and historical change in New England, 1640-1860', dissertation prospectus, University of Massachusetts, Amherst

Frank, A.G. (1966) 'The development of underdevelopment', *Monthly Review, 18,* 4

Gardiner, J. (1975) 'Women's domestic labour', *New Left Review, 89*

——, S. Himmelweit and M. Mackintosh (1975) 'Women's domestic labour', *Bulletin of the Conference of Socialist Economists, 4,* 2 (reprinted in *On the Political Economy of Women*, CSE Pamphlet no. 2, London, Stage One, 1976)

Gimenez, M. (1977) 'Population and capitalism', *Latin American Perspectives*, *4*, 4

Gough, I. and J. Harrison (1975) 'Unproductive labour and housework again', *Bulletin of the Conference of Socialist Economists*, *4*, 1

Harrison, J. (1973) 'Political economy of housework', *Bulletin of the Conference of Socialist Economists*, *3*, 1

Hartmann, H. (1976) 'Capitalism, patriarchy, and job segregation by sex', *Signs: Journal of Women in Culture and Society*, *1*, 3, part 2

Himmelweit, S. and S. Mohun (1977) 'Domestic labour and capital', *Cambridge Journal of Economics*, *1*, 3

Humphries, J. (1977a) 'Class struggle and the persistence of the working class family', *Cambridge Journal of Economics*, *1*, 3

—— (1977b) 'The working class family, women's liberation and class struggles: the case of nineteenth century British history', *Review of Radical Political Economics*, *9*, 3

Lane, A. (1976) 'Woman in society: A critique of Frederick Engels' in B.A. Carroll (ed.), *Liberating women's history: theoretical and critical essays*, Chicago, University of Illinois Press

León de Leal, M. (ed.) (forthcoming) *Informe final del estudio acerca de la mujer rural Colombiana*, Bogota, ACEP

—— and C.D. Deere (1978a) 'Estudio de la mujer rural y el desarrollo del capitalismo en al agro Colombiano', *Demografía y Economía*, *12*, 1: English version forthcoming in *Signs*

—— —— (1978b) 'La proletarización y el trabajo agrícola en la economía parcelaria: estudio de la división del trabajo por sexo en dos regiones Colombianas', paper presented to the Conference on Women in the Labour Force, Rio de Janeiro, November

Levine, D. (1977) *Family formation in an age of nascent capitalism*, New York, Academic Press

Mamdani, M. (1972) *The myth of population control: family caste and class in an Indian village*, New York, Monthly Review Press

Marx, K. (1964) *Precapitalist economic formations*, London, Lawrence and Wishart

—— (1967) *Capital, I*, New York, International Publishers

—— and F. Engels (1976) *Collected works, 5*, London, Lawrence and Wishart

Meillassoux, C. (1975) *Femmes greniers et capitaux*, Paris, Maspero

Pinchbeck, I. (1969) *Women workers and the industrial revolution, 1750-1850*, New York, Augustus M. Kelley

Rowbotham, S. (1973) *Woman's consciousness, man's world*, Harmondsworth, Middlesex, Penguin

Sacks, K. (1975) 'Engels revisited: women, the organization of production and private property' in Rayna R. Reiter (ed.), *Toward an anthropology of women*, New York, Monthly Review Press

Safa, H. (1978) 'Women, production and reproduction in industrial capitalism', mimeo., Department of Anthropology, Rutgers University

Seccombe, W. (1974) 'The housewife and her labour under capitalism', *New Left Review, 83*

—— (1975) 'Domestic labour – reply to critics', *New Left Review, 94*

Tilly, L. (1977) 'Reproduction, production and the family among textile workers in Roubaix, France', paper presented at the Conference on Social History

Van Allen, J. (1974) 'Women in Africa: modernization means more dependency', *The Center Magazine, 12*, 3

White, B. (1975) 'The economic importance of children in a Javanese village' in M. Nag (ed.), *Population and Social Organization*, The Hague, Mouton

Young, K. (1978) 'Modes of appropriation and the sexual division of labour: a case study from Oaxaca, Mexico' in A. Kuhn and A.M. Wolpe (eds.), *Feminism and materialism*, London, Routledge and Kegan Paul

# PART THREE: SOCIAL AND CULTURAL DIMENSIONS INFLUENCING WOMEN'S ROLES

# 5 FEMALE POWER, AUTONOMY AND DEMOGRAPHIC CHANGE IN THE THIRD WORLD

## Constantina Safilios-Rothschild

The recent awareness and concern with women's status in different societies has usually focused on macro indicators at the national level and often only on the few indicators included in census data. These macro-level indicators, such as percentage of girls enrolled in school or percentage of women in the labour force, which may not be the most sensitive measures of women's status, are then used to assess the relationship between status and fertility rates (Mauldin and Berelson, 1978).

Reproduction, however, is a behaviour occurring at the micro level, and it is not necessarily a given that there is a direct relationship between the status of women in the society and women's power within the household. Since women's status is a multidimensional concept based on a wide range of macro, structural indicators, some of these dimensions may be more readily translated than others into female power at the individual level, and some of them may affect women's reproductive behaviour more directly than others.

The purpose of this chapter is to develop a set of indicators of women's power that can be used in conjunction with indicators of women's status to determine how status in society is translated into power at the individual level. Women's *power* can be distinguished from women's *status*, in that status refers to women's overall position in the society while power refers to women's ability to influence and control at the interpersonal level. Power can be defined as 'the ability to control or change the behavior of others' (Mishler and Waxler, 1968; Olson and Cromwell, 1975) and 'the ability to realize one's will even against opposition' (Phillips, 1967). Thus, female power can be defined as women's ability to control or change other women's and men's behaviours and the ability to determine important events in their lives, even when men and older women are opposed to them. At this point we know that as long as marked social inequalities exist between men and women, the probability is low that women can have power. But we do not know what is the *tipping point*, that is, what, how many and to what degree women's status indicators must reflect an equalization trend between men and women before the prevailing ideology changes sufficiently to allow individual women to translate this 'higher' status into actual power in their lives.

As was noted above, the indicators of women's status most often used are not detailed enough to provide an accurate measurement; therefore, a prerequisite of a discussion of the relationship between status and power is the detailing of more satisfactory indicators of status. On the basis of research studies in a number of different countries as well as existing theoretical models of sex discrimination, a list of indicators of women's status can be suggested. The selection of these indicators is based on the notion that (i) the higher women's ability is to control important events in their lives (such as age at marriage, remarriage, etc.), the higher is their status; and (ii) the more women that have the same life options as men in the same age group and social class with respect to food, education and training, occupations, remuneration and occupational advancement, migration, use of time and leisure, land and property ownership, and life expectancy, the higher is their status (Safilios-Rothschild, 1970).[1] The indicators that result from this selection process are as follows:

— Percentage of women 15 to 19 and 20 to 24 years old who never married.
— Percentage of women marrying men younger than themselves.[2]
— Remarriage rates of widowed and divorced women by age group and rural-urban place of residence.
— Men/women ratios in the 30 to 39 and 40 to 49 age groups.
— Percentage of women owning land or businesses.
— Degree of sex segregation in occupations, or degree of concentration of women in a few occupations.
— Percentage of women at high levels of different occupations.
— Ratio of men/women in the informal sector as compared to ratio of men/women in the formal sector.
— Degree of discrepancy between men's and women's wages for the same type of work.
— Sex differences in malnutrition rates among children and adolescents under 15 years of age.
— Division of labour by sex among children 5-12 years old (housework and child-care versus school attendance and schoolwork and/or income-producing activities).
— Ratio of men/women completing elementary school.[3]
— Ratio of men/women farmers receiving agricultural training and credit, and participating in productivity improvement schemes.

- Degree of discrepancy between men's and women's ratio of time spent in productive activities to time spent in leisure.
- Sex ratios of rural-urban and international migrants.
- Existence of women's economic associations (co-operatives, loan associations, etc.).

Some of these indicators are available for most developing countries, either through the regular census or through special census compilations, and many more of the indicators are becoming available through special studies and projects.

In the following sections, I will turn to the development of a set of indicators of women's power – both power as it is derived from men and power as it is a result of women's income-generating activities.

## Power Derived From Men

Women can derive power from men even in societies in which their status is low and when, as we shall see, their own productive activities and other accomplishments cannot be translated into power. This type of power is, however, limited; women may have the power to control the lives and behaviour of younger women and, to some extent, younger men in the household, but they usually do not have the ability to determine their own lives and to make choices not endorsed by the men in the household. In this case, female power could be represented by the following equation:

$$F_P = F_{P1} + F_{P2} + F_{P3} + F_{P4} + F_{P5},$$

in which

$F_{P1}$ = reproductive power ('son' power);
$F_{P2}$ = marital power based on unequal love;
$F_{P3}$ = power based on father's social status/wealth;
$F_{P4}$ = power based on husband's social status/wealth;
$F_{P5}$ = power based on the 'asexual' status of middle-aged and older women.

In those developing societies which are rigidly sex stratified and patriarchal and patrilineal, a secure basis for women's power is derived from their ability to have children, especially sons. In fact, reproduction is the only power base that women in all social classes and marital relationships can more or less control. Hence, they have no motivation to limit the number of children they bear until they have at least two or three sons to consolidate their position in the household (Caldwell, 1976; Okonjo, 1978a).

The other bases of power, although they are potentially important, depend on the husband's feelings (marital power), the father's and/or husband's social class, or the wife's age, and therefore they cannot be manipulated. An exception may be marital power: there is some evidence that in developing countries women who do not have a high social status from their kin can use love as a 'resource' when they marry men who love them more than they love the men (Safilios-Rothschild, 1976). In fact, women may prefer such marriages because the husbands tend to be less adamant about maintaining their dominant position and more willing to grant power to their wives. Women in such marriages feel more confident of their husbands' concern for their feelings and thus can effectively use psychological influence techniques, such as withdrawal of love or affection, crying, etc. (Safilios-Rothschild, 1969; Safilios-Rothschild, 1979b). This power is based on the men's love for them; but even when women have married men who love them more than they love the men, the balance is quite precarious and cannot be always relied upon or controlled at will.

Women can also escape the constraints of the inferior status assigned to them if their social status (inherited from their fathers and other male relatives) is sufficiently high to neutralize their low status in the sex-stratification system. In these cases, a woman can have power *vis-à-vis* her husband if she controls a sizeable dowry (from her father) or if the prestige or powerful connections of her father and brothers can be helpful to her husband's career (Safilios-Rothschild, 1979b). Thus, women are translating resources derived from male relatives into power *vis-à-vis* their husbands, the degree of power varying according to how much lower their husbands' status is than that of their fathers and other male relatives.

In general, power derived from kinship ties (fathers, brothers, uncles) tends to be relatively more secure than that derived from marriage ties, since the economic and social bonds of kinship are more indissoluble. Similarly, in societies in which women's status — or land ownership — is based on having children (especially sons), this power base, once acquired, tends to be secure. In cases in which the father's high social class involves women's control over income (from land, rent, etc.) or large contributions to family income, women may be able to determine the nature of the division of labour in the family by using their resources to buy some services.[4]

Furthermore, a woman may derive power to control other family members' behaviours from her husband's high social status, especially when the husband's social status is clearly higher than that of other male family members in the household. In these cases, the power base is relatively more stable and less strained when the husband-wife bond is based on convenience (in terms of exchanged resources and services) or affection and companionship, rather than on love or sexual attraction (Oppong, 1977).

There is ample evidence from these societies that women who have high social status use birth control mainly because they have satisfactory alternative power bases. Thus, in patriarchal, highly sex-stratified societies, reproduction ceases to be an important power basis for women only when they can derive sufficient status and power from their associations with men. These women, as we shall see below, are also allowed to translate their productive activities into economic power. High social status in this case neutralizes the negative effects of the inferior gender status. Upper- and upper-middle class women, unlike women of lower social status, do not have to rely on reproduction, the one unique gender-related asset of women, in order to diminish their powerlessness and alienation.

In clearly male-dominated and rigidly sex-stratified societies, the prevailing male/female ratio is high (e.g., 930 Indian women to 1,000 Indian men and 900 Pakistani women per 1,000 men) because women's life expectancy is generally low due to a high death rate in childhood, mortality at childbirth, and other adverse life and health conditions (Bose, 1975; Jacobson, 1977). The relatively few women who reach middle or old age are usually granted a special status which provides them with some independence, freedom of movement and control over their lives, as well as authority to control younger female family members' (and, to some extent, younger male family members') lives and behaviours (Okonjo, 1978a). Since they can no longer bear children, they are viewed as 'asexual', and the negation of their sexuality can be translated into power in terms of autonomy and authority (Bart, 1969; Mernissi, 1975; Safilios-Rothschild, 1977a).

## The Limitations of Power Derived From Men

Women's power derived from men has some distinct characteristics which bring into question the validity of using the term 'power'. Because it is derived from men, women are quite aware that their power depends on alliances with and approval of men. It is difficult, therefore, for women to challenge men's decisions or to act in ways that are contrary to men's wishes. A further problem is that because their alliance is with men, such women do not identify with other women or feel the need to help other women free themselves from male domination. On the contrary, women often enforce other women's subjugation to men, an enforcement that gains them men's approval and, thus, enhances their access to status and power. An example is the way in which the cruel, almost inhuman, practice of 'Pharaonic circumcision' of young girls is enforced by mothers, grandmothers and aunts; it is an outstanding illustration of adult women's dependence on, and identification with, men as the powerful, dominant gender (Hayes, 1975).

In some societies women can gain power and status from their productive activities. In patriarchal, traditional societies, however, such activities can be translated into power *only if men allow it* − even if women's productive contribution to the household is equal to, or even greater than, that of their husbands. In such cases, it is still the men who control the wages and decide when the women will start and stop working. The men assert power and dominance over women through restrictions and prohibitions, through the control of women's sexuality and the consequences of their sexuality, and/or through physical force (or threats of physical force) (Moses, 1976; Safilios-Rothschild, 1979a). It can be hypothesized that men exert more control if women earn incomes equal to or even higher than those earned by their husbands, although this is difficult to prove since there is a high degree of sex discrimination in these societies, in terms of occupation, type of position and level of wages. As a result, women are usually involved in auxilliary or marginal occupations and positions, and their wages are but a fraction of those earned by men. Thus, regardless of their working status, women remain socially and economically dependent on men, and there is no ideological support for women's independence, even among the women themselves.

The net result is that women in these societies cannot translate their work and earnings into power; often, in fact, working women have less power and autonomy than women who do not work. This is especially true in households where men have low incomes and marginal occupations, as has been documented among working-class and low-income Greek families (Safilios-Rothschild and Dijkers, 1978), working-class and low-income Black Americans (Hammond and Enoch, 1976) and traditional Igbo families (Okonjo, 1978b). When men have a stable and strong economic base, however, they feel more confident about this dominant position, and their wives' substantial income from work in no way threatens them. In these cases, the women's economic contribution becomes a valuable and powerful resource that wins them more decision-making power, more equality in the division of labour in terms of husband participation and hired help, and more freedom to practice birth control (Okonjo, 1978b; Safilios-Rothschild and Dijkers, 1978).

In developing countries, however, it is more often the case that men have difficulty establishing a stable and adequate financial base and they adapt to the situation in several ways. In the traditional patriarchal societies of Southeast Asia, Southern Europe, North Africa and the Middle East, they assert their dominance over women (Safilios-Rothschild, 1979a). Women's sexuality is controlled and regulated by men, and the family remains stable. An alternative model of masculine adaptation to an unstable and weak economic base is avoidance of permanent, contractual economic responsibilities towards women and children, that is, withdrawal from family power – although not necessarily from domination of women (at least as long as an informal union lasts). This tendency towards unstable relationships often means men must migrate to distant urban areas or emigrate abroad in order to find jobs – as is true in many Caribbean and Latin American societies, as well as North African societies (as the opportunity to emigrate to Saudi Arabia or Iraq has become available). Because this model leads to a series of unstable relationships with men, and because all men express their masculinity and their dominance of the woman by having children, the number of children born to each woman is high. However, the unstable relationships also lead to large numbers of 'female-headed households'; these include households in which men are present but making only marginal financial contributions as well as households where men are entirely absent (Buvinic and Youssef, 1978).

Because the prevailing male-dominance ideology in these highly sex-stratified societies is adhered to by women as well as by men, the women do not seek to become economically independent – rather they become involved in productive activities only by default. They are not socialized to want or enjoy independence, autonomy and power based on their own productive activities. Furthermore, their lack of education and skills and the prevailing sex discrimination and exploitation of women make it very difficult for lower- and working-class women, especially, to survive in female-headed households (Maynard, 1974; Blumberg, 1977; Buvinic and Youssef, 1978). Psychological, social and financial constraints prevent these women from translating their structural position into power and autonomy. Instead, they continue to look for a more permanent relationship with a man who will protect them and dominate them.

## Power Achieved Through Productive Activities

An alternative basis of female power are women's productive, income-generating activities, which, when supported by an ideology of women's economic independence, can be translated into power. The existence of such an ideology of women's economic independence has been well documented. For example, in many West African communities women are expected to have an occupation in order to establish themselves as respectable adults in the community and are held responsible for their personal expenses as well as for a considerable percentage of the expenses related to their children. In this cultural area women are not only allowed to translate their economic activity into power, they are actually expected to be socially and economically independent of men (Oppong, 1974; Simmons, 1976).

Economic independence of women is usually accompanied by a belief that women's sexual needs and urges are real and strong, and that women want and must be able to express and satisfy their sexuality. In societies in which such beliefs prevail, the inheritance laws allow land and other private property to be passed on from mother to daughter, and women are allowed considerable freedom to express and satisfy their sexuality; they have considerable freedom of movement as well as sexual power (what is colourfully called in Ghana 'bottom power') (Little, 1973; Bleek, 1976; Akuffo, 1978; Dinan, 1978). It seems, therefore, that the higher the female power derived from women's economic activities, the greater their freedom of movement and sexual freedom. And the higher the degree of women's power derived from productive activities, the higher the degree of sexual power they enjoy.

Women can also derive power from a matrilineal kinship system that provides them with social, psychological and economic support. When the kinship system is matrilineal, women's autonomy is considerable and is often expressed in terms of high marital instability, because women can leave unsatisfactory marriages and husbands and return to their matrilineage (Bleek, 1975; Oppong, 1978). Furthermore, matrilineage organization structurally renders husbands marginal because they are absolved of the responsibility of being the exclusive or main breadwinners. As Bleek (1975) has very correctly pointed out, men's lesser economic and social responsibility implies lesser power.

In societies in which there is matrilineage organization as well as a social ideology supportive of women's economic independence, the women are more able to find remunerative economic activities, there is a greater degree of marital instability, and it is easier for women to remarry or to find satisfactory sexual/love relationships outside marriage (Gomm, 1972; Little, 1973). Under these conditions, women can translate their power (which is achieved independently of men) into autonomy, which is often expressed in terms of a 'lukewarm' attitude towards marriage and constraining familial responsibilities. Thus women have the option of staying single for as long as they wish in order to build up their economic base, often while having children (Dinan, 1978). Or they may opt for one of a variety of flexible structural arrangements which allows them maximum mobility, autonomy and productive/economic involvement as well as the maintenance of familial roles. Such arrangements may include living in a different town from their husbands (Kumekpor, 1974); accepting, in some African societies, a co-wife so that they have a greater freedom from familial responsibilities and more occupational mobility (Kumekpor, 1974)[5]; or living in a different household from the husband (or lover) and visiting him frequently. In rural Ghana, for example, 40 per cent of the married couples were found to be living in separate households (Bleek, 1975).

While groups that give women psychological and social support can be found in male-dominated, patriarchal societies (e.g., 'sisterhood' groups in Zaire or solidarity groups in Middle Eastern countries [Nelson, 1974; Gould, 1978]), women's informal networks with an economic as well as a social and psychological basis are more often found in matrilineal societies. A variety of women's co-operatives, credit and loan associations, and other organizations help women to translate their individual power into collective power. Women's autonomy from men at the business level is reinforced and sex discrimination is avoided (Grandmaison, 1972; Okonjo, 1978a). All of these groups also aid women in achieving greater freedom of movement and independence from men by supporting them in their choices to remain single, to be divorced, or to have children outside marriage (Gomm, 1972; Little, 1973; Simmons, 1976; Dinan, 1978).

Therefore female power achieved independently of men could be expressed as a function of:

$$F_P = F_{P1} + KF_{P2} + F_{P3} + F_{P4} + F_{P5},$$

in which

$F_{P1}$ = power derived from economic activities, the income of which is controlled by the women;

$F_{P2}$ = power derived from a social ideology supportive of women's economic independence and responsibility – even in the presence of a husband ($K$ is a constant, since this type of power base is necessary regardless of the values of the other power bases);

$F_{P3}$ = sexual power;

$F_{P4}$ = power derived from matrilineage;

$F_{P5}$ = power derived from women's collectives that provide economic as well as a social or psychological support.

The formula indicates that women may accrue power independently of men even when all power bases are not available to them – when, for example, the kinship system is not matrilineal. The ideological power basis must, however, always be present, in order for women to translate potential power bases into actual power, to define themselves in terms of such power, to want such power and to be satisfied holding it.

The idea that women can achieve power independently of men is not meant to imply that they cannot also derive power from men. The two are not mutually exclusive. In many societies, some types of power derived from men enhance women's independently achieved power; similarly, their independently achieved power helps women derive more power from their husbands. Thus, the prestige, wealth and power that women derive from husbands, fathers and other male relatives – especially if much higher than the prestige, wealth or power they can achieve on their own – helps women further enhance their positions in their jobs, and therefore increase their own status (Safilios-Rothschild, 1975). In addition, in societies where women's economic independence is encouraged and admired, economic power can be translated into marital and familial power in terms of influence and decision-making.

Finally, we cannot assume an inverse relationship between productive power and reproductive power. Even where there are matrilineal kinship systems and economic collectives, women still derive power from having children (Oppong, 1978). In rural matrilineal societies, children are women's 'most reliable assets in building up their own farm properties' (Oppong, 1978). In Ghana in 1976, for example, only 2 per cent of married women were known to be accepters or active users of contraception (Oppong, 1978). The economic role is not viewed as an alternative to the mother role (as it has been conceptualized in the Western demographic literature), but rather as a role that facilitates and supports the mother role. No notion of role incompatibility has been envisaged, since women's domestic and child-care duties can be easily performed by female relatives, daughters and other helpers. (It is interesting to note that although women can use economic power within the household to obtain other women's services – paid or unpaid – rarely can they use it to obtain a more egalitarian division of labour between husband and wife for household and child-care tasks (Oppong, 1974; Church, 1978; Nsarkoh, 1978)).

It seems, therefore, that even in societies in which women can translate their productive activities into economic power, the total female power formula should also incorporate bases of power derived from men and from bearing children:

$$TF_P = F_{P1} + KF_{P2} + F_{P3} + F_{P4} + F_{P5} + F_{P6} + F_{P7} + F_{P8} + F_{P9},$$

in which

$F_{P6}$ = reproductive power;
$F_{P7}$ = marital power;
$F_{P8}$ = power based on father's *or mother's* social status/wealth;
$F_{P9}$ = power based on husband's social status/wealth.

The power based on the 'asexual' status of women in middle age has not been included, because it becomes less important as women increase their economic power.

This equation makes it clear that while reproductive power is one of the components of female power, it is not necessarily a crucial one. Depending on the magnitude of the values of the other power bases, it can become less important for women to have a large reproductive power base. In fact, we could hypothesize that when women have several secure power bases, reproductive power may no longer be viewed as important. As has been amply documented, modernization and development often make women's traditional productive roles more insecure and strenuous (Boserup, 1970; Oppong, 1978), and women therefore have come to rely upon their reproductive power for social and economic security. It is only when women can feel socially, economically and psychologically secure in economically productive activities that they may become motivated to use birth control in order to have as many children as they enjoy rather than as many as they need.

## Indicators of Women's Power

At the beginning of this chapter, I tried to devise indicators of women's status in society; now I will turn to indicators of women's power in the household. While the indicators of women's status are important for macro level studies of different societies, the indicators of women's power in the household are important methodological tools for case studies of individual women (or networks of relatives). These indicators are:

— Women's ability to control decisions about their productive and economic activities, including freedom of movement and control over the resulting wages or income.
— Women's ability to control the services of others (unpaid family members or paid help) who substitute for them in household and child-care tasks and responsibilities.[6]
— Women's ability to control the type of household structure in terms of composition (extended or not and with which relatives; female-headed or not; polygynous or not and with second wife, etc.), size or duration.
— Degree of discrepancy between men's and women's ratios of time spent in income-earning activities to leisure time.
— Degree to which the women's time budgets show unreciprocated special services rendered to husbands.
— Percentage of own expenses and children's expenses paid by mother.
— Women's membership in economic and social collectives, and formal or informal groups (credit or loan associations, co-operatives, etc.).
— Degree of discrepancy between men's and women's wages or income from productive activities in the household.
— Women's ability to have an important say (if not make the actual decision) in decisions which affect their lives, such as major purchases, building a house, family size (including having a child at a particular time of life and work), moving or not to another town, etc. Or, in other words, women's ability to play an important role in decisions

which are not stereotyped as 'feminine' — such as what to eat, how to decorate the house, minor household purchases or the rearing of children.[7]

The above indicators are all behavioural, and the assessment of them can be best carried out through brief observation and intensive interviewing of the women being studied. During the intensive interviews, it should be fairly easy to assess the prevailing attitudes towards male supremacy and dominance and towards women's economic, social and psychological independence.

The establishment of two sets of indicators, one at the macro level — women's status in the society — and the other at the micro level — women's power at the interpersonal level within the household — allows the study of the relationships between the two indices. We can hypothesize that because women can derive social status and power from men and from reproduction, they can have power at the household level even when their status at the macro level is quite low. Conversely, individual women may have very little power at the household level, even when the status of women at the macro level is fairly high. This can very easily happen when women are married to men (or into families) who reject the value of women's social and economic independence and who enforce male dominance by controlling the income from women's economic activities, by restricting their freedom of movement or by limiting their choice of jobs. It seems, therefore, that the two sets of indicators presented in this chapter can guide research design so that it will include societies in which the status of women is high, medium and low, and within each society the sample studied will include women with high, medium and low degrees of power at the household level. Such a research design would allow us to determine empirically the ways in which the different profiles of women's status at the macro level can be translated into female power at the interpersonal level.

## Notes

1. It is recognized that a number of societal, economic or political constraints may be operating that limit their ability to determine these events. It is important to assess the extent to which these factors operate equally as constraints in men's and women's self-determination.

2. Marrying younger partners has traditionally been an option only open to men and it has been found that, cross-culturally, the greater the economic

emancipation of women in a society, the more the option of marrying younger men than themselves becomes a reality (Safilios-Rothschild, 1970). The latest trends in developed societies, such as the United States, further support the above generalization (Presser, 1976).

3. Completion data are better than enrolment data because they are more sensitive to the sex differentials in attrition due to the greater responsibilities assigned to girls for housework and child-care as well as other gender-related reasons for attrition (e.g., pregnancy, marriage for Third World women in the 8-19 years age group).

4. In some cases, even inherited high status and prestige may help women escape some household responsibilities because such duties can be relegated to other female family members.

5. Thus, African women realize the wish of successful American women: 'I wish I had a wife' (meaning a traditional housewife).

6. As long as all substitutes are also women, the stereotypic definition of housework and child-care as 'women's work' has not changed, and the sex-stratification system persists, partially because of the even more powerful class-stratification system. It is only when men also substitute for household and child-care tasks and responsibilities that the woman's *power* in the household begins to be translated into an equal *status* with the men in the household.

7. In addition, a few indicators related to what is happening to female children in the household are also important in giving an idea as to whether or not sex-role socialization continues to be clearcut and to perpetuate male supremacy and dominance. These indicators are:

- Division of labour by sex among children in the household, especially those in the 5-12 years age group. The degree of discrepancy between the ratio of time spent in child-care and housework to time spent in income-earning activities or in school for boys and girls is the most relevant.
- Degree of difference between years of formal and nonformal education completed by boys and girls.

# References

Akuffo, F.O. (1978) 'High wastage in women's education: the case of the rural elementary school girls', paper presented at the Conference on Women and Development, Legon, Ghana, 4-9 September

Bart, P.B. (1969) 'Why women's status changes in middle age: the turns of the social ferris wheel', *Sociological Symposium*, *3*, 1-18

Bleek, W. (1975) 'Appearance and reality: the ambiguous position of women in Kwahu, Ghana' in P. Kloos and K.W. van der Voen (eds.), *Rule and reality: essays in honor of Andre J.F. Kobben*, Amsterdam, University of Amsterdam, pp. 50-65

———— (1976) *Sexual relationships and birth control in Ghana*, Amsterdam, Anthropological-Sociological Center

Blumberg, R.L. with M.P. Garcia (1977) 'The political economy of the mother-child family: A cross-societal view' in Luis Lenero-Otero (ed.), *Beyond the nuclear family model. Cross-cultural perspectives*, Beverly Hills, Calif., Sage, pp. 99-163

Bose, A. (1975) 'A demographic profile' in Devaki Jain (ed.), *Indian women*, New Delhi, Patiala House, Ministry of Information and Broadcasting, pp. 127-84

Boserup, E. (1970) *Women's role in economic development*, London, George
  Allen and Unwin
Buvinic, M. and N.H. Youssef (1978) 'Women-headed households: the ignored
  factor in development planning', report submitted to AID/WID, Grant
  AID/otr-G-1593, March
Caldwell, J.C. (1976) 'Fertility and the household economy in Nigeria', *Journal
  of Comparative Family Studies, 7*, 2 (Summer), 193-253
Church, K. (1978) 'A study of socio-economic status and child-care arrangements
  of women in Madina', paper presented at the Conference on Women and
  Development, Legon, Ghana, 4-9 September
Dinan, C. (1978) 'Pragmatists or feminists? The professional "single" women of
  Accra, Ghana', *Cahiers d'Etudes Africaines, 65*, 17, 155-76
Gomm, R. (1972) 'Harlots and bachelors: marital instability among the coastal
  Digo of Kenya', *Man, 7*, 1, 95-113
Gould, T.F. (1978) 'Value conflict and development: the struggle of the
  professional Zairian woman', *Journal of Modern African Studies, 16*, 1, 133-9
Grandmaison, C. le Court (1972) 'Femmes Dakaroises', *Annales de l'Universite
  d'Abidjan*, serie F: Ethnosociologie, Tome 4
Hammond, J. and J.R. Enoch (1976) 'Conjugal power relations among black
  working class families', *Journal of Black Studies, 7*, 1, 107-28
Hayes, R.O. (1975) 'Female genital mutilation, fertility control, women's roles
  and the patrilineage in modern Sudan: a functional analysis', *American
  Ethnologist, 2*, 4
Jacobson, D. (1977) 'The women of North and Central India: goddesses and
  wives' in D. Jacobson and S.S. Wadley (eds.), *Women in India: two perspectives*,
  New Delhi, Manohar
Kumekpor, T.K. (1974) 'Mothers and wage labor employment: some aspects of
  problems of the working mother in Ghana', *The Ghana Journal of Sociology,
  7*, 2, 68-91
Little, K. (1973) *African women in towns*, Cambridge, Cambridge University
  Press
Mauldin, W.P. and B. Berelson (1978) 'Conditions of fertility decline in
  developing countries, 1965-1975', *Studies in Family Planning, 9*, 5, 139-41
Maynard, E. (1974) 'Guatemalan women: life under two types of patriarchy' in
  Carolyn J. Mattiasson (ed.), *Many sisters: women in cross-cultural perspective*,
  New York, The Free Press, pp. 77-98
Mernissi, F. (1975) *Beyond the Veil: male-female dynamics in a modern Muslim
  society*, New York, John Wiley and Sons
Mishler, E.G. and N.E. Waxler (1968) *Interaction in families: an experimental
  study of family processes and schizophrenia*, New York, John Wiley and Sons
Moses, Y.T. (1976) 'Female status, the family and male dominance in a West
  Indian community', paper presented at the Wellesley Conference on Women
  and Development, May, Wellesley College, Wellesley, Mass.
Nelson, C. (1974) 'Public and private politics: women in the Middle Eastern
  world', *American Ethnologist, 2*, 3, 551-63
Nsarkoh, J. (1978) 'Women and home', paper presented at the Conference on
  Women and Development, Legon, Ghana, 4-9 September
Okonjo, K. (1978a) *Aspects of decision-making in the rural Igbo household*,
  Nsukka, Nigeria, University of Nigeria, Institute of African Studies
—— (1978b) 'New wine in old bottles. The changing role of the Igbo women
  in the family – the Nsukka example', paper presented at the Conference on
  Women and Development, Legon, Ghana, 4-9 September
Olson, D.H. and R.E. Cromwell (1975) 'Power in families' in Ronald E. Cromwell
  and David H. Olson (eds.), *Power in families*, New York, John Wiley and Sons,

pp. 3-11

Oppong, C. (1974) *Marriage among matrilineal elite*, Cambridge, Cambridge University Press

——— (1975) 'Nursing mothers: aspects of the conjugal and maternal roles of nurses in Accra', paper presented at the Canadian African Studies Association Meeting, Toronto

——— (1978) 'Modernisation and aspects of family change in Ghana: with particular reference to the effects of work', paper presented at the Aspen Institute/Iran Workshop, Gajereh, Iran, 27 May-2 June

——— (1979) 'Changing family structure and conjugal love: the case of the Akan of Ghana' in M. Cook and G. Wilson (eds.), *Love and attraction*, Oxford, Pergamon Press

Phillips, C.E. (1967) 'Measuring power of spouse', *Sociology and Social Research*, *52*

Presser, H.B. (1976) 'Age differences between spouses', *American Behavioral Scientist*, *19*, 2, 190-205

Safilios-Rothschild, C. (1969) 'Patterns of familial power and influence', *Sociological Focus*, *2*, 3, 7-19

——— (1970) 'Toward a cross-cultural conceptualization of family modernization', *Journal of Comparative Family Studies*, *1*, 1, 17-25

——— (1975) 'Family and stratification: some macrosociological observations and hypotheses', *Journal of Marriage and the Family*, pp. 855-60

——— (1976) 'A macro- and micro-examination of family power and love: an exchange model', *Journal of Marriage and the Family*, pp. 355-62

——— (1977a) 'Sexuality, power and freedom among "older" women' in L.E. Troll, J. Israel and K. Israel (eds.), *Looking ahead*, Englewood Cliffs, NJ, Prentice-Hall, Spectrum, pp. 162-6

——— (1977b) 'The relationship between women's work and fertility: some methodological and theoretical issues' in Stanley Kupinsky (ed.), *The fertility of working women. A synthesis of international research*, New York, Praeger Publishers, pp. 355-68

——— (1979a) 'The demographic consequences of the changing roles of men and women in the 80's', *Proceedings of the 1978 Conference on Economic and Demographic Change: Issues for the 1980's*, Liege, Belgium, IUSSP

——— (1979b) *The dynamics of the husband-wife relationship in urban Greece*, Athens, National Center for Social Research

——— and M. Dijkers (1978) 'Handling unconventional asymmetrics' in Rhona and Robert N. Rapoport (eds.), *Working Couples*, London, Routledge and Kegan Paul

Simmons, E.B. (1976) 'Economic research on women's participation in rural development', paper presented at the Fourth World Congress for Rural Sociology, Torun, Poland, 9-13 August

# 6 FAMILY STRUCTURE AND WOMEN'S REPRODUCTIVE AND PRODUCTIVE ROLES: SOME CONCEPTUAL AND METHODOLOGICAL ISSUES

Christine Oppong

The most harmful distortion [in studies of fertility in the developing world] is probably in the nature of the family both as a social and economic unit. Western sociologists are capable of perceiving that the nuclear (or conjugal) family of the West, with an economic concentration within a group made up of husband, wife and non-adult children and usually residence restricted to the same group, is not universal; that traditionally it may have been a rarity elsewhere. But when carrying out social surveys outside of the West, they tend to treat other types of kinship as if the differences were restricted to having a few more financial responsibilities (Caldwell, 1977).

The neoclassical model has a much more sophisticated disguise for the role of women. That is the household (Galbraith, 1973, p. 36).

This chapter addresses several issues relevant to the development of a research framework for the interdisciplinary and comparative analysis of women's roles as mothers and workers in contrasting cultures. It focuses in particular upon the domestic and familial contexts within which women live and work, and on some of the problems involved in the collection and classification of survey and case study data in the domestic domain. The discussion is based upon the simple premiss that little understanding can be gained of differences and fluctuations in women's productive and reproductive activities, attitudes and aspirations in any cultural context, if critical and more complex analyses of residential patterns and domestic organization (including division of labour, allocation of resources, authority and power, and systems of kinship and marriage) are not carried out. This is a basic point, and one which has been made by a number of those who have written about the sociology of fertility and employment.

Another purpose here is to indicate the contribution that the anthro-political viewpoint can make in the conceptualization of the methodology of a project combining the approaches and techniques of different disciplines and having no ethnocentric biases. As the two quotations at the beginning of the chapter emphasize, the approaches

133

of sociology, demography and economics to the study of women and family systems have often been singularly hampered by their intrinsic sexist and ethnocentric biases. This is partly because the type of ideal family system that is predominant in industrialized capitalist societies has formed the basis for designs used around the world. At the same time, the corresponding concept of the male 'breadwinner' and 'household head' has meant that in many study designs, as Galbraith notes, women have been disguised as dependent members of solidary units called 'households'.

The focus on the domestic group is crucial for two reasons — one practical, the other theoretical. The practical reason is fairly simple: in designing a project in which survey data will play an important part, *units* for study must be selected; typically the units will be either individuals or households. The second, theoretical, reason is that within the context of the domestic domain it may be possible to find links between aspects of women's status and productive activities, and attitudes and behaviour associated with demographic phenomena — such as fertility, mortality and morbidity.

I will begin by noting the methodological and conceptual problem of selecting units for study and will then discuss the reasons for rejecting the unitary . 'household' model of the New Household Economics as an analytical tool in cross-cultural research. Arguing, as have many others, that women are so involved in their familial roles and contexts, and are so constrained or supported by conjugal and kin ties, that to neglect to focus on the latter would seriously prejudice the value of a project (Nash, 1975), I will look at ethnographic evidence on the composition and function of domestic groups that points to the necessity of examining separately ties of kinship and marriage, co-residence patterns, and domestic functions. Data on socialization and care-taking in different cultures will be presented to illustrate that such functions are most often carried out not just by the parents but by a wider group. In the final section, I will outline a simple framework for the analysis of domestic behaviour and familial rights and duties that avoids the pitfalls found in analyses based on the New Household Economics.

## Problems in Selecting Units of Study

Household sample surveys have long provided data for social research in several disciplines focusing on fertility, but, recently, questions have arisen about the basic assumption of such studies. There is a need to re-think the definition of 'household' and the criteria used to decide whether given individuals are included in it. At the same time, it is recognized that 'family structure' must be examined, particularly women's familial rights and obligations and the extent to which families are classifiable as 'extended' or 'nuclear'. There is also a need to go beyond current economic theories of 'household decision-making', in which the family/household is seen as a 'homogeneous unit' (Anker, 1978).

## Inappropriate Assumptions of the New Household Economics

One important reason for not using models based on the New Household Economics in cross-cultural research is that they rest upon a set of culture-bound assumptions about family systems (that is, the allocation of rights, duties, responsibilities, tasks and resources among spouses, offspring, kin and social institutions). Implicit throughout is the notion of bounded conjugal family units — units functioning separately in every sphere of action from other family units — and the assumption that residential boundaries coincide with functional boundaries.

It is assumed in Schultz (1974), for instance, that income to be spent upon a set of siblings is earned only by their biological parents and that the income the parents earn is used *jointly* for satisfaction of their own and their offspring's needs. Such discrete conjugal family units are considered to be coterminous with co-resident, physically identifiable *households*. Again the unit of the conjugal pair is assumed in the discussion of household decision-making; it is implicitly assumed that there is a stable monogamous conjugal pair who together make decisions, carry out actions and manage resources, etc. A further assumption is that a married couple bear the costs of their children *jointly*; at the same time, however, it is assumed that the mother bears the *total costs of time*. This assumption does not take into account the large and growing literature which examines variations on the conjugal-role relationship. Detailed studies of conjugal relationships have revealed that there are differences in the extent to which there is joint responsibility for financial support and management even among couples of the same ethnic or socio-economic group (Oppong, 1974).

The dynamic interaction resulting from the potentially different aspirations of husbands and wives has been inadequately and infrequently accounted for in such models. New Household economists tend to assume syncratic modes of decision-making or husband dominance, perhaps admitting wife dominance for a minority of aberrant cases; but in Ghana, for example, conjugal autonomy is a common phenomenon (Oppong, 1970). It is dangerous, therefore, to assume unity in conjugal family decision-making.

Another basic assumption of these models is that the mothers who bear the children bear the time costs of rearing them. Thus, it is supposed that the value of the time of the women is a major factor affecting fertility, since it is taken for granted that women leave the labour force to bear and care for children (Schultz, 1974). It is argued that the most important factor, at least in a child's early years, in determining the cost of raising a child is the price of the mother's time. The cost of a woman's education, which is an index of her earning power, is often assumed to be the cost (in terms of foregone income) of raising children. Thus, most of the costs (sacrifices) of having children and in caring for them during their infant years is borne by mothers. Indeed, 'the core of the theory is designed primarily to analyze the effects of the differences in the price of time of parents that enter directly into the production of children' (Schultz, 1974). However, as will be discussed below, child-care is often delegated to individuals other than the mother; in such situations time is acquired free or at minimal cost, and time inputs are provided by several individuals rather than only by mothers. Thus the mother's own time may be scarce and valuable and used in remunerative employment, but child-rearing itself may be inexpensive.

At different times and in different cultural settings, time and money may vary in value and scarcity, and therefore the constraints imposed by either will also vary. As has been pointed out elsewhere, time in the domestic domain is cheap and readily available in societies at certain intermediate stages of development (Boserup, 1970). Furthermore, the concept of the housewife role itself is the product of a particular process of economic development (Oakley, 1976). It is a culture-bound phenomenon and cannot be assumed in other societies, especially peasant societies, where household work and productive labour (such as farming, food processing and crafts) are scarcely distinguishable, and all household members play an active role in both. It is necessary therefore in any particular inquiry to examine *whose* time is potentially available and selected for child-care and related *household* activities, and the cost of that time. As a recent study of Akan domestic economy indicates, child-rearing tasks may be passed on to those members of the kin set whose time is least valued for other purposes

(Church, 1978a). Other data from Ghana also call into question the relevance of the assumptions implicit in these theories and raise the issue of what new kinds of data are needed to test them (Oppong, 1976b). There is already considerable evidence that functional bounded-ness of the conjugal family in different areas of behaviour is highly vari-able, both within and between cultures. Only detailed documentation of patterns of time use, money earning and spending, and norms and behaviour regarding actual and potential rights and obligations can distinguish one type from another.

The recent increase in such studies of household behaviour by economists has not yet led to a corresponding increase in analysis of household structure and family relationships, although there are signs of movement in this direction (Ben-Porath, 1978). Research has con-tinued to focus on the nuclear family, which is the more predominant household composition in the high-income areas in which much of the research of the New Household Economics has taken place. (Although even in these areas it has been noted that there are problems with lack of adequate data or of sophisticated techniques for analysis (Schultz, 1978).)

There is recognition in some quarters that all is not well. Field-workers in the Third World, realizing that the nuclear family model does not fit their materials, have attempted to innovate and to increase the sophistication of their analyses by adding another category of household type — 'extended' (Kelly and Swartz, 1978; Singh, 1978). However, the problems involved in these studies, such as the inability to process all the cases of data collected because they do not 'fit' the categories defined, indicate that the simplicity of such solutions is deceptive and that there are still basic problems to be solved.

An approach different from that of the economists has been taken by several prominent social anthropologists who have analyzed domes-tic organization and co-residence patterns. Their findings will be dis-cussed in the next sections.

## Evidence of the Need for a New Framework of Analysis

Ethnographers grappling with the analysis of complex and diverse domestic data from around the world have been continuously impressed by the need to refine the concept of household for research purposes and to distinguish carefully among families, marriage and descent relationships, and co-residential groups, on the one hand, and domestic functions, on the other. As Goody (1972) has pointed out, much of the recent discussion of household composition and familial functions was anticipated two or three decades ago by Fortes' brilliant analyses of domestic groups among the Tallensi and Ashanti in Ghana (1949b). Fortes emphasized the need for quantitative analysis in the study of household composition and domestic organization, the futility of blanket terms, and the importance of seeing domestic organization as the result of a number of factors operating both at a given time and over time. His accounts of Tallensi homesteads and joint families, the domestic family and the developmental cycle of the domestic group provided early models for subsequent ethnographers.

Significantly, among the Tallensi the units of consumption and reproduction were seen to be enclosed within larger dwelling units, while among the Ashanti the reproductive and economic units were found to be usually distinct from the dwelling group at any time. Fortes found, for instance, that the Ashanti 'houseful' was more often based upon the sibling than on the conjugal bond.

Goody's point, in his discussion of the fission of the domestic groups among the Lodagaba (1958), was clearly similar to Fortes' argument, for Goody noted that among neither the Tallensi nor the Lodagaba does the domestic organization focus exclusively on one multifunctional unit. There are a number of such units which function in different situations, the main contexts in which they emerge being the two basic processes of production and reproduction. Goody maintained that previous writers had inhibited analysis of the organization of domestic groups by assuming that the central focus of this process was necessarily the 'nuclear family'. He demonstrated that among the Lodagaba of northern Ghana the 'nuclear family' is the nucleus neither in the productive nor the reproductive process. In the process of reproduction, the smallest unit is the conjugal pair, but in the process of food production, distribution, consumption, etc., different groups are involved. The basic farming unit is a group of agnatically related males, and dependent upon them is a group of women and children who contribute their labour for weeding and harvesting. In the process of distribution, preparation and consumption, the basic unit is the mother and her young children.

Ethnographic data from other regions of the world (such as that collected in the course of the study of West Indian domestic institutions) have also clearly illustrated the problems engendered by the basic failure to distinguish between co-residential groups, units of consumption and production, and the family as a reproductive and child-socializing agency (Smith, 1962). The unique configuration of relationships and the flexibility and variability in family ties and domestic settings encouraged the realization that family organization is not reducible to co-residence patterns. Links between co-resident groups may be just as important as links within co-resident groups. Another point which emerged was the importance of considering and documenting the processes and patterns of parental substitution in a society in which there was substantial evasion of or failure to accept the obligations of parenthood. Women's kin were found to be particularly important in providing parental substitutes. Overall there were found to be both a plurality of mating forms and a diversity and instability of domestic organization. Smith (1962) emphasized that it should be recognized that 'marriage does not exhaust mating, that elementary families may be dispersed as systematically as they are nucleated and that some societies may base the family structure on alternative sets of mating relations and parental roles'.

Examination of these and other materials (Stack, 1974) make clear that several units or sets of networks may be involved in the process of production, maintenance, consumption, reproduction, sexual relations and socialization. The core members of these groups are usually kin or a couple who may live together or close to each other for periods of time. Residential groups may be built around married pairs, parents and children, or siblings, but there may be only one adult. What makes these various sets of people or 'units' overlap in membership is the close relationship usually maintained between sex, reproduction and socialization. Domestic groups may thus be thought of as those basic units that revolve around the processes of reproduction and production, but these processes central to the maintenance of human life are not necessarily all carried out by a single-boundary maintaining unit (Goody, 1972).

The size of the dwelling unit has to be separated from the size of the unit of consumption (one hearth/fire or one board/table/pot) and from the localized groups of kin who co-operate — grandparents who live nearby and share care of children, or large groups jointly concerned with aspects of production. These findings emphasize that meaningful examination of relationships and domestic functions cannot be confined to co-residential groupings but should include exchanges and ties between co-residential groupings. This point is being increasingly recognized.

Thus in any study of women's productive, reproductive and other roles, each set of activities, norms, rights, duties, decisions and relation-

ships must be separately documented before their congruence and interactive effects can be determined. The problem of analyzing such data
will be discussed in the next section.

### Residential Patterns: Census Data

A basic requirement of demographers' descriptions of social systems is
the establishment of the rules of residence or the size and composition
of households on the basis of a house-by-house census. An indication
that this is not a simple or straightforward process is that anthropologists' reports of the same data have varied. Many of the earlier typo-
logies used deal only with ideal types or are ambiguous and may thus
be of limited value when the fieldworker is confronted with the diversity of forms. The limitations of these approaches have been noted and
new, sometimes unwieldy and complex, modes of classification have
been offered as substitutes (Mukherjee, 1972). The size and complexity
of the problem is particularly acute in contexts in which dwelling
groups are particularly large. For instance, Hill (1977) has recorded
dwellings with more than one hundred members.

One point which soon becomes clear from a perusal of some of the
analyses of ethnographic data on residential patterns is that there are
many different ways of sorting data and any number of categories can
result. Dorjahn (1977), for example, developed fourteen different
categories for the classification of his census data from the Temne of
Sierra Leone. Casselberry and Valavanes (1976) classified residence
types on the basis of several different referent groups — the community,
the household and the dwelling. Another significant point which
emerges from a range of studies is the importance of the set of household categories used. Authors note that even rearrangement of subtypes
can lead to very different results in their analyses (Clarke, 1957; Solien,
1970; Goldberg, 1976).

Thirty years ago attempts were made to view changes in co-residential patterns over time using the concept of the developmental cycle in
the domestic group (Fortes, 1949a), by using quantified data that were
essentially synchronic. This was followed by similar attempts in other
cultural contexts (Goody, 1958). At least one research team has
attempted to use data from several points in time to support the
developmental approach (Otterbein and Otterbein, 1977). Recently
Dorjahn (1977) has considered the value of comparing census data
collected at two points in time from the same population and from two
populations at the same time.

The earlier, simpler paradigm of the developmental cycle of domestic groups, however, has been found to be inadequate for more complex situations in which there may be several complementary life cycles (Davenport, 1961). More important to the discussion here is that it also cannot accommodate differences in men's and women's cycles (Sanjek and Sanjek, 1975).

One thing which detailed studies of residence have documented is that actual co-residence patterns may be very different from the ideal (Freedman, Moots and Weinberger, 1978). It has also been demonstrated that an individual's shifts in residence over the life cycle must be taken into consideration. For instance, Bartle (1978) has documented variations in individual residence patterns among the Kwahu of Ghana; residence may be conjugal-, family- or matrilineage-based at different stages of the life and migration cycle.

It has also been found to be necessary to distinguish between the stranger/observer's categorization of household residence patterns and the way in which the individuals in the group describe the system, so that decision models may be based on local knowledge about what kinds of people live in what kinds of situations (Fjellman, 1976).

Another important point made in a recent study by Freedman *et al*. (1978) is that the physical availability of kin needs to be taken into account in measuring the incidence of differential composition of households; retrospective data may show that at some stage many or all houses are 'extended'. Bradley and Mendels (1978) have attempted to distinguish between family composition and family organization, the latter being the fundamental process whereby the former is generated. What is common to these anthropological approaches is the documentation of the *genealogical* relationships of the people who live together and the classification of residential groupings on this basis as well as, in some cases, on the basis of the relationships to people living nearby.

Some recent work has focused on the quantitative estimation of the incidence of certain types of family structures in past societies. For historical periods, synchronic data are of course far more readily available than diachronic data, as well as being much easier to collect and analyze. Historians have therefore tried to infer the latter from the former, a task that is made easier now by the use of computers and population registers (van de Walle, 1976; see also the recent work of Macfarlane, Harrison and Jardine, 1977).

From the above discussion can be seen the complexity of research in the area of documenting co-residence as it has moved beyond the use of data based simply on counting heads found in buildings of a certain type and size. One conclusion that can be drawn from the studies mentioned here is that the standard definitions of household in current international use need to be reconceptualized.

## Socialization

Twenty years ago Levy and Fallers (1959) made the important point, in the debate about the universality of the family, that it seemed untenable to assume that the socialization function is invariably carried out primarily within a single kinship structured unit – the nuclear family or any other type of family – even though they assumed that small kinship structured units are structural prerequisites of any society and that the nature of such units is bound up with the socialization function. They therefore suggested that the concept of 'family' be used for general comparative purposes to refer not to a single social unit in each society, but rather to any small kinship structured unit that carried out aspects of the relevant functions.

An examination of the cross-cultural evidence on socialization supports such an argument, for it shows that parents, particularly mothers, are not the only, or even the primary, care-takers and socializers of children in most societies. It shows that the type of family system that is widely discussed and documented in Western Europe and North America is in fact an aberrant form; therefore findings of research on attachment and detachment of infants in that culture area are inapplicable to the rest of the world (Ainsworth, 1967). Indeed, cross-cultural evidence indicates that nonparental care-taking of children is either the norm or a significant norm in most societies of the world (Weisner and Gallimore, 1977).

Scales of care-taking using a controlled sample of 186 societies have given quantitative evidence of the significance of nonmaternal care for infants and young children (Barry and Paxon, 1971). Nearly 40 per cent of infants in the sample were rated as being cared for by people other than mothers; only 2.7 per cent of infants were cared for almost exclusively by the mother, and there were no societies in this category when the children were past infancy. Other children and other adults were seen to play significant care-taking roles. The conclusion of these ratings was that in the majority of societies mothers are not the principal care-takers or companions of young children. Weisner and Gallimore (1977) note that even in ethnographies that have recognized the importance of multiple care-taking, the diffuse character of interpersonal attachments in such societies, and the fact that children are trained in large and inflexible family groups, there has been little documentation of the different styles of care-taking. An important point, which they stress and which is relevant to future research on women's maternal roles, is the availability of individuals to assume care-taking roles. They note that such availability is a function of many factors, one being the composition and size of the residential domestic group. In cases where a mother lives alone with her children and no kin or other possible care-takers live nearby, it is difficult for the mother to find child-care. Analysis of cross-cultural residential patterns has shown that such situations occur only in a small minority of cultures, however (D'Andrade, 1966).

Whiting and Whiting (1975) have provided evidence from six cultures on the availability of mothers and other care-takers. Their data show the availability of 'housemates' and 'courtyard cousins', and highlight the fact that it is only in their New England sample that the mother is present in the observations more frequently than siblings. Unfortunately, we are given availability in these figures but not a record of the amount of time children actually spend as care-takers. There is indirect evidence, however, that in some of the societies sampled, children were interacting with infants 25 per cent of the time. Minturn and Lambert (1964) also reported from their data in the six cultures study that mothers in the United States spent more of their time in charge of their children  than those in any of the other five societies — 92 per cent of the US mothers usually or always cared for their babies by themselves. In the other five societies there was significantly less maternal care. Continuous sharing of child-care is seen to be the pattern in some communities and supervision by the mother often involves the use of children as assistants. The importance of studying maternal roles in a social context is thus stressed, as well as the need for time-budget data in order to document child-care roles precisely.

In commenting on the traditional West African patterns, Fortes notes that parenthood is 'embedded in a matrix of wider social relations, defined by rules of kinship and descent which determines each person's status in, claims on and responsibilities to society . . . offspring belong not only to their parents but to kinship  and descent groups which stretch to ascendants and collaterals' (1978, p. 27). He goes on to point out that,

[Rearing and socialization] are not confined to the natural parents. In a patrilineal joint family of the type represented by the Tallensi, a child grows up in a domestic group which may number as many as ten coresident kin spread over three generations, and in contact from earliest age with classificatory kin outside the family. A father's

> disciplinary roles may be delegated in part to fathers, brothers; a
> mother's nurturing role to her cowives; and the siblingship that is the
> basis of fraternal trust and cooperation may embrace a range of peers
> . . . Customs of adoption, fostering and apprenticeship . . . extend
> the role of the parents to collateral kin and even to nonkinsfolk . . .
> (pp. 30-1).

He next calls attention to the common occurrence of a number of practices, including pawning, crisis and voluntary fostering, 'housemaids',
educational fosterage, wardship and apprenticeship. These all in one
form or another involve the delegation of parental roles to others.
These patterns of delegation are not simply 'occasional statistical
anomalies in the otherwise even flow of nuclear family life'. They are,
rather, 'formalized institutions with elaborated beliefs, rituals, and sanctions, institutions which have sufficient incidence to form a significant
aspect of childbearing in a given society' (Fortes, 1978).

Societies in which there is considerable delegation of maternal
responsibilities are not limited to those with subsistence economies in
which social organization is based on kinship ties or groups. Innovative
modern societies such as the Soviet Union, China and Israel offer
extensive child-care facilities which effectively provide a system of
maternal role delegation. Both the informal and the formal systems of
delegation of maternal responsibilities in kin and non-kin settings
reflect a family ideology which permits a mother to entrust her children
to others for considerable periods during the day.

The rapidity with which crèches and day-care centres have sprung up
within the private sector in the city of Accra indicates that there may
be little difficulty from a social point of view in urban areas in shifting
to a different type of delegation of tasks, when such a mode of behaviour is already an accepted norm.

A number of recent studies have documented the extent to which
these patterns of parental role delegation continue in new and different
contexts, sometimes involving sending children from rural to urban
communities or from urban to rural communities (Goody, 1978).
Significantly, the lack of such possibilities for parental role delegation
has been cited as a restraint on urban women's ability to earn an income away from the home (Church, 1978b).

Data on socialization underline the importance of looking at kinship and marriage ties, co-residence patterns, and domestic functions
separately. An important variable is the extent to which the connected
activities and rights and obligations are shared by sets of people, and

the extent to which the availability of the latter is affected by residence patterns. One major point to note is that no assumption has been made here about the congruence of socialization activities, rights and duties, and those in any other sphere of domestic activity.

A second major point is the significance of *substitution*; that is, the extent to which a particular right, duty or task is attached to a single individual woman or is shared by several people, and, if shared, the composition of this set of people. In the case of child-care, as noted above, responsibilities were attached to one figure – the mother – in only a few cases; in the majority of cases they were distributed relatively widely among co-resident or neighbouring kin and affines.


## A Framework for Analysis

The framework proposed here allows researchers to focus on women within the domestic context in analyses of domestic behaviour and familial rights and duties but makes no assumptions about the overlap of different areas of domestic functioning.

This approach combines the study of the conjugal division of labour, power, rights and duties in each domestic area with analysis of the extent to which kin or kin substitutes share in such domestic rights, duties and responsibilities. It also facilitates quantification and comparison of the extent to which a woman alone assumes responsibilities or receives support. Figure 6.1 illustrates such an approach. Women in Category A shared a particular domestic task or responsibility or right with both their husbands and their kin. Women in Category B shared with kin but not spouses. Women in Category C shared a particular right, task or duty with their husbands, and women in Category D acted without either husbands or kin.

As I have demonstrated elsewhere (Oppong, 1974), a number of areas of domestic functioning may be chosen – child-care or domestic-chore performance, financial provision for self, spouse, children, kin, etc.; detailed items of data may be classified in such a way as to facilitate both synchronic description of domestic organization and the distribution of selected traits in a given population. The potential relationships between different types of behaviour can also be examined. Sets of Ghanaian data analyzed within this framework have illustrated the potential utility of the method by demonstrating the kinds of simple quantifiable and comparable indices which may be used. In the original study referred to here (Oppong, 1974), precise

**Figure 6.1: Female Familial Support System**

Help from spouse (father of child)

|  |  | Yes | No |
|---|---|---|---|
|  |  | A | C |
| Yes |  | + + | + − |
| Help from kin (or others) |  |  |  |
|  |  | B | D |
| No |  | − + | − − |

Source: Adapted from C. Oppong, *Marriage among a matrilineal elite: a family study of Ghanaian civil servants* (Cambridge, Cambridge University Press, 1974), Table 1.1.

quantified indices of conjugal support and sharing and of the type and content of exchanges with kin were devised on the basis of reports of such behaviour as joint property ownership, requests of help from kin, delegation of child-care, amounts of money sent monthly to kin, numbers of relatives educated, proportions contributed to items of domestic expenditure, the frequency of performance of various household tasks, and ways in   which decisions were made. At the same time an ideal model could be built from the study of prescribed norms (Oppong, 1975).

In the study of urban families, the delegation and sharing of tasks and responsibilities by women was seen to be an important factor in their ability to work full time in jobs outside the home. Subsequent studies of other Ghanaian populations have indicated the relevance of this research approach to the study of innovation in behaviour and attitudes relating to fertility. It was found that the measurement indices could be used to test a number of hypotheses current in the population research literature, hypotheses attempting to link changing aspects of women's status — particularly their positions and resources as wives and kinswomen — with their tendencies to innovate in terms of reproduction, motherhood and child-rearing (Oppong, 1976a, 1977 and 1977b). A number of observers have hypothesized correlations between the division of child-rearing responsibilities and the motivation to restrict family size. Others have noted correlations between the availability of alternative child-care arrangements and the lack of role conflict or stress for working mothers. Both hypotheses have been examined within the framework sketched, using Ghanaian survey and

and case data from mobile migrants, first-generation salary earners, and others of their less socially and spatially mobile peers (Oppong, 1976a; 1977 and 1977b). These studies point to the fact that it is possible to collect both quantifiable and qualitative data on norms, behaviour and the allocation of domestic resources, which, while focusing upon individual women, give relevant information about their domestic contexts – including availability and participation of spouses and kin in domestic activities, and their domestic constraints and supports – and can be used for the exploration of hypotheses linking women's roles and demographic issues.

Ultimately this chapter is a plea for a more 'synthetic' approach to the study of women's (and men's) roles in the two spheres of production and reproduction – 'synthetic' in the sense of combining the concepts and techniques of several disciplines. Such a union would entail some breaking down of disciplinary boundaries in order to achieve the needed interpenetration of theories, concepts and methods. Women's studies may prove to be the field in which a synthesis of approaches could be achieved.

## References

Ainsworth, M.D.S. (1967) *Infancy in Uganda*, Baltimore, Johns Hopkins Press
Anderson, M. (1971) *Family structure in nineteenth century Lancashire*, Cambridge, Cambridge University Press
Anker, R. (1978) 'Demographic change and the role of women: a research programme in developing countries', mimeo., WEP research working paper, restricted, Geneva, ILO
Barry, H. and L.M. Paxon (1971) 'Infancy and early childhood cross cultural codes', *Ethnology, 2*, 10, 466-508
Bartle, P.F.W. (1978) 'Conjugal relations, migration and fertility in an Akan community Obo Ghana' in Oppong, Adaba, Bekombo-Priso and Mogey
Ben-Porath, Y. (1978) 'Family functions and structure and the organization of exchange', paper presented at IUSSP Conference on Economic and Demographic Change: Issues for the 1980s, Helsinki
Berkner, L.K. (1972) 'The stem family and the developmental cycle of the peasant household: an eighteenth century Austrian example', *American Historical Review, 27*, 2, 398-418
——— (1975) 'Use and misuse of census data for the historical analysis of household structure', *Journal of Interdisciplinary History, 5*, 4, 721-30
Blake, J. (1961) *Family structure in Jamaica: the social context of reproduction*, New York, Free Press of Glencoe
Bohannan, P. (1957) 'An alternative residence classification', *American Anthropologist, 59*, 126-31
Boserup, E. (1970) *Woman's role in economic development*, London, George Allen and Unwin
Bradley, B.P. and F. Mendels (1978) 'Can the hypothesis of a nuclear family organization be tested statistically?' *Population Studies, 32*, 2

Burch, T.K. (1970) 'Some demographic determinants of average household size: an analytic approach', *Demography*, 7, 1
—— and M. Gendell (1970) 'Extended family structure and fertility: some conceptual and methodological issues', *Journal of Marriage and the Family*, 32, 2
Caldwell, J.C. (1976) 'Measuring wealth flows and the rationality of fertility: thoughts and plans based in the first place on African work', paper presented at the Conference on the Economic and Social Supports for High Fertility, Camberra, 16-18 November
—— (ed.) (1977) *The persistence of high fertility: population prospects in the third world*, Changing African Family Series, monograph 3, Canberra, Australian National University Press
—— (1977) 'Towards a restatement of demographic transition theory' in Caldwell
Casselberry, S.E. and N. Valavanes (1976) 'Matrilocal Greek peasants and a reconsideration of residence terminology', *American Ethnologist*, 3
Church, K.V. (1978a) 'Women and Family Life in an Ashanti Town', MA thesis, Accra, Institute of African Studies, University of Ghana
—— (1978b) 'A study of socio economic status and childcare arrangements of women in Madina', paper presented at the Conference of the National Council on Women and Development, Accra, September
Clarke, E. (1957) *My mother who fathered me*, London, George Allen and Unwin
D'Andrade, R. (1966) 'Sex differences and cultural institutions' in E.E. Maccoby (ed.), *The development of sex differences*, Stanford, Stanford University Press
Davenport, W. (1961) 'The family system in Jamaica', *Social and Economic Studies*, 10, 420-54
Dorjahn, V.R. (1977) 'Temne household size and composition: rural changes over time and rural urban differences', *Ethnology*, 16, 2
Fjellman, S.M. (1976) 'Talking about talking about residence: an Akamba case', *American Ethnologist*, 3
Fortes, M. (ed.) (1949a) *Social structure*, Oxford, Oxford University Press
—— (ed.) (1949b) *The web of kinship among the Tallensi*, Oxford, Oxford University Press
—— (1970a) 'The submerged descent line in Ashanti' in I. Schapera (ed.), *Studies in Kinship and Marriage*, occasional paper no. 16, London, Royal Anthropological Institute
—— (1970b) *Time and social structures and other essays*, London, Athlone Press
—— (1970c) 'Social and psychological aspects of education in Taleland' in *Time and social structures and other essays*, London, Athlone Press
—— (1978) 'Family marriage and fertility in West Africa' in Oppong, Adaba, Bekombo-Priso and Mogey
Foster, B.L. (1978) 'Socioeconomic consequences of stem family composition in a Thai village', *Ethnology*, 17, 2
Freedman, R.B., T.H.S. Moots and M.B. Weinberger (1978) 'Household composition and extended kinship in Taiwan', *Population Studies*, 32, 1
Galbraith, J.K. (1973) *Economics and the public purpose*, Boston, Houghton Mifflin
Goldberg, R.S. (1976) 'The concept of household in East End Grant Cayman', *Ethnos*, 41
Goodenough, W.H. (1955) 'Residence rules', *Southwestern Journal of Anthropology*, 12, 22-37
Goodman, L., A.N. Keyfitz and T.W. Pullman (1974) 'Family formation and the

frequence of various kinship relationships', *Theoretical Population Biology, 5,* 1-27

Goody, E.N. (1978) 'Some theoretical and empirical aspects of parenthood in West Africa' in Oppong, Adaba, Bekombo-Priso and Mogey

Goody, J. (ed.) (1958) *The developmental cycle in domestic groups,* Studies in Social Anthropology no. 1, Cambridge, Cambridge University Press

——— (1972) *Domestic Groups,* Anthropology Module 28, New York, Addison Wesley

——— (1976) *Production and reproduction: a comparative study of the domestic domain,* Studies in Social Anthropology no. 17, Cambridge, Cambridge University Press

———, J. Thirsk and E.P. Thompson (eds.) (1976) *Family and inheritance,* Cambridge, Cambridge University Press

Handwerker, W.P. (1977) 'Family fertility and economics', *Current Anthropology, 18,* 2

Hill, P. (1977) *Population, prosperity and poverty,* Cambridge, Cambridge University Press

Kelly, A.C. and C. Swartz (1978) 'The impact of family structures on micro-economic decision making in developing countries: a case study of nuclear and extended families in urban Kenya', paper presented at IUSSP Conference on Economic and Demographic Change: Issues for the 1980s, Helsinki, September

Laslett, R. and R. Wall (eds.) (1972) *Household and family in past time,* Cambridge, Cambridge University Press

Levy, M.J. and L.A. Fallers (1959) 'The family, some comparative considerations', *American Anthropologist, 61,* 647-51

Macfarlane, A., S. Harrison and J. Jardine (1977) *Reconstructing historical communities,* Cambridge, Cambridge University Press

Minturn, L. and W. Lambert (1964) *Mothers of six cultures,* New York, John Wiley and Sons

Mukherjee, R. (1972) 'Concepts and methods for the secondary analysis of variation in family structures', *Current Anthropology, 13,* 3-4

Nag, M. (1967) 'Family type and fertility', *Proceedings of world population conference,* New York, UN, *II,* 160-3

Nash, J. (1975) 'The integration of women in the development process as equal partners with men', prepared for the United Nations Conference on International Women's Year, Mexico City, June; Doc. E/CONF/66/4

Oakley, A. (1976) *Woman's work,* New York, Vintage Books

Oppong, C. (1970) 'Conjugal power and resources: an urban African example', *Journal of Marriage and the Family, 32,* 4, 676-80

——— (1971) 'Joint conjugal roles and extended families: a preliminary note on a mode of classifying conjugal family relationships', *Journal of Comparative Family Studies, 2,* 2, 178-87

——— (1974) *Marriage among a matrilineal elite: a family study of Ghanaian civil servants,* Cambridge, Cambridge University Press

——— (1975) 'Norms and variations' in C. Oppong (ed.) *Changing Family Studies,* Institute of African Studies, University of Ghana, Accra

——— (1976a) 'Financial constraints and family size', *Canadian Journal of African Studies, 10,* 3, 403-8

——— (1976b) 'Ghanaian household models: data for processing by the New Home Economists of the developing world', paper presented at a Seminar on Household Models of Economic Demographic Decision-Making, IUSSP Committee on Economics, Mexico City

——— (1977) 'The crumbling of high fertility supports' in Caldwell

—— (1977a) 'A note on chains of change in family systems and family size', *Journal of Marriage and the Family* (August) pp. 615-21

—— (1977b) 'Family type and size: some recent evidence from Ghana' in L. Ruzicka (ed.), *Social and Economic Supports for High Fertility*, Canberra, Australian National University Press

—— (1978) 'Property, power and time' in Oppong, Adaba, Bekombo-Priso and Mogey

—— (1978a) 'Modernization and aspects of family change in Ghana, with particular reference to the effects of work', paper prepared for the Aspen Institute/Iran Workshop on Modernization and Cultural Change, Gajereh, Iran, May/June

—— (1978b) 'Household economic demographic decision making', introductory statement, IUSSP Conference on Economic and Demographic Change: Issues for the 1980s, Helsinki, September

——, G. Adaba, M. Bekombo-Priso and J. Mogey (eds.) (1978) *Marriage, fertility and parenthood in West Africa*, Canberra, Australian National University Press

Otterbein, K.F. and C.S. Otterbein (1977) 'A stochastic process analysis of the developmental cycle of the Andros household', *Ethnology, 16,* 4

Paydarfar, A.A. (1975) 'The modernization process and household size: a provisional comparison for Iran', *Journal of Marriage and the Family, 37,* 2, 446-52

Sanjek, R. and L. Sanjek (1975) 'Notes on women and work in Adabraka', *African Urban Notes*, series B2, 1

Schultz, T.W. (ed.) (1974) *Economics of the family: marriage, children and human capital*, Chicago, University of Chicago Press

Schultz, T.P. (1978) 'Current developments in the economics of fertility', paper presented at IUSSP Conference on Economic and Demographic Change: Issues for the 1980s, Helsinki

Singh, K.M. (1978) 'Population pressure and labour absorbability in agriculture and related activities', paper presented at IUSSP Conference on Economic and Demographic Change: Issues for the 1980s, Helsinki

Smith, M.G. (1962) *West Indian family structure*, Washington, DC, University of Washington Press

Smith, R.R. (1973) 'The matrifocal family' in J. Goody (ed.), *The character of kinship*, Seattle, University of Washington Press

Snyder, D. (1974) 'Economic determinants of family size in West Africa', *Demography, 2,* 4

Solien, N.L. (1970) 'Towards a definition of matrifocality' in N.E. Whitten and J.F. Szwed (eds.), *Afro-American Anthropology*, New York, Free Press

Stack, C.E. (1974) *All our kin*, New York, Harper and Row

van de Walle, E. (1976) 'Household dynamics in a Belgian village 1847-1886', *Journal of Family History*, 1, 1

Vercruijsse, E. (1974) 'Composition of households in some Fanti communities', Legon, Family Research Papers, no. 1

Weisner, T.S. and R. Gallimore (1977) 'My brother's keeper: child and sibling caretaking', *Current Anthropology, 18,* 2

Whiting, B.B. and J.W.M. Whiting (1975) *Children of Six Cultures*, Cambridge, Mass., Harvard University Press

Wong, F.M. (1975) 'Industrialization and family structure in Hong Kong', *Journal of Marriage and the Family, 37,* 4, 985-1000

# 7 A SOCIAL ANTHROPOLOGICAL APPROACH TO WOMEN'S ROLES AND STATUS IN DEVELOPING COUNTRIES: THE DOMESTIC CYCLE

T. Scarlett Epstein

## Introduction

The object of this chapter is to discuss the role of social anthropology in interdisciplinary studies of women's roles and status in developing countries. The focus here is on women's position in rural African and Asian societies, and the variables which affect both status and changing attitudes towards fertility control and participation in the labour market.

In the first section a brief description of method in social anthropology is presented as preparation for the theoretical framework that follows. The basis for that framework is the argument that women's position in a society changes as they pass through different phases of the life cycle. Their roles differ in each succeeding phase: early in life they are being trained by older women to accept social and cultural norms of behaviour; at marriage, they must adapt to the role of young wife; as their children begin to leave home, and as they grow older, the constraints on their behaviour lessen and they begin to influence the training of succeeding generations; in the final phase, when their children are married with children of their own, these women perpetuate cultural traditions and norms.

The conclusion thus states that more attention must be paid to the way in which women's attitudes vary with the constraints of the domestic cycle and especially to the role of older women in structuring the behaviour of younger women.

## The Cross-cultural, Holistic Approach

Anthropological studies reveal the great diversity of social structures and behaviour patterns existing in different societies as well as those within different categories or groups of people belonging to the same society.[1] These studies dissect the different variables which interact in a social system, and illustrate the dangers and pitfalls involved in the

151

aggregation of social data. Though these studies focus on social behaviour at grass-roots levels, this must not be taken to imply that social anthropology is not concerned with studying broader regularities.[2] Large-scale, quantitative studies which aim at determining regularities in the pattern of social behaviour and lend themselves for cross-cultural comparison can be found in the anthropology literature. These anthropological generalizations differ from macro-economic studies in that the latter are based on aggregations, usually of quantitative data, whereas the former refer not only to the qualitative aspects of social processes but also use a holistic approach to concentrate on the interrelationship of multiple variables.

Anthropological studies start with the assumption that societies constitute very complex systems. For practical purposes a social system can be defined as a group of individuals among whom the frequency and intensity of interaction is greater than between them and outsiders. There exists, thus, an intricate interaction and interdependence between the different types of relationships within a social system. A change in one affects other components, though not necessarily in the same way, at the same time or with the same force. By contrast, most of economic analysis assumes 'that all other things remain equal' if there is a change in one variable.

With their focus on behaviour patterns, anthropological studies can show the full implications of introducing a specific change into societies of different types (e.g., nomads or peasants, rural or urban dwellers). Policies for change, while desirable at face value, fail in practice because the target society cannot or does not want to accept some of the secondary or tertiary effects which had escaped the consideration of policy-makers. For instance, in South India new agricultural methods were rejected by farmers because male extension agents from outside villages were needed to train women labourers (Epstein, 1962). Thus to an uninformed outsider the rejection was irrational while to the people concerned it was based on sound reasoning.

It is the holistic approach underlying anthropological studies which can help to show the rationale behind decisions which otherwise would appear to have been randomly made without any good reason. Anthropology therefore always seeks to discover *order* in what at face value may seem to be complete chaos in social life.

Second, and implicit in what has already been said, social anthropologists study not only the immediate effects of change in one variable but trace secondary 'ripple' effects found in other parts of the social system. In doing so, not only quantifiable but more important, as we have just seen, qualitative variables also have to be examined.

## Qualitative Nonrandom Data

Statistically estimated values rest on the assumption that only data that has been collected on a random sample basis lends itself for valid generalizations. Little anthropological data falls into this category simply because the micro societies studied are never selected by means of random sampling. Unlike many economic and sociological inquiries which use large-scale surveys for macro generalizations, anthropological studies aim to discover regularities with a view to providing a typology of social behaviour patterns through in-depth analysis of relatively small groups.

Because of the vast number and great variety of social systems, most 'anthropological generalizations' are expressed in a strictly circumscribed and hypothetical manner. Validity, then, lies in testing the hypotheses in different settings. For example, the hypothesis I have put forth elsewhere, that the more diversified a village economy, the greater the displacement of the ritual by the economic aspect of prestige (Epstein, 1962), must be tested by additional studies of economic development and social change.

Statistical surveys can indicate *how* things change, but the reasons for the changes can be inferred only from the findings. By contrast, social anthropological studies examine processes of change and therefore can attempt to answer directly the question of *why* changes occur the way they do.

Recently there has been a growing interest in quantification among social anthropologists. Many of their studies now include a large number of tables, but, to repeat, this data does not readily lend itself to macro generalization because it is not statistically reliable. What is often not sufficiently appreciated is that the basic data collected in many large-scale surveys is frequently highly suspect. There is plenty of evidence to show, for instance, that under survey conditions many informants are tempted to give the answers which they think are expected of them. Even if questionnaires are designed to test the internal consistency of informants' answers, there is no way in which the reliability of the basic data can be satisfactorily checked. This is particularly so because large-scale surveys rely on the participation of many investigators who usually differ in training and degree of committedness.

### 'In-depth' Studies: Participant Observation

Anthropological studies are usually conducted personally by senior investigators in one small society. The researchers have knowledge of the local dialect and rely heavily on participant observation for the collection of data. This facilitates careful checking and cross-checking of data collected. Though questionnaires are also used, they are never completed in front of the informant nor in the course of one interview.

The anthropological method of 'participant observation' is particularly useful in investigations of sensitive areas of human life, such as for instance 'fertility behaviour'. The continuous and close contact of social anthropologists with their informants is likely to produce more meaningful and reliable data on the knowledge, attitude and practice of contraception than can be expected to emerge from say surveys of the KAP type. Therefore, while social anthropological studies lack breadth, they make up for this by producing highly reliable in-depth data. There is thus a need for complementarity between large-scale random sample surveys and social anthropological micro studies.

Another anthropological method useful in the study of social change is the analysis of case studies (van Velsen, 1967) in terms of social dramas (Turner, 1957). This tool can expose much of the myth of change and report the actual situation. In India, for example, concern with population growth has led to a legally stipulated minimum marriage age for girls. In spite of this law, social anthropologists have shown that many villagers concerned with population growth attach more importance to the perpetuation of traditional social and moral norms, according to which it is more important now that a girl be betrothed before she reaches puberty. 'It appears that social legislation has not had a very significant effect in raising the age at marriage, giving us a good example of the divergence between law and custom, which is so common in all societies' (Beteille, 1975).

The above discussion indicates the kind of data and theoretical framework social anthropological studies may contribute to a multidisciplinary approach to development problems. However, it must be mentioned here that social anthropological studies have until recently been sadly deficient in examining women's roles and status. There has been a heavy male bias in data collection and analysis among female as well as male anthropologists. It is only during the last few years that the societal models based on male perception have begun to be questioned.[3]

As yet there are too few reliable studies available which show in detail how different sets of social conditions affect the position of women. Little knowledge often goes with a lot of speculation. This seems to be the case with women's studies. Glib generalizations abound while hard facts are few to come by.[4] Discussions on women's roles and status have often taken on an ideological stance, and argue what *ought* to be rather than exploit the reasons for the way traditional gender roles are being perpetuated in different cultural settings.

The recent Feminist and Women's Liberation movements are products of Western cultures. Though they are performing a laudable task in stressing the need of integrating women in development programmes, which was first indicated by Boserup (1970), many of their arguments are ethnocentric with applicability only to Western culture and frequently only to certain sections of women within developed countries; they bear little, if any, relevance to the lives of most women in less developed countries.

The anthropological perspective warns against the use of ideological approaches in the study of social relationships, and prescribes the detailed examination and analysis of the many different variables which affect the functioning of social systems. This anthropological approach has not only theoretical validity but is of practical importance, particularly with regard to fertility behaviour: policies aiming to encourage lower fertility can be expected to be successful only if their design and implementation are based on a thorough knowledge and understanding of the total socio-cultural nexus of customs, beliefs and relationships which is bound up with the roles and status of these women.

## Women's Roles and Status

Roles and status are situation-specific, yet defined in such a way that they retain meaning in different contexts. The *International Encyclopedia of the Social Sciences* specifies that a role provides 'a comprehensive *pattern* for behavior and attitudes; it constitutes a *strategy* for coping with a recurrent situation; it is *socially identified*, more or less clearly, as an entity; it is subject to being played recognisably by *different individuals* and it supplies a major basis for *identifying* and *placing* persons in society' (Turner, 1968, *13*). *Status* connotes evaluation, hence *honour, esteem, respect* and *prestige* are its synonyms. Status in this sense is a gratification, and its loss, a deprivation (Zelditch, Jr, 1968). Accordingly, a woman's role refers to the way she is expected to behave in certain situations and her status indicates the esteem in which she is held by the different individuals and groups who come in contact with her. Therefore, the same woman is likely to behave differently in different situations as she proceeds through the different phases in her life cycle and be awarded different prestige ranking by different people within her social range.

Biological endowment and environmental conditions impose certain constraints on women's behaviour. Women's reproductive and mothering roles affect the division of labour between the sexes. Moreover, women, like men, have to adapt to their environmental conditions. Nomadic women have to spend a lot of their time gathering food, thus requiring them to space the births of their children (Lee, 1972). By contrast, a peasant woman needs more children to help with domestic and agricultural tasks, and therefore is not so worried about birth spacing and has more children than her nomadic counterpart (Lee, 1972; White, 1976). Women in regular formal employment, particularly professional women with control over their income, usually resent the loss in their earnings due to frequent pregnancies and therefore tend to control their fertility (Chaudhury, 1974).

These are examples of the way women may adapt their child-bearing to different socio-physical environments. But even within this apparent overall homogeneous process of adaptation, women in different social positions play different roles and enjoy different esteem. Within the same social group, for instance, an old childless woman may be despised − often she is regarded as a witch − a Hindu widow is treated as inauspicious, while an elderly mother of many sons and daughers whose husband is still alive is often seen to have authority not only over her young female affines but even over her husband and younger male kin (Gough, 1975). Yet the same woman will have enjoyed only little prestige when she was a young bride. This indicates that a woman's role and status varies directly not only with the way she fulfils her reproductive designation but also with the different phases in the domestic cycle.

## The Domestic Cycle

Some anthropologists have long recognised the importance of the household as a unit of social analysis and the domestic cycle as a means by which the different and changing lives of individuals are adjusted to the more orderly and continuous life of the community. 'In all human societies the workshop, so to speak, of social reproduction is the domestic group. It is this group which must remain in operation over a stretch of time long enough to rear off-spring to the stage of physical and social reproductibility if a society is to maintain itself' (Fortes, 1966). Various phases are attributed to the life of the domestic group (e.g., 'expansion', 'fission' and replacement (Fortes, 1966)). The specific division into phases of the domestic cycle tends to depend on the social phenomenon it is used to investigate. The following five phases: 'preparation', 'adaptation', 'expansion', 'consolidation' and 'dispersal' are used here for the study of how and why women's roles and status change as they pass through the domestic cycle.

In the following pages, I elaborate it with reference to rural women in less developed countries (LDCs) and in particular the poorer strata, because the large majority of LDC women come within this category. The ethnographic details indicated relate to Africa and Asia only, but the theoretical framework developed is likely to apply to all LDC rural areas. Some comments on urban women are added because they often act as a reference group for rural women.

From time immemorial the physiology of human reproduction and the need to care for young children have tied women to domestic activities and allocated to men the tasks of protection and providing for women and children. The different tasks assumed by men and women not only served to complement each other but helped to keep a harmonious balance in the family. Gender-specific specialization of work is thus a key factor in determining a woman's role. Upon this fundamental role segregation between men and women there rests a whole superstructure of cultural elaboration and belief systems: in many cultures role/task separation is viewed as part of the order of the universe ordained by supernatural forces. Attempts to vary this are regarded as a threat to the order within society and punished accordingly. Many witchcraft accusations may be explained in terms of the accused woman having tried to break into the male sphere of activity.

Recent changes in the social adaptation of sex differences, as for instance bottle-feeding of babies, and, more important still, the changes in resource base resulting from new economic opportunities have produced some changes in social practices. Yet at the same time there is considerable cultural continuity even during a period of rapid economic development. In most less developed countries the majority of women continue to predominate in the domestic sphere and men in the public domain. The traditional gender-role specificity seems to reassert itself even more under the new conditions, though they have made biological and environmental factors less imperative in necessitating a division of labour between men and women. This cultural continuity may be seen as a function of the persistence of the domestic cycle as an ordering mechanism in society. As already mentioned, I discuss here the changing roles and status of women as they pass through the five phases in their domestic cycle. Figure 7.1 illustrates the interrelationship between the different phases in the domestic cyle.

*Preparation Phase*

During this phase the young generation is being initiated into the cultural heritage of its society by the socializers who are then in their 'consolidation phase'.

The preparation for the establishment of a new family unit begins early in the life of a child. Boys and girls are informally educated by their mothers and grandmothers, and taught the practices, values and beliefs of their society — an ancestral legacy, handed down from generation to generation.

Marriage

For large numbers of people, particularly in Asia, marriages are still arranged by the kin of the bride and groom. Different societies have different preferred patterns of marriage: some have exchange marriages, according to which a brother and sister from one kin group marry a sister and brother of another kin group. Cross-cousin unions are another marriage pattern widely practised in Asia and Africa; it reduces the social radius of marriage ties. Many marriages are negotiated with the objective of forging new or reaffirming already existing social or political links (Ahmed, forthcoming). Marriage is thus an event which involves the entire kin group of the spouses and is therefore preceded by lengthy and protracted negotiations between the parties concerned. The young bride-to-be is rarely consulted; she has been brought up to believe that her elders are better equipped than she herself is to find her a suitable marriage partner.

Among upper-caste and upper-class Hindus and Muslims in the Indian subcontinent prepuberty marriage has been the norm; the bride is betrothed before the onset of her menarche. These social groups attach great value to virginity and prepuberty marriage is rationalized in terms of making sure that the bride meets her husband as a virgin. Prepuberty marriage is also linked with lack of education for girls.

**Figure 7.1: The Different Phases Through which Women Pass in the Domestic Cycle**

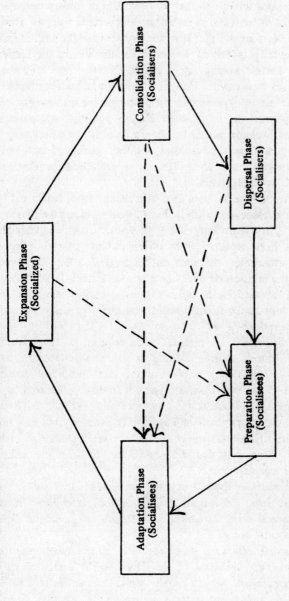

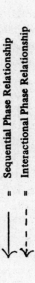

= Sequential Phase Relationship

= Interactional Phase Relationship

Many marriages involve either bridewealth or dowry payments. Bridewealth has often been regarded as the purchase price of a bride, though it has been argued that it is not payment for the girl but rather for her reproductive potential. Evidence for this lies in the fact that the kin of a barren woman are expected to return the bridewealth or provide a substitute wife. However, since an increasing number of Asian societies are substituting dowry payments for bridewealth, even though control over the bride's reproductive potential still passes on marriage to her husband and his kin group, this may be a necessary but certainly not a sufficient explanation for the transfer of cash and/or goods from the groom's to the bride's kin, nor should it be taken as an indication of a woman's status.

It is significant here to note that the chánge from bridewealth to dowry is usually associated with increased wealth among the parents of the brides, who no more know how, or want, to work outside their home. It has been reported from different parts of Asia (Epstein, 1973; Nath, forthcoming; Abdullah and Zeidenstein, 1981) that women withdraw from work outside their home as soon as their family's wealth permits hired labour. South Indian farmers proudly claim that their daughters do not know how to weed, transplant or carry out other agricultural operations. .

The girls themselves are pleased to be relieved of these arduous tasks. Thus, in purely economic terms, a wife changes from an asset into a liability, which may be one of the most important variables accounting for the change from bridewealth to dowry reported for an increasing number of Asian societies; another being the fact that dowry has been an Indian upper-caste and upper-class practice for a long time. Therefore, sanskritization, namely the link between secular and ritual rank (Srinivas, 1969), may also be a contributory factor in the changing pattern of marriage payments.

Prepuberty marriage severely restricts the chances that a young girl has to benefit from education. A girl's school attendance is also affected by several other variables; for instance, the economic conditions in her parental home.

Though formal education represents one of the most important factors in reshaping the lives of the Third World communities, its focus and organization, which largely replicates the Western model, accounts for its failure up to now to realize its potential. Formal education could be more effective in helping to change women's roles and status if it could be moulded into the existing informal socialization of young boys and girls during the 'preparation phase', when the new generation forms its attitudes under the influence of the ancestral cultural legacy.

*Adaptation Phase*

In the course of this phase the socialization of the young generation crystallizes in the establishment of new domestic units.

Monogamy and Polygamy

Most marriages are monogamous unions. Even where religious beliefs allow polygamy, as for instance Hinduism or Islam, the actual proportion of polygamous marriages is comparatively small.

In monogamous marriages the wife does not have to compete with co-wives for her husband's favours, but if she has to join her husband's extended family, she has to contend with her female affines. It is impossible to say *a priori* whether polygamy or extended families offer more freedom of action to the individual young wife. The actual arrangements depend on the specific cultural setting. For instance, many Muslim women in Bangladesh dread the possibility of their husbands marrying a second wife, and that their husbands will ignore their own and their children's needs while they lavish attention on their second and in most cases much younger wives (Abdullah and Zeidenstein, 1981).

By contrast, 'Many market women in Africa argue in favour of polygamy. A survey conducted in the Ivory Coast in the 1960's found that 85 per cent of the women came out in favour of polygamy. According to Dobert the women believe that in a monogamous marriage power accrues to the man as head of the household whereas formerly both men and women had to defer to the head of the lineage. Furthermore, co-wives shared the burden of household work and cooking; one woman could go to trade while another stayed at home to do the household tasks' (Tinker, 1976). In monogamous unions each wife has to look after her husband, children and home as well as do the necessary kitchen gardening for subsistence consumption, unless the women in an extended family divide their labour more rationally, which is often what they do.

Family Structure and Female Affines

The adaptation of a new household is directly affected by the family structure into which it has to nestle. The nuclear family composed of parents and their offspring plus single or widowed near-kin predominates among landless labourers and marginal farmers. Young girls from these families live in their husbands' homes at marriage. They are then less subject to the control by female affines and more concerned to ensure a livelihood for their husbands and new families. Coming from a poor background and joining an equally poor husband does not radically change a girl's life style. To move into an extended family causes a much more serious problem of adjustment for the young bride. She has to exchange the comparative freedom she enjoyed in her natal home for the often strict regime by her mother-in-law. Polygamous marriage also constitutes a type of extended family because it involves a degree of co-operation between individual co-wives' domestic units.

Women's roles and status are amenable to change during the 'preparation phase' in the domestic cycle. It may also be possible to introduce such changes during the 'adaptation phase', before a girl enters the reproductive span of her life. Poor girls, for whom marriage maintains poverty, may be influenced by education and income-earning opportunities to consider family planning. These girls may also be influenced by their grandmothers. Paradoxically, this means that grandmothers may have to be convinced of the efficacy of family planning before young women can be expected to use contraceptives.

## Expansion Phase

Reproduction is the central concern in the process of family formation and culminates in the 'expansion phase' of the domestic cycle. Reproduction ensures parental immortality (Mbiti, 1969) and perpetuates social groups. Birth is usually the occasion of religious and ritual observances which are different for boys and girls.

## A Woman's Dilemma

Households with limited resources are often hard-put to meet the increased demand resulting from many children. Among the many poor households in LDCs, it is often impossible for the men to increase the supply of resources to their family. Therefore, at a time when young women want and ought to spend more time on caring for their children, which incidentally may be a factor in reducing infant mortality, they are forced to do more work outside their home so as to help provide the minimum necessities for their children. Women's wages tend to be lower than men's; moreover, agricultural labour requirements are seasonally peaked. Many landless women therefore face the dilemma of either working and thereby neglecting their infants, or remaining at home, thereby foregoing the possibility of earning money for basic needs.

To assume that most women enjoy doing the laborious and unskilled tasks which fall within their sphere of specialization is a fallacy. Nath found in Rajasthan that 'agricultural working women of both agricultural and non-agricultural households expressed a strong desire to be able to afford the leisure of preparing two hot meals and looking after the health and personal hygiene needs of their children as could the high caste, higher income grou, of women of the area who were not working. It was observed further that women of the non-agricultural group, in which both men and women were workers in a cement factory, withdrew from work as soon as the husband or one of the sons became a permanent worker with higher wages in the factory' (1970).

Dixon (1978) is convinced that work participation is corrc'ated to lower fertility and uses this hypothesis as justification for a policy stressing programmes designed to increase women's productivity outside the home. This hypothesis fails to take into account women's own perception of their role and their attitude towards work that takes them away from their domestic sphere. Purdah, the seclusion of Muslim women, is often claimed by observers to represent an extreme deprivation, while many of the women in purdah regard themselves as being privileged by being able to enjoy the relative cool of their compound while their menfolk have to face the heat of the day. A recent study among Hausa women in Nigeria found that 'most women interviewed claimed they preferred to be kept in seclusion on the grounds that it reduced their work load and raised their prestige' (Tinker, 1976).

For other women child-care takes up a major portion of their time; yet more children are desired for the future contributions to the household. For example, five Taita women from Kenya, aged between 20 and 25 years old, averaging four to six children, spend about two-thirds (67 per cent) of their daily activities working in the home, and only 10 per cent on gardening and animal husbandry, while the rest (23 per cent) they devote to church activities and social intercourse. They explain that it is easier to take small children along to church or when visiting friends than it is to take them along for work in the kitchen garden or cattle-grazing. The daily time allocation accounted for the average day of these five Taita women amounts to almost 14 hours, of which nine hours are spent on food preparation, child-care and cleaning.[5] They rely heavily on their husbands for the provision of food.[6]

Each of these five women lives in a nuclear family and none of them intends to use birth control. Quite the contrary, they look forward to producing more offspring in the hope that their children will help relieve the work burden which they presently carry on their shoulders. Mkangi (1978) blames the break-up of the extended family among the Taita for their high rate of population growth by explaining that nuclear families lose the advantages of economies of scale which extended families enjoy. Domestic activities are particularly subject to economies of scale. Therefore, so Mkangi argues, married couples living in nuclear families are likely to want and have more children than if they are embedded in extended families.

To advocate encouraging or forcing women within the reproductive age span to enter formal employment, as some economists and planners are apt to do these days, is not going to improve the welfare of families in LDCs nor is there much evidence to suggest that it will reduce fertility. On the other hand, the positive correlation between infant mortality and fertility is now generally established.

These accounts illustrate the need for proper child-care if the welfare of the society is not to suffer. The full implications pushing women who are in the 'expansion phase' into paid employment must be pointed out. In order that women in particular and society in general should derive the benefit from increased female labour force participation, special care needs to be taken that the social framework within which women operate enables them to have more options without jeopardizing the welfare of their own families.

Once women come into the 'expansion phase' of their domestic cycle they have been thoroughly socialized into following traditional norms. Moreover, they are usually preoccupied with trying to meet their families' daily requirements, which places a heavy demand on their time. They are, therefore, least prepared to respond to exogenous changes. They are too set in their ways to change their behaviour, particularly their fertility aspirations, and too young and insecure to be in a position to effect changes in the socialization of the succeeding generation of girls.

*Consolidation Phase*

A household enters its 'consolidation phase' when its children are old enough to contribute to its livelihood and the older ones begin to get married.[7] Women need less time for child-care than during the 'expansion phase' and are freer to contribute to the satisfaction of other family needs. A comparison of the average daily time allocation of five Taita women (discussed above) in the 'expansion phase' of their domestic cycle with that of six Taita women in their 'consolidation phase' indicates their different roles. The two sets of women belong to the same socio-economic stratum; each of them has a small garden and one or two head of cattle. The ages of these six Taita women range between 42 and 50 years old; all of them have passed their menopause. Three of them have eight surviving children, two have six and one has four offspring alive. The six women altogether gave birth to 46 children of whom six died in infancy. Four of them are already grandmothers. None of these women used birth control nor do they advise their daughters or granddaughters to do so. Now that they are getting older they depend on the help from their children and grandchildren, and therefore do not want to have them deprived of this support when they will need it.

These women daily spend about one-third (32 per cent) of the time for which they accounted on gardening and animal husbandry, and only 44 per cent on work in their homes, as compared to the 67 per cent spent by their younger counterparts. It is interesting to note that both sets of women spend about the same proportion of their daily time allocation on church activities and social intercourse.

The often severe social constraints which operate on younger women are usually relaxed for women once they pass their menopause and reach the 'consolidation phase' of their domestic cycle. There are accounts from many different cultures which indicate the greater freedom and higher prestige enjoyed by women in well-established households. As Thai 'women grow older their freedom to comment on social, personal and sexual affairs of the community is relaxed. There is a marked contrast between the prudish behaviour of younger women and crude language of older women' (Chutikul, 1975, p. 7). In the African urban environment, too, the status of a woman changes as she passes through the domestic cycle; 'whereas an older woman with experience of town life can perhaps look after herself and support children, a younger and less experienced woman or girl may require not only economic opportunities but physical protection' (Little, 1973). Similarly, Strathern, writing on New Guinea women, states that 'with age a Hagen woman seems to find it easier to manipulate the court system . . . older women . . . are both able to apply more pressure when aggrieved and are themselves more likely to yield to pressure in the informal settlement of disputes. This is a direct result of their growing importance and stature' (1972). Though the stress here is on age, age alone without the concomitant social position is unlikely to have much impact on a woman's status. In most societies, particularly among the poorer groups, a woman must first fulfil her role as mother before she can expect to enjoy higher prestige and possibly occupy a position of authority once her children are grown up.

Mature women in the 'consolidation phase' of the domestic cycle, who are responsible for socializing their children and grandchildren, may be more amenable to responding positively to exogenous changes than is usually assumed. These women who are managers of the domestic sphere of large households could possibly be made the agents of change. According to Islam, 'a woman's heaven is under the feet of her husband — a man's heaven is under the feet of his mother' (Abdullah and Zeidenstein, 1981). Women in the 'consolidation phase' of their domestic cycle may thus be in a position not only to affect a change in the role of their succeeding generations of females but also to influence the esteem which men attach to their wives.

*Dispersal Phase*

The dispersal phase begins with the marriage of children. In many cases only one parent is still alive by the time a new family is fully established, and in turn produces children. The presence of grandparents, in particular grandmothers, plays an important role in the perpetuation of traditional customs and norms. All cultures, however, are continuously changing in the process of succeeding generations trying to adapt to changing socio-environmental conditions. It is the interplay between alternate generations which tends to determine the pattern of social change. The absence of grandparents as cultural intermediaries is likely to result in identity crises among the young (Epstein, 1978) and possibly in a state of social disorder as Mkangi (1978a) is arguing for the Taita.

## Conclusion

In the preceding discussion I have tried to give an example of the contribution social anthropological studies can make to an interdisciplinary study of women's roles and status. My analysis refers mainly to the rural areas of LDCs, and in particular to the poorer families. I suggest that this is a valid approach because the large majority of LDC women still live in an agricultural setting and belong to the lower socio-economic strata.

The main thrust of my argument here has been to indicate the intricate and complex interaction of some of the most important variables which affect women's position in society, and to show that there exist regularities as women pass through the different phases in the domestic cycle. This approach provides a framework for the study of women's roles and status by using women rather than men as focal points in the examination of social relationships. It also has important policy implications, particularly for population programmes. If what I have been arguing is correct, and there is evidence to suggest that it is, then phases in the domestic cycle are critical not only in determining women's roles and status but more important in determining their readiness to accept social change. Accordingly, women in the 'consolidation phase' together with their daughters and granddaughters in the 'preparation and adaptation phases' are likely to be the ones most amenable to adopt a changed pattern of behaviour. Yet the younger women lack the freedom from social constraints and the time to calculate the advantages and disadvantages of suggested innovations enjoyed by women in the later phases. On the other hand, women in the 'expansion phase' have usually come to be set in their ideas; moreover, the heavy demand which frequent pregnancies, child-care, domestic and other duties make on their energies leaves them little chance to consider alternative ways of life.

The holistic anthropological approach to the study of women's roles and status thus indicates that women in the later phases of their domestic cycle occupy key positions as 'socialisers'. Moreover, it suggests that the 'socialisees', rather than the already 'socialized', represent the potential agents of change.

## Notes

1. See Firth (1968) for a thorough description of anthropology and the anthropological approach.

2. For example, see Gluckman (1950) for the detailed analysis of different kinship systems and the divorce rates associated with the lower frequency of divorce with patrilineal kinship; see also the investigation of the relationship between economic development and social change, which hypothesizes that there is a consistency in economic, political, ritual and organizational change, while familial change may take place without any corresponding structural change (Epstein, 1962, p. 334). These provide but a few examples of hypotheses which suggest certain regularities in the pattern of social behaviour and lend themselves for cross-cultural comparison.

3. 'The fact is that no one could come back from an ethnographic study of "the x", having talked only to women, and *about* men without professional comment and some self-doubt. The reverse can and does happen constantly . . . Models of society that women can provide are not of the kind acceptable at first sight to men or to ethnographers . . . they do not see society bounded from nature' (Ardener, 1975).

4. There exists a great deal of information on women 'but it frequently comes from questions asked of men about their wives, daughters and sisters, rather than from themselves. Men's information is too often presented as a group's reality, rather than as only part of a cultural whole' (Reiter, 1975).

5. The individual time budgets indicate that there is only little variation from the average. The five women all display similar patterns of time allocation.

6. I am indebted to Dr George Mkangi for allowing me to use here some of his as yet unpublished field data.

7. The end of the expansion phase does not necessarily have to coincide with the end of a woman's reproductive period. In India, for example, it is regarded as morally wrong for a woman to produce a child after the birth of her first grandchild.

# References

Abdullah, T.A. and S. Zeidenstein (1981) *Village women of Bangladesh: prospects for change*, Oxford, Pergamon Press

Ahmed, A. (forthcoming) '"Mor" and "Tor" binary and opposing models of Pukhtun womanhood' in T. Scarlett Epstein and Rosemary A. Watts (eds.), *The endless day: some case material on Asian rural women*, Oxford, Pergamon Press

Anwar, S. and F. Bilquees (1976) 'The attitudes, environment and activities of rural women: case study of Johk Sayal', research report no. 98, Pakistan Institute of Development Economics

Ardener, E. (1975) 'Belief and the problem of women' in Shirley Ardener (ed.), *Perceiving women*, London, J.M. Dent & Sons Ltd

Bangun, M. (1978) 'The importance of education and credit facilities for rural women to improve their standard of living', unpublished paper, University of Sussex

Beteille, A. (1975) 'The position of women in Indian society' in Devaki Jain (ed.), *Indian women*, New Delhi, Ministry of Information and Broadcasting, Government of India

Boserup, E. (1970) *Women's role in economic development*, London, George Allen and Unwin

Chaudhury, R.H. (1974) 'Labour force status and fertility', *Bangladesh Development Studies*, 2, 4, 819-38

Chayanov, A.V. (1966) 'Peasant farm organization' in D. Thorner, B. Kerbley and R.E.F. Smith (eds.), *The theory of peasant economy*, Homewood, Illinois, The American Economic Association

Chutikul, S. (1975) 'Women in rural northeast society in Thailand', unpublished paper, Khon Kaen University

Das, V. (1975) 'Marriage among the Hindus' in Devaki Jain (ed.), *Indian women*, New Delhi, Ministry of Information and Broadcasting, Government of India

Dasgupta, M. (1976) 'Ladies first', paper presented to the Fourth World Congress for Rural Sociology, Poland

—— (1977) 'From a closed to an open system: fertility behaviour in a changing Indian village' in T.S. Epstein and D. Jackson (eds.), *The feasibility of fertility planning – micro perspectives*, Oxford, Pergamon Press

Dixon, R. (1978) *Women's co-operatives and rural development: a policy proposal*, Resources for the Future, Baltimore, Johns Hopkins University Press

Engels, F. (1972) *The origin of the family, private property and the state*, edited and with an introduction by Eleanor Burke Leacock, New York, International Publishers

Epstein, A.L. (1978) *Ethos and identity*, London, Tavistock Publications

Epstein, T.S. (1962) *Economic development and social change in South India*, Manchester, Manchester University Press

――― (1973) *South India: yesterday, today and tomorrow*, London, Macmillan

――― (1977) 'From "accommodation" to "intervention": socio-economic heterogeneity and demographic patterns' in T.S. Epstein and D. Jackson (eds.), *The feasibility of fertility planning – micro perspectives*, Oxford, Pergamon Press

Faithorn, E. (1975) 'The concept of pollution among the Kafe of the Papua New Guinea Highlands' in R.R. Reiter (ed.), *Toward an anthropology of women*, New York, Monthly Review Press

Firth, R. (1968) 'Social anthropology' in D.L. Sills (ed.), *International encyclopedia of the social sciences*, New York, The Macmillan Company and The Free Press

Fortes, M. (1966) 'Introduction' in J. Goody (ed.), *The developmental cycle in domestic groups*, London, Athlone Press

Gluckman, M. (1950) 'Kinship and marriage among the Lozi of Northern Rhodesia and the Zulu of Natal' in A.R. Radcliffe-Brown and D. Forde (eds.), *African systems of kinship and marriage*, Oxford, Oxford University Press

Gough, K. (1975) 'The origin of the family' in R.R. Reiter (ed.), *Toward an anthropology of women*, New York, Monthly Review Press

Jahan, R. (1975) 'Women in Bangladesh' in R. Rohrich-Leavitt (ed.), *Women cross-culturally – change and challenge*, The Hague, Mouton Publishers

Lee, R.B. (1972) 'Population growth and the beginnings of sedentary life among the Kung Bushmen' in B. Spooner (ed.), *Population growth: anthropological implications*, Cambridge, Mass., MIT Press

Levinson, F.J. (1974) *Morin da: An economic analysis of malnutrition among young children in rural India*, MIT International Nutrition Policy Series, Cornell University Press

Little, K. (1973) *African women in towns: an aspect of Africa's social revolution*, Cambridge, Cambridge University Press

Longmore, L. (1959) *The dispossessed*, London, Cape

Mbiti, J.F. (1969) *African religions and philosophy*, London, Heinemann

Mkangi, G.C. (1978) 'Population growth and the myth of land reform in Taita', unpublished doctoral thesis, University of Sussex

――― (1978a) 'Taita: neighbourhood hegemony and population control', unpublished paper, University of Sussex

Nath, J. (forthcoming) 'Beliefs and customs observed by Muslim rural women during their life cycle' in T.S. Epstein and R.A. Watts (eds.), *The endless day: some case material on Asian rural women*, Oxford, Pergamon Press

Nath, K. (1970) 'Women, work and growth', *Economic and Political Weekly*, V, 45

――― (1977) 'Work participation and social change among rural women: a case study in Eastern Rajasthan, India', unpublished paper

Nelson, N. (1977) 'Dependence and independence: female heads of households in a Nairobi squatter settlement, Mathere Valley', unpublished doctoral thesis, University of London

――― (1979) *Why has development neglected rural women? – a review of the Asian literature*, Oxford, Pergamon Press

Okonjo, K. (1975) 'The role of women in the development of culture in Nigeria' in R. Rohrich-Leavitt (ed.), *Women cross-culturally – change and challenge*, The Hague, Mouton Publishers

Onwuazor, S.N. (1977) 'Continuity and change: abortion and family size in a Nigerian village' in T.S. Epstein and D. Jackson (eds.), *The feasibility of fertility planning – micro perspectives*, Oxford, Pergamon Press

Parvathama, C. (1976) *Socio-economic survey of the scheduled castes and tribes in Karnataka*, Mysore, University of Mysore

Radcliffe-Brown, A. (1952) *Structure and function in primitive society*, London, Cohen and West

Reiter, R.R. (1975) 'Introduction' in R.R. Reiter (ed.), *Toward an anthropology of women*, New York, Monthly Review Press

Robertson, A.F. and G.A. Hughes (1978) 'The family farm in Buganda', *Development and change*, London and Beverley Hills, Sage, *9*, 415-38

Rousseau, I.F. (1975) 'African women: identity crisis? Some observations on education and the changing role of women in Sierra Leone and Zaire' in R. Rohrich-Leavitt (ed.), *Women cross-culturally: change and challenge*, The Hague, Mouton Publishers

Sahlins, M (1972) *Stone age economics*, Chicago, Aldine

Shanin, T. (1972) *The awkward class: political sociology of peasantry in a developing society: Russia 1910-1925*, Oxford, Oxford University Press

Schuster, I. (1979) *The new women of Lusaka*, Palo Alto, Mayfield Publishing Company

Ssennyonga, J.W. (1977) 'The traditional cultural inventory versus the elite roadside ecology' in T.S. Epstein and D. Jackson (eds.), *The feasibility of fertility planning – micro perspectives*, Oxford, Pergamon Press

—— (1978) 'Population growth and cultural inventory: the Maragoli case', unpublished doctoral thesis, University of Sussex

Srinivas, M.N. (1969) *Social change in modern India*, Berkeley and Los Angeles, University of California

Strathern, M. (1972) *Women in between – female roles in a male world: Mount Hagen, New Guinea*, London, Sominar Press

Tinker I. (1976) 'The adverse impact of development on women' in Irene Tinker, Michèle Bo Bramsen and Mayra Buvinić (eds.), *Women and world development*, New York, Praeger Publishers

Turner, R.H. (1968) 'Role, sociological aspects' in David L. Sills (ed.), *International encyclopedia of the social sciences*, New York, The Macmillan Company and the Free Press

Turner V.W. (1957) *Schism and continuity in an African society – a study of Ndembu village life*, Manchester, Manchester University Press

Van Velsen, J. (1967) 'The extended-case method and situational analysis' in A.L. Epstein (ed.), *The craft of social anthropology*, London, Tavistock Publications

Wallman, S. (1977) *Perceptions of development*, Cambridge, Cambridge University Press

White, B.N.F. (1976) 'Production and reproduction in a Javanese Village', unpublished doctoral thesis, Columbia University

—— (1977) 'Rural household studies in anthropological perspective', mimeo., Agricultural Development Council, Indonesia

Zelditch, Jr., M. (1968) 'Social evaluation' in David L. Sills (ed.), *International encyclopedia of the social sciences*, New York, The Macmillan Company and The Free Press

# PART FOUR: WOMEN'S ROLES AND THEIR RELATIONSHIP TO FERTILITY AND MORTALITY

# 8 THE INTERRELATIONSHIP BETWEEN THE DIVISION OF LABOUR IN THE HOUSEHOLD, WOMEN'S ROLES AND THEIR IMPACT ON FERTILITY

Nadia H. Youssef

## Introduction

Most analyses of fertility behaviour focus on three aspects of women's status: education, employment and the husband-wife relationship. Few of them point out, however, that the relationship between each of these variables and fertility is neither direct nor simple. Each variable affects the others as well as fertility: employment opportunities are affected by education, conjugal interaction is influenced by the education and employment of the wife (and husband), and vice versa (Piepmeier and Adkins, 1973). In addition, there may be other variables that have an equal impact on fertility behaviour; this chapter explores one such possibility — the division of labour between the sexes within the rural household. In order to determine the effect of the sexual division of labour on fertility, several key questions must be looked at:

(i) Under what conditions does a specific patterning in the sexual division of labour within the household generate a resource base for women?

(ii) Under what conditions are resource bases for women translated into power in other spheres and into the development of higher status for women?

(iii) How do specific patternings in the sex-based division of labour interact with components of women's status to influence reproductive behaviour?

In the discussion that follows, I will put forward some possible answers to these questions, drawing upon studies of women's activities and their findings. Some of the hypotheses presented are based on such work, others are a natural outcome of the particular approach taken here.

It is only recently that the literature on women's activities has included studies of women's non-wage earning economic activities in rural settings: their participation in agricultural activities, in marketing, in home production of goods and in small-scale petty trade (Deere,

1978). Macro-level information may acknowledge women's economic role in labour-intensive activities such as ploughing, planting and harvesting — all of which are performed outside the household — but in order to assess the contribution of women (and children) to household income or resources, economic activities must be defined more broadly to include such activities as agricultural and pastoral labour, fishing, hunting, poultry-raising, house-building, tool-making, spinning and weaving, other arts and crafts, marketing, shopping, transportation, fuel-collecting, water-carrying, food preparation and processing, washing, etc. (Nag, 1976). Such activities have not been considered to be 'productive' and therefore, in most cases, have not been included in census data or labour force statistics. If women who perform these tasks have been included in the data at all, they are most likely to have been classified under the general rubric of 'unpaid family workers', which is a poorly measured and imprecisely defined category.

An attempt to encompass in the definition of economic activities those activities assigned to women on the basis of sexual division of labour within the rural household should contribute to a more complete profile of the total range of women's economic roles. It should also underline the strong links that exist between the subsistence economy and the market economy. Because the majority of women in the developing world still live in rural areas where wage earning opportunities for either sex are relatively restricted, exploration of the possible influence that these 'other' economic activities may exert upon fertility behaviour seems especially important (Mason, 1971).

One of the more consistent findings in demographic literature has been that women's employment in agricultural (rather than non-agricultural) activities and in work at or near the home (rather than work outside the home) has a neutral if not a positive effect on fertility. I would like to extend these ideas to make a finer division within rural economic activities — one that goes beyond the broad distinction between agricultural/nonagricultural activity, and work away from home and in and around the home. Conceivably, a close analysis of the sexual division of labour within rural households might give us a better idea of the total work that women perform than do the current definitions of work which exclude house-based activities. Because of the strong interrelationship in rural households between housework that is not directly productive (i.e., income-generating) and productive labour, analysis of the linkage between the sexual division of labour within the household and reproductive behaviour may help to explain differential fertility patterns.

Because little or no work has been done on the links between household work and fertility, there is little evidence on which to base hypotheses about the effect of household roles on fertility. Studies of women's employment in the labour market are available, however, and an analysis of them may show how their findings might apply to work in the rural household as well. (The review of the literature that follows is intended to be only suggestive of trends rather than to reflect the whole range of research on this subject.)

## The Relationship Between Women's Work and Fertility

Research to date has failed to provide a clear and consistent explanation of the relationship between women's employment and fertility, and has not confirmed the causality. Do fertility levels affect women's involvement in economic activities rather than vice versa? Do women work only until they have children or because they cannot have children at all, or does working cause them to delay or even forego child-bearing? Significant effects work in both directions. Recent studies have leaned heavily towards the interpretation that fertility influences labour force participation more than labour affects fertility (Dixon, 1978).

It has also been suggested that if and when a negative association between the two variables occurs, it is because employment affects child-spacing, not total fertility. There is evidence for the United States that women's labour force participation is indeed directly related to the length of the interval between births (Namboodiri, 1964), but whether the woman who works ever 'catches up' to those who do not work in terms of total number of children is unclear. Namboodiri argues they do not; Freedman (1963) argues that they do, basing her conclusion on the fact that while work participation is one of the strongest predictors of fertility for US women married less than ten years, it is one of the weaker predictors for women married ten years or more (Mason, 1971).

Theoretical statements postulating an inverse relationship between female employment and fertility have been advanced by economists and sociologists. The former have attempted to explain fertility as a function of rational economic choice within the household by husband and wife. The New Household Economics offers a theory that begins with the assumption that children, like other goods, involve cost and benefits. Therefore, it is argued, an increase in the wife's market wage rate could have two economic effects. One is that the increase in household income would make it possible for a couple to have a larger family; this 'income effect' would favour increased fertility. On the other hand, an increase in the wife's wage could increase the opportunity cost of the wife's time spent in non-market activities, inducing her to reallocate her time in favour of market activities. If child-care is more time-intensive for the wife than are other non-market activities, the opportunity cost of children will increase more than will that of other demands on her time, and she will choose to have a smaller family (Ridker, 1976).

Sociologists would argue that the pure income effect could also predict that female employment would have an 'indirect' influence on fertility. Because of a working daughter's economic contribution to the home, for instance, parents may find it advantageous to postpone the daughter's marriage, and they may decide to have fewer children themselves as they become less dependent on sons for economic survival (Dixon, 1978).

The sociologists' argument, which is grounded in the experience of Western Europe and the United States where there has historically been an inverse relationship between female labour participation and actual family size, and family size expectation/desires, postulates that employment outside the home provides satisfaction, alternatives to children, or the means to such satisfaction in the form of financial remuneration. Foregoing employment will often be experienced as a cost — one of the costs — of having children. Thus employment is a means of introducing into women's lives the subjective awareness of the opportunity costs involved in child-bearing, an awareness that traditional feminine roles and activities seem designed to circumvent (Blake, 1965).

Contradictions in the empirical relationship between the two variables have led both economists and sociologists to include certain specifications in their postulates about the influence of female employment on fertility.[1] These specifications address the central question of why and under what conditions employment would affect fertility patterns.

Stycos and Weller (1967) developed the concept of role compatibility and designed a hypothetical matrix defining the relationship of fertility to female employment under varying societal conditions. They chose compatibility of mother-worker roles and availability of contraceptive devices as two factors that determine the existence of and direction of a relationship between fertility and women's labour force participation.

Birdsall (1975) argues for the need to conceptualize a cost-reward ratio in women's employment as being more or less favourable to child-bearing in both economic and psychological terms. The bulk of conventional economic or socio-economic research on fertility has assumed a commonality or congruence of interest between husband and wife in desiring a child. This is grounded in the principle that it is the household that maximizes its utility. The introduction of psychological variables into the equation assumes that differences can arise between husband and wife with regard to interest in children. Such variables include 'role extensiveness' of males and females, the nature of the relationship between husband and wife, 'machismo', type of marriage, sexual gratification, etc. These variables refer to family and individual characteristics and distinguish thereby among couples who share a common socio-economic background (Goldberg, 1974). Leibenstein's theory of selective rationality, although not specifically addressed to the issue of the employment-fertility relationship, proposes the need, in the analysis of fertility-related behaviour, to focus on the individual (not the household) as the basic decision-making unit and to assume that differential interests (as opposed to identity of interests) prevail within the household regarding the decisions related to fertility. Family size may be determined by 'a lack of calculation of considerations; or by extremely gross calculations; or by a lack of caring of the connection between current behavior and future consequences' (Leibenstein, 1977).

## The Evidence for a Negative Association Between Female Employment and Fertility

A negative association between female employment and fertility in developing countries was found in the 1950-60 Puerto Rican data (Carleton, 1965; Weller, 1968; Nerlove and Schultz, 1970) and corroborated by findings in Costa Rica and Chile (Carrajal and Geithmann, 1973; DaVanzo and Lee, 1978), Colombia (Chi and Harris, 1975), elsewhere in Latin America (Requeña, 1965; Stycos, 1965; Miro and Mertens, 1968; Gendell, Maraviglia and Kreitner, 1970) and in the Philippines (Harman, 1970). All indicate that women's past, present or expected labour force participation is inversely associated with their fertility behaviour or directly associated with use of contraception and abortion.

Studies that distinguish between rural and urban residence have shown that for urban women in modern labour force occupations, work decreases fertility at both the individual level (Kupinski, 1971; Miro and Rath, 1965) and the aggregate level (Jaffe and Azumi, 1960; Collver and Langlois, 1962; Heer and Turner, 1965). The Centro Latinoamericano de Demografia (CELADE) data – which covers Rio de

Janeiro, Bogota, Caracas, Panama City, Mexico City, San Jose and and Buenos Aires -- indicate in all comparative fertility studies that urban working women at the aggregate level have a lower average number of children than nonworking women. These findings are confirmed for others parts of Latin America by Heer (1964), Stycos (1965), Stycos and Weller (1967), Miro and Mertens (1968), Weller (1968), and Gendell *et al.* (1970); for Egypt by Bindary, Baxter and Hollingsworth (1973), and for Bangkok by Goldstein (1972).

More specific evidence of the negative relationship between female employment and fertility is provided by disaggregating employment data to distinguish between occupational categories according to sector and place of employment. Such analysis shows that it is only when the roles of worker and mother are incompatible that employment status will affect fertility. In what is now considered a seminal work, Jaffe and Azumi (1960) demonstrated that in Japan and Puerto Rico fertility of women who work at home is highest among agricultural workers and only slightly lower among cottage industry workers, as compared to women who do not contribute to family income. It is women who leave their home for work whose fertility is lowest, regardless of residence or age (Jaffe and Azumi, 1960). There are similar findings for Turkey (Stycos and Weller, 1967), Colombia (Chi and Harris, 1975) and in metropolitan areas of Latin America (Hass, 1971).

Analysis of the CELADE data on urban female employment by specific occupational categories indicates that the lowest fertility levels are found among women who are professionals, administrators or white-collar workers (Stycos and Weller, 1967; Weller, 1968; Hass, 1971; Goldstein, 1972). In Lima, Peru, professionally and technically employed women average 14 per cent fewer births than non-white-collar workers and 43 per cent fewer births than housewives (Stycos and Weller, 1967). Except for Mexico City and Caracas, women in Latin American cities who work full-time outside the home have lower fertility than part-time workers (Hass, 1971).

The trends in fertility of women who are in domestic service are unclear. The Collver and Langlois analysis (1962) excludes domestic service from their metropolitan employment figures, on the assumption (later confirmed by Stycos and Weller, 1967) that domestic servants display high fertility because live-in arrangements provided for the accommodation of working and maternal roles. More recent findings, however, seem to contradict this assumption: they indicate that domestic servants display lower fertility than any other economically active urban group of women and mothers (Chaplin, 1968; Gendell *et al.*, 1970).

Are specific occupations, place of employment and employment status in any way reflected in women's decisions about contraceptive use? The data on this question is not consistent from one Latin American city to another. In Rio de Janeiro, Bogota, San Jose and Panama City, white-collar employees use contraceptives earlier and more frequently than non-white-collar workers and housewives (Hass, 1971). Full-time work status is in no way linked to extent and timing of contraceptive usage. Work outside the home and longer work hours do affect contraceptive use in San Jose and Panama City in the expected direction. In Mexico City, Caracas, Brazil and Colombia, neither employment status nor place of employment influence contraceptive use (Hass, 1971; Chi and Harris, 1975).

## The Evidence for a Neutral or a Positive Association Between Female Employment and Fertility

Another body of research reveals either no association or a positive association between female labour force participation and fertility. This is most true among rural women workers and among urban women who are involved in marginal income-earning activities.

There are several reasons for there being a positive relationship between the two variables in developing countries. First, the income effect (desire to have more children as income rises) could be strong at low levels of income, as is suggested by an analysis of the Egyptian data (Bindary *et al.*, 1973). Second, poverty forces women into the labour market because their families need additional income; they work because they have to, not necessarily because they want to, therefore their work may not affect their fertility decisions (Chai and Cho, 1976). Third, the opportunity costs of children in some circumstances are low. Large families and extended families make it easier to find substitutes for the mother's time in child-rearing. The jobs set aside for women in developing countries are often compatible with child-care — or at least are less incompatible than are jobs in formal 'modernized' work settings.

The effect of work upon fertility may also differ according to a woman's stage in the life cycle. Using age-specific data, Goldstein (1972) finds for Thailand a negative association between work status and fertility for women up to the age of 30, but a positive association thereafter, with the differential between Thai working and non-working women aged 45 and over as high as 15 per cent.

That there are unmeasured influences or structural conditions independent of employment status that operate to counteract the expected effect of female employment upon fertility is suggested by a comparative analysis of the data from Middle Eastern Muslim countries and the Soviet Central Asian Republics. Despite substantially higher rates of economic participation among women in the Soviet Republics, these women displayed both higher fertility levels and higher fertility ideals than did Muslim women in the Middle East and North America, whose economic activity rates are extremely low (Heer and Youssef, 1977). Zarate (1967), in a sample of Mexican males, finds a relationship between the wife's work prior to marriage and subsequent fertility of the husband, but none between work experience after marriage and fertility. Minkler (1970), in a study of New Delhi teachers and uneducated women, finds no association between ideal family size and work status, but the less educated women do have much higher actual fertility than do the women teachers. A study done in Central India finds a positive relationship between employment status and fertility, but this relationship is reduced to zero when age is controlled for (Driver, 1963).

Several studies have shown that the fertility of working women in rural areas is higher than the fertility of nonworking women in urban areas. This is true in some European countries, as well as in developing countries. In Italy, the greatest differentials in fertility in the north occurred between women doing permanent agricultural work (fertility rate, 135.0) and women doing permanent nonagricultural work (fertility rate, 75.0), with housewives in between (fertility rate, 117.6) (Pinelli, 1971). In Japan, rural women in agricultural work who averaged 3.5 children (compared to 2.8 for nonworking women) had a higher fertility than rural nonworking women, because larger families created a need for more household income. In Thailand, rural agricultural female workers registered a higher number of children-ever-born to 1,000 ever-married women (4.5) than did urban housewives (3.8) or Bangkok housewives (3.7). Rural agricultural women workers in Thailand also had a higher fertility rate (4.5) than rural women who were not agricultural workers (4.3) (Goldstein, 1972).

## The Effect of Work Satisfaction and Work Commitment in Reducing Fertility

Female employment is expected to lower fertility if the nature of work is such that the woman's interest in having a large family is reduced. That notion may be true for middle- or upper-class women with considerable education who can aspire to well-paid and/or highly satisfying jobs. For most women in developing nations such work opportunities are not available. Nevertheless 'attitude towards work' is important in understanding the dynamics between women's work and fertility behaviour.

In urban Greece, women with a high work commitment have fewer children and use birth control more effectively than women with low work commitment; working women who had a low work commitment had about as many children as housewives (Safilios-Rothschild, 1972a). In Italy, women who worked because they wanted to be independent and were interested in their work had fewer children than women who stated that they worked only because of economic need (Pinelli, 1971).

That job satisfaction influences a couple's fertility decisions, even when a large number of socio-economic, modernity and birth control variables are controlled for, is borne out by Tunisian data (Suzman, Miller and Charrad, 1976). Results of that study support the hypothesis that a woman's job satisfaction is inversely related to fertility.

A woman's conception of appropriate sex-role behaviour, particularly with respect to maternal roles, is important and should be taken into account regardless of whether she conforms to such standards herself. Women who approve of nondomestic roles, even if they do not work outside the home, appear to have a greater desire to limit fertility. When Hass (1972) introduced controls such as female education, age at first sexual union and variables related to attitude to sex roles (particularly degree of approval of maternal employment), the fertility differential initially ascribed to place of employment and type of occupation disappeared. Education and approval of nondomestic activities for women seemed to be as effective as incompatibility of work and maternal roles in explaining differences in fertility behaviour among urban Latin American women. Similarly, women employed outside the home who disapproved of nondomestic roles for women had the lowest score on the contraceptive usage index.

## The Complex Relationship Between Division of Labour, Status and Fertility

Several important facts have emerged from the preceding discussion. One is that the bulk of research on the economic activities-fertility relationship has studied reproductive behaviour and fertility-related attitudes among a 'working' female population that is linked to a formal, or at least an identifiable, labour market. A second is that the effect of women's work upon fertility varies according to the specific type of work performed and the woman's place of employment. Another is that women's work in rural areas, specifically in the agricultural sector, appears to have a neutral, if not in fact a positive, effect on fertility.

It was proposed above that the division of labour between the sexes within rural households might be a more comprehensive concept than the currently measured work activities of rural women, and one which might provide a linkage to motivations related to fertility behaviour. Specifically, there is a need to pursue the flow of the relationship between the sexual division of labour and variables related to women's status in the rural community, and how these all might combine to interact and influence fertility.

## Definitional Issues

It is important to acknowledge that such a division of labour is by no means a given. Specific patterns of the division of labour within the family unit and degrees of sex-role specialization are dynamic and reflect responses to both endogenous and exogenous social, economic and political pressures. I will address myself to three major determinants, with particular focus on the implication these have upon labour allocation decisions for rural women:[2] (i) the level of agricultural complexity and differentiation; (ii) the level of hierarchization of the community, particularly in land ownership; and (iii) the purpose and scale of the economic activity performed.

For what I consider to be distinct aspects of the core concept 'status', particularly as it refers to rural women, I will use some of the measures proposed by Whyte (1978), which I believe are congruent with Dixon's definition of status as 'a broad and inclusive term that may cover the differential power, prestige, rights, privileges and importance of women relative to men' (Dixon, 1978).[3] From the several measures proposed by Whyte (1978), I consider the following to be crucial, although they by no means reflect the entire range of aspects of status/power: property control; power of women in kinship context; value placed on lives of women; value placed on labour of women; domestic authority; control over women's marital and sexual life; female solidarity; and male/female joint participation. Each of these variables has intrinsic power or status implications, but there is no guarantee that each and every single aspect will be highly related to the other. In fact, aspects of status are often found to be largely independent of each other, so that no one particular variable, if known, can predict how women fare on other measures (Whyte, 1978). It is therefore difficult to arrive at final definitions of 'high status', 'low status', 'power', etc.[4]

Fertility measures should encompass the conventional measures — i.e., actual fertility behaviour (number of children-ever-born, controlled by the woman's age and duration of marriage); expressed attitudes towards additional births (births expected or wanted, ideal family size); and attitudes towards, and knowledge of, fertility control. The basic unit of analysis that is proposed here is not conventional, however. It is the individual fertility of the woman; the woman, not the couple or the household, is the basic unit of analysis.

## Determinants of the Division of Labour Between the Sexes

*Level of Agricultural Complexity and Differentiation.* The extent and type of female family labour in agricultural work are conditioned by the interaction between differences in the technical nature of farming operations and systems of cultivation. As agricultural complexity and differentiation increase, the demand for female labour in agriculture decreases and the role of women in the agricultural production process becomes less visible. Boserup (1970) classifies systems of subsistence farming according to whether fieldwork is done almost exclusively by women, predominantly by women, or predominantly by men. In systems of shifting cultivation where the plough is not used, women play a very active part in agricultural production. In areas of low population density it is not necessary to have a large crop in order to survive, therefore there can be less labour input per unit of agricultural output and most farm work can be left to women. In densely populated regions, subsistence agriculture demands much more labour, and men have to do much of the work.

When the ploughing of permanent fields is introduced in lieu of shifting cultivation, a radical shift in sex-role specialization occurs. Basically, female farming systems disappear. The plough is used by men; women are left to perform some hand operations. In densely populated regions, where there is extensive plough cultivation (such as Arab and Latin American countries), there is little demand for female labour except to help with the harvest and to care for domestic animals. Women (and children) come to constitute a marginal labour force utilized to meet peak seasonal labour demands and needs (Boserup, 1970).

The productivity of women's agricultural labour is further reduced with the introduction of improved agricultural technology and cash crops, for men are thought to be primary income-producers. They are taught to apply modern methods of agriculture, particularly in the cultivation of cash crops, and to use part of their earnings from cash crops to invest in the improvement of production. Women who only raise crops for family use continue to use traditional methods of cultivation and are thus unable to derive cash income for eventual improvement of their farming technique. The relative status of women in agriculture declines sharply.

The sexual division of labour is conditioned by variations in the *demand* for labour. This, in turn, is dependent upon the particular crops that are grown. Because vegetables, cotton and irrigated rice are very labour-intensive crops, there is a large demand for female labour where they are grown. In grain agricultural economies female labour demand is seasonal and concentrated in brief time periods. In plantation zones, where men are employed, it is the women who have to take over subsistence production.

*Level of Hierarchization of the Community*. Deere (1978) and Young (1977) argue forcefully that it is important to recognize social differentiation among the peasantry (which is based upon differential access to the means of production) and the form of integration of the household into the wider economy as factors conditioning the sexual division of labour. Access to the means of production determines the structure of the particular process of appropriation and distribution of the surplus generated by familial labour after basic requirements to reproduce the household level of subsistence consumption have been fulfilled. Lack of land requires the poorest peasant strata to depend on nonagricultural activities for their livelihood and forces them into the sale of labour power for a wage. Access to sufficient resources allows other elements of the peasantry to purchase wage labour to carry out productive activities and to engage in petty commodity production (crop- or animal-raising, artisanship, etc.).

The implications of this social differentiation process for the economic role of women are far-reaching, since different opportunity costs by sex in the labour market operate to influence the division of labour between the sexes within the household among different strata (Deere, 1978). Larger farmers use the labour of the women and children in the household as much as do small farmers, but they can now hire wage labour for most of the agricultural work. Female family members of farmers who own land are the ones who benefit most from the availability of the landless peasantry who work for wages (Boserup, 1970). For a large percentage of these 'upper strata' women, agricultural work comes to be defined as 'inappropriate' work for women. The result is that they are able to devote themselves largely to work within the home and to leave work in the fields to male family members and hired labour.

Land ownership operates to bring about significant cleavage between strata in terms of the degree of sex-role specialization. Among the poor and landless, few economic activities are defined as inappropriate for women. Sex-role differentiation is blurred. Among the landless farmers, female family workers participate equally in all kinds of agricultural activities (except ploughing), use most tools and implements, and have equal control with men over the disposition of both produce and the proceeds from its sale (Young, 1977; Deere, 1978). It is these women who become involved in artisan production and supply the bulk of female wage labour.

Among the upper strata of the peasantry, by contrast, a high degree of segregation of work roles is evident. Restrictions are imposed upon women's use of implements and tools, on their participation in decisions related to agricultural production and on their responsibility and/or control over marketing or any other kind of commercialization of commodities which they have aided in producing (Young, 1977; Deere, 1978). The only activity outside of agriculture which women from these strata are likely to pursue is trade, where they attain a considerable degree of autonomy.

It has often been stated that restriction on labour is grounded in economics and not in culture. When there is surplus of labour and marginal productivity is consequently low, culture 'restricts' the effective labour force. Manual labour comes to be thought of as demeaning for the upper classes; therefore it is socially inappropriate for all but the poorest to work (Mueller, 1976).

*Purpose and Scale of Economic Activity.* There is a distinction between activities associated with domestic use (use-value) and those which are associated with the marketplace (exchange-value). By and large, women are the major, if not the only, producers of use-value activities (those needed for maintenance of familial labour power on a daily basis), but are increasingly isolated from activities — agricultural or nonagricultural — related to exchange-value.

When agriculture is the major source of livelihood, males play the more active part in the production of cash crops. Women are charged with those artisan activities that generate goods for the family's consumption (spinning, weaving and sewing). Men predominate when the activity is a full-time occupation (tailoring, brickmaking, carpentry, pottery, basket-weaving) (Deere, 1978). When farm production is an income-generating activity (rather than only a subsistence activity), men control the marketing of produce which women help to produce.

However, there are differences among strata in the *degree* to which labour is divided according to the purpose of the activity. Among the poor and landless, women are more active in production, whether for use-value or exchange-value. Among the upper strata, however, labour is divided in terms of who controls the outcome of the activity. Men control the marketing of cattle and of milk, even though women share responsibility for care of cattle; in landless families, women participate in the marketing of cattle, however small the sale (Deere, 1978).

The following working hypotheses are suggested:

(i) Women will be assigned important agricultural tasks where subsistence is based on shifting cultivation, and, conversely, minor and only seasonal tasks where subsistence is based on plough cultivation.

(ii) Women will be assigned important agricultural tasks in sparsely populated regions where subsistence is based on intensive cultivation.

(iii) Women will be assigned agricultural tasks that are equally as important as those of men in regions of intensive cultivation of irrigated land.

(iv) Women will be assigned to minor agricultural tasks in societies where cash crop cultivation has been introduced.

(v) Women will be assigned to minor agricultural tasks in societies where farm mechanization has been introduced.

## Sexual Division of Labour Within the Household and Status of Women

The major thrust of the inquiry in this section is the following: *under what conditions does the sexual division of labour 'generate a resource base for women that can be translated into power in other spheres?'* (Dixon, 1978). The linkage between the sexual division of labour and female power is well stated by Young (1977):

> I wanted to analyze the sexual division of labor, meaning by this a system of *allocation* of agents to positions within the labor process on the basis of sex and a system of *exclusion* of certain categories of agents from certain positions within the social organization on the basis of sex, and lastly a system of *reinforcement* of the social

construction of gender (emphasis added).

Do women derive power, status and privileges by virtue of the system of allocation within the labour process? Are they denied power, status and privileges by virtue of the system of exclusion? What type of productive roles might be linked to female power variables by virtue of their valuation, the income derived (directly or indirectly) from them, the level of skill involved? In the literature on women and development, the range of indices for power is considerable.

Boserup's (1970) positive evaluation of women's traditional roles in the productive process suggests the following proposition: *the more highly valued the economic activity performed by women, the greater will be the woman's power within the community and the family.*

Women's power (as measured by mobility, independence, etc.) is linked to the female farming system. The gradual displacement of that power comes about with the use of technology (plough cultivation, farm mechanization, cash crops). Women's status varies with the combined effects of the system of cultivation and stratification variables associated with appropriation of land.

*Shifting agricultural systems* combined with low population densities do not yield class differences based on differential land ownership. Status concerns are not important here. Marriages are not controlled, bridewealth is common; sexual life is freer, polygamy is frequent; women are not secluded in the home; the conjugal unit is not emphasized in economic life; women are assigned their own domains of familial responsibility; sex-role specialization is de-emphasized; women have some control over proceeds from the sale of their own crops; women are valued as workers and mothers (Boserup, 1970; Whyte, 1978).

*Plough cultivation and private ownership of land* are associated with decreasing demand for female labour, parental control over marriage choices, emphasis on female purity, payment of dowry, female seclusion and veiling, women's economic dependency on husband, valuation of women in their mother role (Boserup, 1970), less domestic authority and female solidarity, and more unequal restrictions on sex lives (Whyte, 1978).

The linkage between women's traditional roles and power has been challenged with the argument that women's participation in agriculture and stock-raising economies does not necessarily lead to power (Chinas, 1973; Moses, 1977). Thus, participation in economic production is a necessary but not a sufficient condition of high female status; low levels of female economic participation correlate with low female status, but so do high levels of participation (Sanday, 1973).

It is argued that the contribution of women to subsistence could be seen as an indication of their subordination to less diligent men, rather than of the value of women to society. When women have a near monopoly on the production of subsistence goods, they may be far more dependent on men for nonsubsistence needs than men are on women for subsistence needs (Sanday, 1973). Huntington (1975) argues that female farming systems are male dominated and serve male interests in that it is women's labour that provides men with a livelihood and leisure. Female farming systems characterized by polygamy and recognition of the economic worth of women only further women's subordination. First wives exploit second wives and female children have important roles, so that 'men subjugate women and women subjugate other women and their own female children in a system of thoroughgoing and self-perpetuating exploitation' (Jacquette, 1978).

There is controversy as to the importance of areas of female power associated with domestic/relational capacities, female networks and female solidarity groups. The feminists discount these sources because they directly or indirectly legitimize male domination. But in traditional, and more particularly in rural, societies there may be need to explore arenas of power and influence that lie outside dominance structures and which are not hierarchically ordered; because they are informal and private, they can give women considerable autonomy with regard to decisions affecting their own lives; they obviously carry the potential of influencing male decisions as well.

In the final analysis, concepts of power and prestige take on meaning only in the context of group interaction and women's perception of their own power and self-esteem — hence the need to devise a way of measuring women's general feelings of control over major decisions of their lives (Dixon, 1978).

The following working hypotheses are suggested:

(i) In societies where women contribute much to subsistence production, their status will be the same or higher than in societies where they contribute little.

(ii) Women will have lower status in societies possessing significant private property rights (in the means of production) than in societies where there are no such rights.

(iii) The greater the control women have over the valuable property in a society (inheritance rights, etc.), the higher is their status (Whyte, 1978).

(iv) Women's status will be higher in societies where they have sub-stantial control over the fruits of their productive labour than it will be in societies where they have little control (Whyte, 1978).

(v) Women's status will be higher in societies where women have sub-stantial control over the fruits of male labour than it will be in societies where they have little control (Whyte, 1978).

(vi) In societies where women have substantial control over the fruits of joint labour, their status will be higher than in societies where they have little control (Whyte, 1978).

(vii) Where women's control over property (land) is restricted, women have limited rights in the product of their labour.

(viii) In societies where women are organized collectively for economic activities, their general status will be higher than in other cultures (Whyte, 1978).

## A Framework of Analysis

This section brings together the ideas developed in the previous discus-sion in order to suggest a framework of analysis and propose some research strategies to explore the relationship between the sexual division of labour in the household, stratification variables and aspects of the status of women, and the impact these may have either separate-ly or combined upon reproductive behaviour.

*The Sexual Division of Labour.* With respect to the interrelationship between the labour allocation process among the sexes within the domestic unit and fertility behaviour, two arguments can be made. Both raise important questions regarding the flow of causality. Do women's productive undertakings determine the degree to which women can be committed to a reproductive role or is the reverse true?

The first argument proposes that fertility is a woman's individual response to her perceived private value of children as substitutes for the workload allocated to her by the intra-familial division of labour. The second argument proposes that fertility levels are a response to differen-tial demands for female labour in the rural sector. Such demands, rooted in political and economic forces, exert an independent influence upon the structuring of the sexual division of labour and upon the importance bestowed upon women's reproductive role (Young, 1977).

*Fertility as a response to women's workload.* The literature reviewed earlier stresses the compatibility of work and family roles and the household-based maximum utilization principle as major determinants of reproductive behaviour. High fertility among rural women is seen to be a result of the perceived economic value of children to the household and of the nature of the work opportunities available to rural women, most of which appear to be compatible with family responsibilities.[5]

I propose that fertility behaviour can also be seen as a conscious response reflecting the value women place on children as substitutes for the workload assigned to them by the intra-familial labour allocation process. Certain patternings in the sex-based division of labour are thus expected to be associated with a high preference for children, because numerous children are perceived to lessen the burden of women's tasks in household enterprises, domestic chores and productive activities.

This approach to fertility is somewhat different from the traditional 'economic value of children' approach in that it stresses a linkage to *women's workload* (both home and productive activities), draws upon a maximization of utility model based *on the mother (woman) as the basic unit of analysis* (as opposed to the household) (Leibenstein, 1977), and allows for the specification of *differential interests in children* among household members (Birdsall, 1975), since it grounds fertility behaviour in *the woman's rational calculation of perceived benefits*.

In an attempt to establish a relationship between the two variables, the following questions need to be answered: *under what conditions does the intra-familial division of labour between the sexes generate conditions favourable to women's motivation for large families? Under what conditions does it generate conditions favorable to women's motivation for small families?* These questions in turn suggest two interrelated lines of inquiry for researchers:

(i) Itemization and classification of the different activities allocated to women and careful measurement of the extent to which specific groups of activities are associated with specific kinds of reproductive behaviour and fertility-related attitudes (of individual women).

(ii) Assessment of the 'objective' advantages of large and/or small families in relation to the accomplishment of the workload assigned to women. Are there specific tasks allocated to women that might be facilitated by the presence of numerous children? For example, in which of the numerous activities allocated to women do children help their mothers? In which do they substitute for their mothers? How are women's assigned tasks carried out if there are no children in the home?

*The demand for labour and fertility behaviour.* The second argument postulates a much more complex interrelationship between women's productive and reproductive roles. Young (1977) identifies differential labour demands, which are created by political and economic forces, as the mechanisms behind the way labour is divided between the sexes, how a woman's status and position in the community is defined, and the emphasis given to women's reproductive functions. Merchant capital is associated with an increased demand for labour, a reallocation of labour resources, the entry of many more women into the productive process, and, eventually, an increase in fertility at the household level to meet the need for an absolute increase in available manpower. Women's relegation to the function of reproducing the labour force diminishes their involvement in other social (labour/productive) roles and lessens their control over social resources.

Commercial capital restructures local economies away from self-provisioning, fosters differentiation of the local community, creates private appropriation of land, accelerates the 'freeing' of labour, and brings about the emergence of a wage labour class. It can have one of two effects on fertility, depending on whether labour is redundant or more labour is required. For families dependent on a wage, the amount of the wage as well as the possibility for augmenting it by selling familial labour power provide the boundary conditions for family size. The cost of raising children rises substantially under commercial capital, and restrictions on family size become imperative. Women have to take on labouring work in addition to their heavy burden of household duties when men's wages are insufficient for household needs. The effect may be to reduce the number of children, although dependency on child labour is still great.

*Women's Status.* One of the prerequisites for unravelling the complex relation between the sexual division of labour and fertility is an understanding of the effect of socio-economic status on rural women (Hull, 1977). Earlier we discussed the structural linkages that exist between social differentiation in the community, the sexual division of labour and the position women occupy in the community. These three interact in a very dynamic way to affect reproductive behaviour.

A variety of comparative work and arguments presented earlier in this chapter yield several propositions and hypotheses.

*Women of the upper and middle strata of peasantry will have a higher fertility than women of the landless peasantry and the wage labour class.* This propositional statement rests on the notion that women from the landless and/or wage labour classes may be forced by necessity to curtail their fertility, and is based upon several empirical findings. The first is the positive relationship between class and fertility (Hull, 1977).[6] The second is the previously discussed influence of the emergence of private appropriation of land and consequent creation of a landless/wage labour class upon the role and position of women from the upper and middle strata of the peasantry.

In an earlier discussion of the combined effects of stratification factors and variables related to women's status, we saw that very poor women are less economically dependent on and subordinate to their menfolk than are those from better-off households (Boserup, 1970; Young, 1977; Deere, 1978). These women work in relative equality with men; they are not secluded in the home, are valued in the community as workers and mothers, experience less sex-role specialization in the labour allocation process, are assigned to and actively involved in extra domestic activities, and have some economic independence. Although there is considerable debate as to whether all these attributes reflect higher status for women, it is nevertheless obvious that the economic role and responsibilities that these women are called upon to assume will build in constraints to the bearing of many children.

By contrast, for women from the upper and middle strata of peasantry, one may hypothesize the following effects:

(i) Diminishment of women's roles in the economic productivity process, by strictly defining what are 'appropriate' activities for women;

(ii) Exacerbation of women's economic dependency on and subordination to their menfolk (through parental control of marriage, the dowry system, etc.);

(iii) Fostering of a highly sex-segregated division of labour, which relegates women to home activities and encourages seclusion and veiling practices;

(iv) Loss of women's control over the proceeds of their productive work and over vital input into the household;

(v) Reinforcement of an ideology in which women become valued solely because of their reproductive capacities.

In separate and/or combined form, these factors are expected to foster high fertility levels.

*Women who have lost access to and control over the productive process will display higher fertility rates than women who have not experienced that kind of loss.*[7] This statement rests on findings that the shift from communal ownership of land with usufruct rights to private ownership has had drastic effects on women. As land passes into private ownership, women are squeezed out of independent access to land and to the means of production. The result in terms of women's power and status is disastrous.

The marginalization of women as a result of this process is associated with high fertility. Incentives for numerous children are expected to be rooted in a woman's search to gain power in the domestic arena once she has lost her productive resource base in the economic sphere. Among other strategies utilized by women to gain domestic power will be the control of men (through sex and children) and the direct control of children.

*Family Decision-Making.* Those who theorize a direct linkage between variables related to women's status and fertility behaviour often do not take into account the fact that the critical element in fertility decisions and behaviour is usually, though by no means always, the husband-wife relationship. This relationship does not exist in a vacuum, but is influenced by a couple's socio-economic status and their place in the kinship system as well as by the personal characteristics and values each spouse brings to the union (Mason, 1971).[8] The classical hypothesis about the effect of marital relationships upon fertility behaviour is that 'The more egalitarian, companionate, and communicative the husband-wife relationship, the lower the fertility and the higher the contraceptive usage and efficacy' (Mason, 1971). It stems from the notion that greater equality between spouses should be associated with greater ability to achieve common goals of all kinds, including fertility goals (Mason, 1971). Several assumptions are built into this hypothesis, however, and these *must* be tested in the field before we can predict whether the woman's domestic authority in family decision-making is a necessary or sufficient condition for changing reproductive behaviour and fertility ideals. These are:

(i) The assumption that one of the main obstacles to the adoption of contraception stems from the unwillingness or indifference of the husband and that the dominance of the male in traditional societies precludes the wife taking an equal part in decision-making (Piepmeier and Adkins, 1973).

(ii) The assumption that the goal of all couples is to restrict their fertility, rather than to expand it.

(iii) The assumption that the wife is committed to fertility control and that she must engage in mutual decision-making with her husband in order to control it.[9]

(iv) The assumption that egalitarian relationships are linked to inter-spouse communication (Mason, 1971).

(v) The assumption that women's domestic authority is necessarily the same as mutuality of decision-making (Mason, 1971).

(vi) The assumption that women's lack of control over fertility decision-making is an example of male dominance.

Furthermore, when operationalizing the concept 'domestic power', particularly in relation to family decision-making, it is crucial to distinguish between family power and marital power, between family power and decision-making, and between female autonomy and decision-making (Safilios-Rothschild, 1970). Egalitarian relationships are not necessarily companionate relationships and interspouse communication is not necessarily highest when wife and husband are equal (Mason, 1971). Dixon (1971) cautions that family power must be studied within the extended family context and suggests guidelines for cross-cultural research. Her recommendations yield insight into the position of women in the family, but these should not necessarily be equated with the woman's power or influence in relationship to her husband.

Given all these cautionary notes, what is known about women's influence in family decision-making and its relation to fertility, and what might be some of the areas of inquiry to pursue?

There is some evidence to suggest that employment outside the home is associated with considerably greater female autonomy and influence in family decision-making than is work within the home (Piepmeier and Adkins, 1973). This evidence has been found in the industrialized West and in some urbanized modern segments of the female population in developing societies.

Greater influence of the wife in family decision-making and verbal communication between husband and wife have been empirically associated with contraceptive usage in Hong Kong (Mitchell, 1972); with adoption of family planning and desire for lower family size in the Philippines (Goldberg, 1974); and with lower fertility in Brazil (Rosen and Simmons, 1971).

Some findings indicate that women with greater economic independence are better able to control their fertility because of greater autonomy and influence in family decision-making. However, the proposition does not appear to hold in most parts of the developing world, among the poor, and probably not in rural areas, because of the intervention of cultural forces which depress the material resource effect of the employed wife (Oppong, 1970; Mukherjee, 1974; Salaff, 1976).[10]

In pursuing the relevance of the decision-making variable to fertility behaviour in the context of the rural population, two directions should be taken: the first is directed towards discovering whether or not a relationship can be traced between specific labour allocation patterns and aspects of female status and female influence in family decision-making. (Do certain tasks bestow a greater power on women than other tasks, and does increased power also give women greater influence with respect to decisions concerning reproductive behaviour?) The second is whether or not the fact that a woman may have influence or power in family decision-making is a sufficient condition for changing her fertility behaviour. (How do these two levels interact to influence the power women have in family decision-making?)

The following working hypotheses are suggested as guidelines to exploring some of the linkages between these variables:

(i) Differential patterns of labour allocation between the sexes are associated with greater or lesser participation of the woman in family decision-making.

(ii) Women who perform activities of economic value to the household will have greater power in family decision-making than those who do not perform such activities.

(iii) Women have greater power in family decision-making in societies where there is little differentiation in sex roles with respect to the division of labour.

(iv) Women have little power in family decision-making in societies where there is a strict sex-segregation principle in the division of labour within the household.

(v) In societies where strict segregation of sex roles exists, women will have higher incentives for fertility than in societies where role differentiation between the sexes is de-emphasized.

(vi) The greater the influence or power of women in the family decision-making process, the greater their sense of power and control over their child-bearing.

(vii) Work that produces income over which women have some control will be associated with women's greater influence or power in family decision-making — in particular, in decisions related to fertility.

## Conclusions

Rather than accept the sexual division of labour in the rural household as a given, this discussion began with an analysis of some of the determinants of the labour allocation process between the sexes because of the need to understand the structural context in which intra-familial decisions regarding the work women are to perform take place. Social differentiation processes within the rural community were shown to play a crucial role, particularly those which stem from private appropriation of land, in simultaneously acting upon the labour allocation process and upon aspects related to women's institutional position in the social structure.

Clearly, there is no causal sequence through which the sexual division of labour and/or different aspects of the role and status of women can separately influence fertility behaviour. All interact in a dynamic way with stratification variables to structure requirements and constraints related to reproductive behaviour.

I have suggested consideration of certain relationships between the sexual division of labour and fertility, and between certain aspects related to women's power and fertility, in an endeavour to begin to single out some central areas of inquiry that might be pursued at both the macro and micro levels of analysis before an actual model might be constructed. One of these treats fertility as a woman's direct response to the sex-based labour allocation process; the other sees a causal flow between sex-specific demands for labour (emerging from economic and political forces), the sexual division of labour and fertility levels. With respect to aspects of a woman's position, I have singled out domestic power as one variable and examined critically its relevance to a clearer understanding of the status-fertility relationship in developing societies.

## Notes

1. Dixon rightfully points out that contradictory findings are partially due to the use of different methodological approaches:

> Some studies use aggregate national or subnational data in ecological correlations; others use census data for comparisons across major population sub-groups or for analyses of aggregate changes over time; still others are based on lengthy personal interviews, including work and pregnancy histories. The dependent variables also differ. Some use actual measures of fertility, i.e., number of children ever born; others use number of additional births expected or wanted, ideal family size, or family planning knowledge, attitudes and practices (Dixon, 1978).

2. For discussion of the impact that the needs of the international market have upon shaping agricultural policies of production relations, the sexual division of labour within the household, and the particular manner in which women are thereby affected, see United Nations Research Institute for Social Development (1978). For an excellent analysis of the intervention of two different types of capital — merchant capital and circulation capital — and the different effects such intervention can have on the sexual division of labour, see Young (1977).

3. For other attempts to develop indicators of the status of women, see Mukherjee (1974) for Indian society; Sanday (1973) for tribal and agrarian societies; Dixon (1976) and Safilios-Rothschild (1972b) for industrialized societies.

4. The complexity of the relationship between status variables and marital power is best illustrated in Kofyar society in the Jos plateau of Nigeria. Women there have considerable independence and social power, despite the fact that their institutionalized roles in patrilineal kin groups and village politics are minimal. They own little property, marry virilocally and play a subordinate role in religious observances. They do, however, make important economic decisions in allocating their own incomes and labour services. They also have the right to either terminate their marriages or to accept lovers in a socially recognized relationship. With a relatively unimportant sexual division of labour and limited marital and economic control, husbands are able to achieve little domestic authority over their wives. The indications are that male dominance is asserted chiefly, though not entirely successfully, in symbolic terms through sex-segregated rites and ritual injunctions (McNetting, 1969).

5. DaVanzo and Lee (1978) demonstrate through their careful work in Malaysia that agricultural tasks involving female labour are not as compatible with child-care as has always been assumed, however.

6. The negative effect of poverty on fertility (independent of women's status and work roles) is in part due to other factors associated with poor women which depress reproduction, such as high frequency of marital disruption, secondary sterility, miscarriages, stillbirths and post-partum abstinence (Concepcion, 1974; Hull, 1977).

7. A distinction is made between the landless peasantry, part of whom become a wage labour class, and women who have lost traditional access to land, as has happened in parts of Africa.

8. This chapter does not address the issue of the significance of the size and structure of the family in determining the status of women and fertility. I make the assumption that the influence of greater internal family hierarchy and more narrow division of labour favouring males (both of which are associated with extended family structure) will be reflected in the scope and degree of female influence and power in family decision-making. For a fresh approach to the continuing debate on the interrelationship between types of family structure and fertility, see Ryder (1976). He distinguishes between extended/joint family structure along the following lines: relationship of individuals to the household head in terms of descent; quantity and quality of interaction characterizing relationship between household members; arrangements of and authority over living units and over production and distribution of economic resources.

9. A surprisingly high percentage of Egyptian women said 'Yes' when asked: 'Do you agree that a woman should go ahead and use a contraceptive even if her husband disagrees?'. About 30% of the total rural and urban sample agreed. Literate wives were more likely than illiterate wives to agree with the statement (Dixon, 1978). The reverse is also true. A sterilization operation on a village wife in India took place after a decision was made by her husband and his mother. The wife was operated upon and did not know that a tubectomy had been

performed until she was told afterwards (Poffenberger, 1975).

10. Mukherjee finds no significant correlation between women's employment status and their role in household decision-making in three states in India. Of the 150 unskilled women labourers on nine major construction sites in Delhi, almost all of whom earned as much income as their husbands, only 8% stated that they participated in decisions regarding education and marriage of their children, selection of jobs, etc. (Mukherjee, 1974).

# References

Bindary, A., C. Baxter and T.H. Hollingsworth (1973) 'Urban rural differences in the relationship between women's employment and fertility: a preliminary study', *Journal of Biosocial Sciences*, *5*, 2

Birdsall, N. (1975) 'How many babies: to each his/her own', mimeo., Washington, DC, Interdisciplinary Communications Program, Smithsonian Institute

Blake, J. (1965) 'Demographic science and the redirection of population policy', *Journal of Chronic Diseases*, *18*

Boserup, E. (1970) *Woman's role in economic development*, New York, St. Martin's Press

Boulding, E. (1977) *Women in the twentieth century*, New York, John Wiley and Sons: Halsted Press Division

Carleton, R. (1965) 'Labor force participation: a stimulus to fertility in Puerto Rico?', *Demography*, *2*, 1

——— (1969) 'Fertility trends and differentials in Latin America', *Milbank Memorial Fund Quarterly*, *43*, 2

Carrajal, M. and D.T. Geithmann (1973) 'Economic aspects of fertility and alternative approaches: Costa Rica, case in point', mimeo., Gainesville, Florida, University of Florida

Chai, L.H. and M. Cho (1976) 'Fertility and women's labor force participation in Korea', in *Recent empirical findings on fertility: Korea, Nigeria, Tunisia, Venezuela, Philippines*, Smithsonian Institution Interdisciplinary Communications Program, monograph series no. 7, Washington, DC, Smithsonian Institution

Chaplin, D. (1968) 'Labour turnover in the Peruvian textile industry', *British Journal of Industrial Relations*, *6*, 1

Chi, S.K.P. and R. Harris (1975) 'Interaction between action programs and social structural variables: a study of family planning and fertility differentials in four Colombian cities', paper presented at the annual meeting of the Population Association of America, Seattle, Washington

Chinas, B. (1973) *The isthmus Zapotecs: woman's roles in cultural context*, New York, Holt, Rinehart and Winston

Collver, A. and E. Langlois (1962) 'The female labor force in metropolitan areas: an international comparison', *Economic Development and Cultural Change*, *10*, 4

Concepcion, M. (1974) 'Female labor force participation and fertility', *International Labour Review*, *109*

DaVanzo, J. and D.L.P. Lee (1978) 'The compatibility of child care with labor force participation and non-market activities: preliminary evidence from Malaysian time budget data', paper presented at the Conference of the International Center for Research on Women: 'Women in Poverty: What Do We Know?', Belmont, Maryland

Deere, C.D. (1978) 'Intra familial labor deployment and the formation of peasant household income', paper presented at the Conference of the International Center for Research on Women, 'Women in Poverty: What Do We Know?', Belmont, Maryland

Dixon, R. (1971) 'Explaining cross cultural variations in age at marriage and proportions never married', *Population Studies, 25,* 2

—— (1976a) 'Women's rights and fertility', *Report on population family planning,* New York, Population Council

—— (1976) 'The roles of rural women: female seclusion, economic production and reproductive choice' in Ridker

—— (1978) *Rural women at work: strategies for development in South Asia,* Baltimore, Johns Hopkins University Press

Driver, E.D. (1963) *Differential fertility in Central India,* Princeton, Princeton University Press

Freedman, D.S. (1963) 'The relation of economic status to fertility', *American Economic Review, 55,* 3

Gendell, M., M.N. Maraviglia and P.C. Kreitner (1970) 'Fertility and economic activity of women in Guatemala City, 1964', *Demography, 7,* 3

Goldberg, D. (1974) 'Modernism: the extensiveness of woman's roles and attitudes', *World Fertility Survey,* occasional paper no. 14

Goldstein, S. (1972) 'The influence of labor force participation and education on fertility in Thailand', *Population Studies, 26,* 3

Harman, A. (1970) *Fertility and economic behaviour of families in the Philippines,* Santa Monica, The Rand Corporation

Hass, P. (1971) 'Maternal employment and fertility in metropolitan Latin America', PhD dissertation, Durham, North Carolina, Duke University

—— (1972) 'Maternal role incompatibility and fertility in urban Latin America', *Journal of Social Issues, 28,* 2

Heer, D. (1964) 'Economic development and fertility', *Demography, 3,* 2

—— and E. Turner (1965) 'Areal differences in Latin American fertility', *Population Studies, 20,* 2

—— and N. Youssef (1977) 'Female status among Soviet Central Asian nationalities: the melding of Islam and Marxism and its implications for population increase', *Population Studies, 31,* 1

Hull, V.J. (1977) 'Fertility, women's work and economic class: a case study from South East Asia', in Stanley Kupinski (ed.), *The fertility of working women: a synthesis of international research,* New York, Praeger Publishers

Huntington, S. (1975) 'Issues in woman's role in economic development: critique and alternatives', *Journal of Marriage and the Family, 37,* 2

Jacquette, J. (1978) 'Women and development in Latin America: the problem of power', paper presented at the annual meeting of the American Political Science Association, New York

Jaffe, A.J. and K. Azumi (1960) 'The birth rate and cottage industries in under-developed countries', *Economic Development and Cultural Change, 9,* 1

Kaberry, P. (1952) *Women of the grass fields: a study of the economic position of women in Bambenda, British Cameroons,* London, HMSO

Kupinski, S. (1971) 'Non-familial activity and socio-economic differentials in fertility', *Demography, 8,* 1

Leibenstein, H. (1977) 'Beyond economic man: economics, politics and the population problem', *Population and Development Review, 3,* 3

Mason, K.O. (1971) 'Social and economic correlates of family fertility: a survey of the evidence', North Carolina, Research Triangle Institute

McNetting, R.C. (1969) 'Marital relations in the Jos plateau of Nigeria', *American Anthropologist, 71,* 6

Minkler, M. (1970) 'Fertility and female labor force participation in India: a survey of workers in Old Delhi Area', *Journal of Family Welfare, 17,* 1

Miro, C. and W. Mertens (1968) 'Influences affecting fertility in urban and rural Latin America', *Milbank Memorial Fund Quarterly, 46,* 1

—— and R. Rath (1965) 'Preliminary findings of comparative fertility in three Latin American cities', *Milbank Memorial Fund Quarterly, 43,* 2

Mitchell, R.E. (1972) 'Husband-wife relations and family planning practices in urban Hong Kong', *Journal of Marriage and Family, 34,* 1

Moses, Y. (1977) 'Female status, the family and male dominance in a West Indian community', *Signs, 3,* 1

Mueller, E. (1976) 'The economic value of children in peasant agriculture', in Ridker

Mukherjee, B.N. (1974) 'The status of married women in Haryana, Tamil Nadu, and Meghalaya', *Social Change, 4,* 1

Nag, M. (1976) 'Economic value of children in agricultural societies' in John Marshall and Stephen Polgars (eds.), *Cultures, natality and family planning,* Chapel Hill, University of North Carolina Press

Namboodiri, K. (1964) 'The wife's work experience and child spacing', *Milbank Memorial Fund Quarterly, 42*

—— (1976) 'On the relation between economic status and family size preference when status differentials in contraceptive instrumentalities are eliminated', *Population Studies, 24,* 2

Nerlove, M. and Schultz, T.P. (1970) *Love and life between the censuses: a model of family decision making in Puerto Rico, 1950-1960,* Santa Monica, The Rand Corporation, RM-6322-AID

Oppong, C. (1970) 'Conjugal power and resources: an urban African example', *Journal of Marriage and the Family, 32,* 4

Piepmeier, K.P. and T.S. Adkins (1973) 'The status of women and fertility', *Journal of Biosocial Science, 5*

Pinelli, A. (1971) 'Female labor and fertility in relationship to contrasting social and economic conditions', *Human Relations, 24*

Poffenberger, T. (1975) *Fertility and family life in an Indian village,* Michigan papers on South and South East Asia, no. 10, Ann Arbor, University of Michigan

Repetto, R.G. (1976) 'Direct economic costs and value of children' in Ridker

Requeña, M. (1965) 'Social and economic correlates of induced abortion in Santiago, Chile', *Demography, 2*

Ridker, R. (ed.) (1976) *Population and development: the search for selective interventions,* Baltimore, Johns Hopkins University Press

Rosen, B.C. and A.B. Simmons (1971) 'Industrialization, family and fertility: a structural psychological analysis of the Brazilian case', *Demography, 8,* 1

Ryder, J.M. (1976) 'The interrelations between family structure and fertility in Yucatan' in Bernice A. Kaplan (ed.), *Anthropological studies of human fertility,* Detroit, Wayne State University Press

Safilios-Rothschild, C. (1970) 'The study of family power structure: a review 1960-1969', *Journal of Marriage and the Family, 32,* 4

—— (1972a) 'The relationship between work commitment and fertility', *International Journal of Sociology and the Family* (Lucknow, India)

—— (1972b) 'Methodological problems involved in the cross-cultural examination of indicators related to the status of women', paper presented at the Population Association of America annual meetings, Toronto

Salaff, J. (1976) 'Working daughters in the Hong Kong Chinese family: female piety or a transformation in the family power structure?', *Journal of Social History, 9,* 4

Sanday, P. (1973) 'Toward a theory of the status of women', *American Anthropologist, 75*, 5

Stycos, J. (1965) 'Female employment and fertility in Lima, Peru', *The Milbank Memorial Fund Quarterly, 43*, 1

—— and R.H. Weller (1967) 'Female working roles and fertility', *Demography, 4*, 1

Suzman, R., K.A. Miller and M. Charrad (1976) 'Employment effects on fertility control in Tunisia' in *Recent Empirical Findings on Fertility: Korea, Nigeria, Tunisia, Venezuela, Philippines*, Smithsonian Institution Interdisciplinary Communications Program, monograph series no. 7, Washington, DC, Smithsonian Institution

United Nations Research Institute for Social Development (1978) *The impact on women of socio-economic changes*, UNRISD/78/c.16/Rev. 1

Weller, R.H. (1968) 'The employment of wives, role incompatibility and fertility: a study of lower and middle class residents of San Juan, Puerto Rico', *Milbank Memorial Fund Quarterly, 46*, 4

Whyte, M.K. (1978) *The status of women in pre-industrial societies*, Princeton, Princeton University Press

Young, K. (1977) 'Modes of appropriation and the sexual division of labour: a case study from Oaxaca, Mexico', paper presented at the Latin American Studies Association Meeting, Houston, Texas

Zarate, A.O. (1967) 'Fertility in urban areas of Mexico: implications for the theory of·demographic transition', *Demography, 4*, 1

# 9 WOMEN'S WORK AND THEIR STATUS: RURAL INDIAN EVIDENCE OF LABOUR MARKET AND ENVIRONMENT EFFECTS ON SEX DIFFERENCES IN CHILDHOOD MORTALITY

T. Paul Schultz

## Introduction: A General Hypothesis

One direct indicator of the relative status of women and men can be found in a comparison of their survival prospects. Since adult occupational roles influence mortality risks, childhood sex-specific survival differences are perhaps a better indicator of male and female status within the family. Biological differences between the sexes may explain the level and age structure of childhood mortality differences by sex, but variation across regions and across households in a society should reflect more clearly the intra-family allocation of investments towards child survival. The hypothesis examined here is that in those regions and households where women are likely to play an economically more active role, the family has a stronger incentive to invest in girls to assure their survival.

It is generally observed that survival is greater for women than it is for men, or at least this tendency is noted in populations of European descent and in many other parts of the contemporary world. Also, female life expectancy at birth, a summary measure of survival prospects or mortality risks, has risen more rapidly for women than for men in this century in most industrially advanced countries.

A notable exception to this pattern is India, where male life expectancy at birth currently exceeds female life expectancy, and where survival rates have recently increased more for males than for females. Can this regional reversal in sex mortality differentials and change be linked to the lower, and possibly deteriorating, status of women in India? Does the proportion of women reported as economically active in India help account for variation in sex differentials in childhood mortality? What conditions in the productive environment of the family are associated with variation in women's economic activity rates and their survival prospects? Do these empirical associations alter our perspective on desired economic and demographic development policies in a country such as India?

It is widely believed that the productivity and participation of women in the labour force are primary determinants of women's status. One school of economic thought argues further that the economic value of women's time has a role in guiding the more general allocation of household resources, including decisions regarding fertility and investments in the nurture of children. If women's status significantly affects the reproduction and improvement of populations over time, it may be worthwhile to seek a better understanding of how social, economic and demographic developments impinge on women's productivity and status. Do social interventions aimed at strengthening the position of women have systematic consequences over time on demographic and economic behaviour and outcomes within their households? Can these consequences be predicted from analysis of cross-sectional patterns among status, productivity, behaviour and welfare outcomes? What linkages between social policy, the productive roles of women in society, and women's status relative to men are suggested by these cross-sectional studies?

Social status is, of course, a complicated and many-sided concept. It is not surprising that sociologists, psychologists and economists often describe different aspects of the phenomenon, and expend relatively little time grappling with quantitative measurement of status, replication of studies in different cultures, or testing of hypotheses that discriminate among competing theories. Clearly, the conventional economic measures of market productivity and labour force participation are limited aspects of the economic contribution of women to their families, to the economy and to society; nor are these patterns of market productivity and participation adequate for appraising the contribution of children or men to both current and future production. To obtain a more comprehensive, intertemporal economic and social accounting of the contribution of persons to the welfare of their family, a means of combining these market-oriented production activities with the host of non-market home activities must be found. Also, the investment attributes of many activities in market and non-market contexts, such as on-the-job training and nutrition, should in principle be estimated and separated from pure consumption.

Measures of a broader concept of economic and social productivity for women and men are not generally available. A few surveys have begun to develop instruments designed for low-income societies that seek to elicit information on the productivity of each member of the family, at least in certain activities, and how all members of the family allocate their time among market and non-market activities.[1] These expanded time-budget surveys first served as a descriptive accounting framework, as in the classic anthropological study, *Penny Capitalism* (Tax, 1953). Analyses of these massive collections of household inform-ation should now begin to sharpen their focus and provide new bases for considering the questions posed above. But to proceed at this time with an investigation of the linkages between labour market activities of women and their status, it is necessary to work with existing data across a diversity of cultural settings. India provides comparably collected data on broadly defined economic-activity levels of men and women from states, districts and households. But obtaining sex-specific measures of status and welfare present special problems that are discussed later.

## Labour Force Behaviour

When people first enter the labour force, the market wage rate exerts only a substitution effect on their behaviour, inducing them to work longer hours when they work. But further increases in the market wage also generate an income effect that tends to induce people to work less time in the market and to demand more time in non-market activities. This negative income effect is proportional to the number of hours worked and may therefore eventually entirely offset the positive substitution effect on labour supply behaviour; in this case, individuals confronted by a higher wage will tend to work fewer hours. Economic theory of demand, therefore, offers no clear predictions as to how an increase in market wage opportunities will affect labour force partic-ipation rates or hours worked in the market. If other sources of income are held constant, women often exhibit the tendency to work more of their time in the market as their market wage increases. Men, on the other hand, display the reverse tendency; as their market wage rate increases they reduce their market labour supply.

The market productivity of husbands and family nonearned income sources, such as land and other forms of material wealth, also influence the labour market behaviour of wives. The spouse-wage (cross-substitution) effect of a change in the husband's wage rate on the wife's labour supply, holding income constant, is negative if the time of husbands and wives are substitutes in non-market activity – that is, the more the wife works at home the less productive is her husband's home time. Alternatively, if the income-compensated spouse-wage effect is positive, the husband's and wife's time are complements in non-market activity. These cross-wage effects should be comparable for husbands and wives, if a fully joint optimization for the family replaces individually different valuations of inputs (i.e., each person's leisure) and outputs. Some empirical evidence would suggest that individuals matter in this respect, and that the convenient abstraction of an integrated family decision-maker must be used with caution. With regard to the wife's labour supply, empirical studies generally find that the income-compensated husband's wage effect is negative, implying that the non-market time of husband and wife are substitutes, at least over most of the life cycle.

The point of this examination of the general factors affecting women's labour market behaviour is to illustrate that rising incomes and economic development can be associated with increasing or decreasing levels of women's labour force participation. A high-income country in which women participate infrequently in the labour force may provide women with high consumption standards, but not high economic status relative to men. Since the level of fertility has fallen in high-income countries and the market has subsumed an increasing share of total production, female labour force activity is likely to increase if women's status is to be maintained. Child-care and non-market home services provided by housewives may still be highly valued.

The reverse case is somewhat more difficult to defend for two reasons. In low-income countries the proportion of women engaged in labour force activities is measured with greater error; subjective custom may influence substantially the implementation of a common concept of labour force as defined by a census bureau (Durand, 1975). How much of the observed variation in female labour force participation rates across countries is real, particularly for the agricultural and rural sectors, remains unclear. The validity of any exercise that compares female labour force participation rates across countries is, therefore, doubtful, whereas more insight may be obtained from analysis of variation within countries over time or across subnational regions. The research methodology followed here is to examine the empirical evidence for a single country — India — but to seek parallel information at both the aggregate district level and the individual household level. In this single country a relatively broad definition of economically active worker is employed that includes persons generally working at least one hour per day in the market labour force or in family-based agricultural activities or household industry.[2] The hypothesis is elaborated and then tested against these data to determine if increased economic activity of women enhances their economic status in the family and community. It is also anticipated that where women are economically more active, they will have command over more resources for their own consumption and for investment in their own health, nutrition, nurture, schooling, training and migration. Survival in childhood is employed as a proxy for this difficult-to-observe intra-family allocation of resources between men and women.

## Childhood Mortality

There are few data on the intra-family allocation of resources that can confirm whether women's greater participation in the labour market actually is associated with women receiving a larger share of household resources earmarked for either consumption or investment. For this reason, I have decided to examine the ratio of male-to-female child mortality.

The first working hypothesis is that *given the biological predisposition of boys and girls to survive in a particular environment, the allocation of more consumption and investment resources to girls relative to boys should contribute to a decrease in the male-to-female child survival ratio*. Parents derive from their children benefits associated with the productive capacity of their children to effect transfers (positive or negative) to the parents. Parents also derive direct consumption benefits or satisfaction from their children. The productive returns of boys relative to girls are directly influenced by the relative participation in economic activity of adult men and women, and are likely to be reflected in the difficult-to-measure dowry and brideprice associated with marrying off daughters.[3] The consumption benefits of children are assumed to be approximately equal for boys and girls, though a preference for sex balance in offspring is probably widespread (Ben-Porath and Welch, 1972).

The second working hypothesis is that *as income or wealth of parents increases, the importance of the consumption component of children increases relative to the production-transfer component*. For this reason, increasing incomes will tend to reduce the imbalance in the resources that parents allocate to boys versus girls, holding constant the labour force participation of mature men and women in the society.

To treat sex differentials in mortality as an indicator of relative economic status, it is desirable (i) that the particular aspect of mortality be relatively *unresponsive* directly to the production and reproduction roles assigned to males and females in the household, and (ii) that the mortality be relatively *responsive* to the allocation of household resources to the consumption of and investment in specific persons.

In an environment where large families are an asset, women are encouraged to bear more children, elevating female mortality risks relative to males, at least during the child-bearing years. The type of labours undertaken by males and females is also likely to affect sex-specific survival prospects. On the whole, the shift from agricultural pursuits to urban economic activities is associated with decreases in adult female mortality relative to male mortality. These rural-urban sex differentials in mortality can be traced to rural-urban sex differences in the cause structure of death, e.g., urban increase in cardiovascular disease and cancer which predominantly strike men (Preston and Weed, 1976), but this does not indicate what aspects of the two environments and of the behavioural patterns that the environments encourage actually produce the differences in mortality – or even why sex differentials within specific disease groups exist in the first place. In order that male and female labour market and reproductive roles do not *directly* influence sex differentials in mortality, which I would prefer to interpret as a measure of the relative welfare of women, I shall restrict my analysis to mortality among children less than ten years of age.

A second problem in measurement of sex differentials in mortality as an indicator of women's welfare is that mortality in the first month of life (neonatal) may respond differently to environmental conditions than post-neonatal mortality; by its nature, neonatal mortality cannot directly respond to the economic preferences of parents for boys or girls to the same degree as mortality risks at later ages. Mortality of the infant in the immediate aftermath of birth tends to be related to sequelae of the birth trauma, including the resolution of congenital defects, which may be affected by prenatal care and attendance at delivery. The conditions for neonatal mortality are not likely to reflect clearly the intra-family allocation of resources between boys and girls. As a consequence, patterns of sex differentials in child mortality in poor countries in the first month of infancy (neonatal) are distinctly different from patterns that emerge in the second month to the tenth year of life.[4] For example, in some poor populations in which women's status is relatively low, such as Egypt, the ratio of male-to-female mortality is highest in the first weeks of life and declines in the months that follow, rising in some again after the age of ten (Hammoud,

Table 9.1: Child Mortality by Age of Death and Sex by States, Rural, 1969

| Age/Sex | Deaths per thousand individuals | | | | | | |
|---|---|---|---|---|---|---|---|
| | Kerala | Assam | Jammu & Kashmir | Punjab | Rajasthan | Uttar Pradesh | All pooled |
| **Less than 7 days** | | | | | | | |
| Male | 23.9 | 46.6 | 37.1 | 27.2 | 49.6 | 51.3 | 44.1 |
| Female | 17.0 | 28.8 | 32.1 | 38.6 | 41.0 | 44.7 | 41.0 |
| **7-28 days** | | | | | | | |
| Male | 17.0 | 37.3 | 29.9 | 16.8 | 27.3 | 37.1 | 29.4 |
| Female | 8.3 | 28.5 | 33.4 | 16.4 | 29.1 | 59.6 | 34.9 |
| **1-6 months** | | | | | | | |
| Male | 15.3 | 54.1 | 26.9 | 27.8 | 62.6 | 39.2 | 38.1 |
| Female | 15.5 | 38.9 | 23.5 | 25.8 | 61.4 | 64.8 | 47.7 |
| **7-12 months** | | | | | | | |
| Male | 8.6 | 16.2 | 12.4 | 9.1 | 28.1 | 26.3 | 20.4 |
| Female | 7.7 | 8.2 | 9.9 | 35.1 | 38.7 | 36.8 | 24.5 |
| **1st Year** | | | | | | | |
| Both sexes | 56.8 | 129.5 | 102.9 | 97.6 | 168.8 | 178.7 | 139.9 |
| **Age 0-4** | | | | | | | |
| Male | 23.9 | 49.2 | 37.8 | 24.3 | 84.8 | 74.8 | 58.3 |
| Female | 22.3 | 39.8 | 34.5 | 37.2 | 100.5 | 111.3 | 70.2 |
| **Age 5-9** | | | | | | | |
| Male | 2.17 | 4.97 | 1.63 | 2.66 | 8.28 | 7.30 | 5.79 |
| Female | 3.56 | 6.17 | 3.62 | 3.15 | 9.88 | 11.57 | 7.71 |

Source: India, Office of the Registrar General, *Measures of fertility and mortality in India*, SRS analytical series, no. 2 (New Delhi, 1972).

Table 9.2: Child Mortality by Age of Death and Sex by States, Urban, 1969

| Age/Sex | Deaths per thousand individuals | | | | | |
| --- | --- | --- | --- | --- | --- | --- |
| | Assam | Jammu & Kashmir | Punjab | Rajasthan | Uttar Pradesh | All pooled |
| Less than 7 days | | | | | | |
| Male | 39.8 | 29.6 | 27.9 | 30.3 | 42.8 | not reported |
| Female | 19.1 | 12.4 | 14.8 | 24.3 | 30.3 | |
| 7-28 days | | | | | | |
| Male | 20.7 | 6.5 | 8.2 | 17.1 | 29.3 | not reported |
| Female | 9.3 | 16.1 | 18.1 | 13.0 | 26.0 | |
| 1-6 months | | | | | | |
| Male | 36.6 | 37.5 | 18.4 | 32.0 | 30.4 | not reported |
| Female | 47.1 | 8.7 | 36.0 | 33.0 | 30.2 | |
| 7-12 months | | | | | | |
| Male | 13.6 | 5.4 | 15.8 | 17.2 | 16.7 | not reported |
| Female | 16.9 | 3.3 | 17.8 | 13.9 | 13.5 | |
| 1st Year | | | | | | |
| Male | 110.7 | 79.1 | 70.3 | 97.0 | 110.2 | not reported |
| Female | 92.4 | 40.5 | 86.7 | 84.2 | 99.7 | |
| Age 0-4 | | | | | | |
| Male | 40.5 | 21.2 | 19.5 | 51.2 | 47.2 | 43.2 |
| Female | 32.6 | 13.0 | 32.0 | 51.9 | 52.7 | 47.1 |
| Age 5-9 | | | | | | |
| Male | 4.36 | 2.42 | 1.68 | 3.66 | 4.17 | 3.67 |
| Female | 2.21 | 0.62 | 2.20 | 6.66 | 6.56 | 5.45 |

Source: India, Office of the Registrar General, *Measures of Fertility and Mortality in India*, SRS analytical series, no. 2 (New Delhi, 1972).

1977). This would suggest that the environment rather than the biological make-up of the species is more favourably disposed towards the male child, but this environmental disposition of resources in the family is less effective in modifying the sex pattern of neonatal mortality than that at later ages. The sex differentials in childhood mortality by cause also suggest the importance of a bias towards the male offspring in the provision of family inputs. Mortality of children from enteritis and other diarrhoeal diseases is more severe for females than males, whereas the reverse is often true for tuberculosis. Nutritional neglect can selectively increase the risk of enteritis, but within the common dwelling place, selective attention appears unlikely to influence the contraction of tuberculosis (Hammoud, 1977).

The optimal period for measuring sex differentials in mortality as a social indicator of women's status in the family should be obtained, therefore, from the mortality experienced from the second month to the tenth year of life. But for many of the countries where this indicator of women's status might exhibit the greatest variation and be most responsive to labour market and wealth conditions, the underlying vital registration systems are most incomplete and unreliable. For example, Tables 9.1 and 9.2 report child mortality rates for 1969 in India by age and sex only from the sample registration system for rural areas of six states and urban areas of five states that are thought to provide the most reliable Indian information.

The small size of the sample and the infrequency of events generate much sample variability in these rates, but some tendencies may be noted, especially in the pooled results (which are heavily weighted by results from Uttar Pradesh). In the first weeks of life, infant mortality for males exceeds that for females except in the extreme case of rural Punjab. The balance appears to shift against females in the first month of life, or at least before a child reaches his or her first birthday. In the urban areas, girls fare slightly better, but the mortality is overall still heavier for girls than boys aged 0 to 4. The urban cross-over point when female mortality exceeds male is probably towards the end of the first year. In order to extract reliable information on sex differentials in child mortality other data sources are needed that can also be disaggregated down to the district and household level.

## Derivation of a Measure of Sex-specific Child Mortality

The age distribution of a stable population is given by the following equation:

$$c_i(a) = b_i e^{-r_i a} p_i(a)$$

where $c(a)$ is the proportion age $a$, $b$ is the birth rate, $r$ is the annual rate of increase, $p(a)$ is the proportion surviving from birth to age $a$, and the subscript $i$ can represent either male, $m$, or female, $f$.

First a sex ratio of the number of males to females of a specific age is constructed:

$$\frac{\bar{C}_m(a)}{\bar{C}_f(a)} = \frac{b_m e^{-r_m a} p_m(a) \bar{P}_m}{b_f e^{-r_f a} p_f(a) \bar{P}_f}$$

where $\bar{P}_i$ is the total number of males or females in the population and $\bar{C}_i(a) = c_i(a)\,\bar{P}_i$.

Rearranging terms, several components in this sex ratio are evident.

$$\left( \frac{b_m \bar{P}_m}{b_f \bar{P}_f} \right) \left( e^{(r_f - r_m)a} \right) \left( \frac{p_m(a)}{p_f(a)} \right)$$

*The first term is the sex ratio at birth; the second term is the differential population growth of females to males over 'a' years; and the third term is the sex ratio of survival rates.* Constructing a ratio of the sex composition of two adjoining age groups yields the following equation:

$$
\begin{aligned}
R(a+t, a) &= \frac{\bar{C}_m(a+t)/\bar{C}_f(a+t)}{\bar{C}_m(a)/\bar{C}_f(a)} \\[2mm]
&= e^{(r_f - r_m)t} \times \frac{p_m(a+t)/p_f(a+t)}{p_m(a)/p_f(a)} \\[2mm]
&= e^{(r_f - r_m)t} e^{\int_a^{a+t} [\mu_f(x) - \mu_m(x)]\, dx}
\end{aligned}
$$

or taking natural logarithms,

$$\ln R(a+t, a) = (r_f - r_m)t + \int_a^{a+t} [\mu_f(x) - \mu_m(x)]\, dx,$$

where $\mu_i(x)$ is the sex-specific death rate at age $x$.* The log of the ratio of the sex ratios of adjacent age groups in a (sex-specific) stable population is a function of possibly distinct sex-specific rates of growth of the population and the difference between the survival rates of females and males in the relevant age interval. The former effect is likely to be negligible in most populations even when survival rates generally favour males, as in India, and the latter sex-specific differential mortality is the primary factor I wish to measure. The natural logarithm of a number close to one is approximately equal to the difference between that number and one. Thus, a regression of the log or linear form on determinants of sex mortality differentials should yield similar results, except for a shift of one in the constant term.

This ratio of adjacent sex ratios in the child population cannot be measured satisfactorily at the individual family level. This is obvious since the family must have at least one girl age $a + t$ and at least one boy and girl age $a$ in order to obtain a definite value for the proxy. Therefore, at the individual level, one might shift to the consideration of the difference of the sex ratios of adjacent age groups:

$$D(a + t, a) = \frac{b_m \bar{P}_m e^{(r_f - r_m)(a + t)} p_m(a + t)}{b_f \bar{P}_f p_f(a + t)}$$

$$- \frac{b_m \bar{P}_m e^{(r_f - r_m)a}}{b_f \bar{P}_f p_f(a)}$$

$$= \frac{b_m \bar{P}_m}{b_f \bar{P}_f} \left( e^{(r_f - r_m)a} \right) \left[ e^{(r_f - r_m)t} \frac{p_m(a + t)}{p_f(a + t)} \right.$$

$$\left. - \frac{p_m(a)}{p_f(a)} \right]$$

where again the first term is the sex ratio at birth, the second term is a sex-specific differential stable growth rate to age $a$, and the difference in sex ratios of survival rates between age $a$ and $a + t$, adjusted for differential stable growth rates, is in brackets. Though less neatly decomposed than the ratio formulation, the difference in the sex ratio for adjacent age groups in the population has analogous components and is likely to behave similarly in a cross-section. For individual

---

* from the definition, $p_i(a) = e^{-\int_0^a \mu_i(x)dx}$ (Coale, 1972).

household data, the information actually examined here is the difference, D, between the ratio of the male child survival rate and the female child survival rate.

$$D = \frac{p_m b_m - p_f b_f}{b_m \qquad b_f}$$

Since this still requires the sample to be restricted to couples with at least one male and one female child, there is a selective-based sampling problem, but probably not a severe one for rural India, since sex of offspring is a random variable.

In analyses dealing with small regional populations, the stable population model is rarely appropriate because of internal migration. Where attention is focused only on the sex composition of children less than age ten, there is less reason to expect migration would be sufficiently sex- and age-selective to distort interregional comparisons. There is also the possibility that under-enumeration of children differs from region to region and perhaps embodies a non-uniform error for boys and girls. Again, the construction of the ratio or difference form of the measure of child mortality is such that sex-specific errors that persisted from one age group to the next would be offset, and any systematic omission of very young or older children would not be a problem unless it were more common for one sex.

Finally, the typical problem in using the stable population model for study of demographic processes is that the assumption of past constancy of the fertility and mortality schedule is not valid. In this case, a change over time in fertility presents no problem unless it implies a change in the sex ratio at birth or sex ratio of child mortality. The former appears unlikely, and the latter would involve the behaviour process I seek to characterize. Likewise, an independent change over time in the sex-specific incidence of mortality, such as might occur due to a change in disease patterns, would be a real change that would be captured by this measure and might indeed be specific to some regions but not others for reasons of climate, ecology, or socio-economic characteristics of the population. Estimates of these linkages are sought here.

## Sources of Mortality Change

Several sources of change in mortality are outlined below: public health services, incomes, prices, returns on human capital and individual efficiency in producing good health. Depending on interactions among public health system, the market system and the household sector, it may be more or less difficult to infer how the individual or society is affected by mortality differentials across social and economic groups at one point in time, or by changes in mortality over time within appropriately defined groups.

Public health activities may *reduce the exposure* of all individuals to disease, without substantially changing personal economic resources, relative prices or individual behaviour. Personal welfare and behaviour changes as individuals experience less disease, which is assumed to occur independently of personal characteristics or behaviour. In this instance, the reduction in mortality is *exogenous to individual behaviour*; the improvement in health resulting from public health activity can be studied without extensive analysis of the demand for health at the individual or household level. Smallpox or malaria eradication may be an example.

More common are public health activities that *subsidize the cost* of preventative and curative medical services, information and supplies. They thereby encourage people to utilize these inputs with the anticipated result of reducing mortality. These interventions are often treated as though they were exogenous to the community and individual served, but generally they are not. The geographic distribution of public health activities is conditioned by political, social and economic factors, and may even reflect the communities' preferences for and priorities among health and social services. At the individual level, the subsidized services are sought differentially by individuals who command different amounts of economic resources, enjoy different endowments of ability and have acquired different educational advantages. Health clinics, family planning activities, home hygiene and health education extension activities all fall in this category of the interactive process involving both non-market subsidies and the characteristics of the demanders of health care. Evidence that the level of services provided by such public health activities is associated with change in mortality or other individual or community outcomes is a weak basis for inferring that the particular public-health activity has *caused* these changes.

The responses of individuals and families to changes in incomes, prices, returns to survival and productive efficiency together influence the expected incidence and pattern of mortality.

Increases in *income* or command over economic resources systematically influence the level and pattern of allocation of money expenditures, but more generally income affects the underlying allocation of one's time among leisure, non-market work and market work activities. These income-conditioned demand functions have direct and indirect repercussions for health and mortality. Direct outlays on health services increase with income – perhaps, in some instances, more than proportionately. Indirectly, expenditures on food, clothing, shelter and sanitation can reduce mortality (Wrigley, 1969), whereas other forms of consumption – of tobacco and alcohol, for instance – can increase mortality.

No new techniques are required for the study of private demand patterns and health outcomes. These relationships may be estimated from cross-sectional household survey data on mortality, health, time allocation, income and expenditure patterns. The infrequency of death suggests the need for large samples, however, and experimentation may be needed to improve instruments for eliciting reliable retrospective information on the incidence of mortality among household members' own children, or relatives.

*Relative market prices* may also account for differences in private behaviour that influence mortality. The measurement of these price differences across households at one point in time and within households over time may call for innovative research methods. It has been common to stress the opportunity value of time required to make use of medical services in high-income countries (Acton, 1973). These time costs are undoubtedly important in a poor country as well, where trained health workers are scarce and transportation systems are often primitive. Changes in the value of service can also be viewed as a change in its relative price. For example, a five-mile trek with a feverish child to a village clinic might not have repaid a mother's effort in many poor countries before the advent of antibiotics. Similarly, medical advice on methods of birth control might not have been of substantial value before the 1960s, when the IUD and pill first became widely available.

Changes in the expected *returns on investment in survival* may also affect how people allocate their time, expenditures, savings and investments. With an increase in the value of time (reflected in rising wage rates), there is also an increase in the return on investments in reducing morbidity and enhancing health. As life expectancy increases, so do the returns on all forms of human capital investments: basic nutrition, schooling, health care, vocational training and migration. Employers who share the costs of and returns on investment in specific training might also be expected to increase their commitments to vocational training for their workers as the prospects that an individual will die by a given age or will be unable to work decrease. Similarly, as the need to spread risks due to frequent mortality becomes less important, investments can become more concentrated in the smaller nuclear family, rather than dispersed in the extended family.

If the nature of the development process and associated technical change alters the mix of employment opportunities for men and women, this is reflected in wage rates received by men and women in the open labour market. Where women's wages are relatively high compared with men's, the returns on investment in survival should be more favourable for girls relative to boys, and the intra-family allocation of resources should reflect this difference in returns to survival by sex. The employment conditions in the labour market may thereby affect the consumption and investment resources provided to boys and girls within the family. These intra-household allocations of resources among children may in turn affect the health, future productivity and survival prospects of men and women.

Finally, *people's skills* may influence their capacity to deal with exposure to the risks of mortality, given subsidized public health services, personal income, market prices and the returns to survival. For lack of a better term, economists refer to these skills as enhancing the *efficiency of the individual in producing 'good health'* (Grossman, 1972). The most common hypothesis in this regard is that certain basic levels of schooling permit people to produce for themselves better health without increasing their expenditure of time and market goods, and thereby to reduce their risks of mortality. As in other areas of behaviour where education is thought to enhance the market and non-market productive capacity of the individual, these gains in labour productivity can be divided into a static increase in output per hour of work and a dynamic gain in allocative efficiency in dealing with an environment in which inputs and prices are subject to change (Welch, 1970; Schultz, 1975). Mothers — and perhaps fathers — may be assumed to use their educational efficiency in the production of health to increase not only their own prospects for survival but also the prospects for survival of their offspring.

The determinants of mortality change in this century and the causes of the substantial social and economic differentials observed across low-income countries are not well understood. Mortality is still relatively high among infants and preschool-aged groups in low-income countries (relative to that achieved in high-income countries). It is among this age group that increasing analysis of socio-economic differentials in mortality may shed light on which environmental constraints are responsible for the higher level of mortality in the Third World.

The orthodox interpretation of declining mortality rates in the low-income world is set forth by Stolnitz (1955, 1956, 1965, 1975) in a series of articles beginning almost 25 years ago. He argues that the evidence of widespread declines in mortality in countries at very different levels of development and experiencing different rates of growth suggests that the socio-economic setting is of minor significance in explaining what has occurred, and that credit should be given to international and national applications of new public health technology. In other words, the mortality transition is due largely to changes in public health techniques that have not relied upon changes in economic conditions and individual behaviour. He restated his viewpoint ten years after the first article appeared: 'Mortality trends are remarkably neutral with respect to economic events — economic misery as such is no longer an effective barrier to the vast upsurge in survival opportunities in the underdeveloped areas' (1965). Though this remains the common view, growing doubts are emerging that we can as yet attribute the decline in death rates to *any* particular cause.

In comparing the nonlinear relationship between life expectancy and *per capita* income in 1930 and 1960, Preston (1976a) could explain less than a quarter of the difference between the two years by the increase in income occurring in the 30 years between them. Another effort to perform this exercise with more recent and perhaps better cross-sectional data suggests more of the change could be explained by gains in income, literacy and nutrition (Preston, 1976b). Regardless, it would be unwise to attribute all the events that income cannot explain to 'technical change in public health'. Simply adding education to income as an explanatory variable, for instance, substantially reduces the shift in life expectancy that remains unaccounted for across countries (Chao, 1979). Thus, Stolnitz's view needs at least a re-evaluation.

All possible sources of mortality change need to be studied together in order to determine with any confidence how any specific factor has influenced the level of mortality. In many populations for which direct vital registration systems are incomplete, it appears more difficult to measure accurately the *level* of mortality than to obtain indirectly an indicator of the *sex differential* in mortality. Many of the sources of mortality change should be relatively neutral to sex differentials, and, thus, public health exogenous interventions, medical service subsidies, changes in market prices and gains in educational efficiency of parents may not notably affect sex differentials in survival (or mortality). But if sex differentials in survival are related in the hypothesized manner to (i) indicators of household wealth and its productive environment, and to (ii) labour market opportunities for male and female workers, this empirical evidence will reinforce the belief that economic returns to investment in survival and household wealth influence the intra-family allocation of resources, and thereby child mortality. It also suggests a linkage between the productive roles of men and women in a society and the investments that parents decide to make in offspring, by sex. Evidence of economic factors constraining the household's allocation of resources to activities that promote child survival would also confirm the need for further studies of mortality determinants conducted in an economic framework.

## A Statistical Model and Its Empirical Implementation

The factors affecting labour force behaviour and mortality have to some degree a common origin; both outcomes are conditioned by shared aspects of the economic environment in which people live. Furthermore, the decisions made by the family that determine who produces what, how much of each commodity thus produced is marketed, and how much is consumed by each member may link the survival prospects of each person to the economically productive tasks each engages in. Labour market decisions can be interpreted in terms of traditional demand equations, embodying income and substitutional effects. The demand for child survival is treated as a good valued partly for the child's future productive contribution to the family, and partly in terms of immediate satisfactions and consumption goals. It is hypothesized that in poor societies, increasing wealth levels reduce disparities between the resources allocated to girls and boys, even if productive roles of men and women are held constant. If women's participation increases relative to men's, the resources available to girls relative to boys will be further increased, and, accordingly, the survival prospects of girls relative to boys will be improved.

It is beyond the scope of this chapter to determine the conditions under which parents are willing to make greater sacrifices to increase the survival prospects of their offspring. Only the sex ratio of these demands is analyzed. It is assumed that the productive contributions of family members are treated as a durable asset with a lifetime of service. The current value of children in a poor society reflects, therefore, the promise of adult productivity. The final valuation of children depends on many issues, including the exchange arrangements surrounding marriage and the extent to which the husband's or the wife's parents exercise claims for support from the younger generation.

In order to estimate how labour force behaviour of men and women affect the welfare and survival prospects of boys and girls, it is first necessary to account for the variation in labour force behaviour. It may then be feasible to determine if the environmental and wealth factors exert an additional effect on sex pattern in child mortality, holding constant the predicted labour market patterns of participation by men and women.

*The Statistical Framework*

More formally, three relations are to be considered:

$$(1) \quad L_f = \alpha_o + \sum_{i=1}^{z} \alpha_i X_i + e_1$$

$$(2) \quad L_m = \beta_o + \sum_{i=1}^{z} \beta_i X_i + e_2$$

$$(3) \quad R_{mf} = \delta_o + \sum_{j=1}^{p} \delta_j X_j + \delta_r L_f + \delta_s L_m + e_3$$

where $L_f$ and $L_m$ are female and male adult labour force activity rates, $R_{mf}$ is the ratio (or difference) of male to female child survival rates, the $X$'s are conditioning variables which are assumed uncorrelated with the disturbances, i.e.,

$$E(e_i X_j) = 0 \quad i = 1,2,3; \quad j = 1, \ldots, z$$

and the disturbances are not independent (across equations), because unobserved factors that would influence one class of outcome would affect the other forms of household allocative behaviour,

$E(e_i e_j) \neq 0 \quad i,j = 1,2,3.$

In order to estimate equation (3) of the sex differential in child mortality as conditioned by the labour market behaviour of men and women in a society, some exogenous variables must influence the labour market behaviour of men and women but not *directly* influence sex differentials in child mortality. In other words, there must be at least two variables, $X_q$ to $X_z$, that enter equations (1) and (2) but do not directly enter equation (3). These crucial identifying restrictions on the model permit one to obtain consistent estimates of the $\delta$'s, and with a sufficiently large sample (asymptotically), these $\delta$'s will also be unbiased.

*Data*

The district-level sample of India used here is drawn mainly from rural district tabulations of the 1961 census (India, 1964, 1965, 1970). The working sample includes all 230 districts of the states of Andhra Pradesh, Assam, Bihar, Gujurat, Kerala, Madhya Pradesh, Madras, Maharashtra, Mysore, Orissa, Punjab and portions of Uttar Pradesh. Labour market behaviour of men, women and children in this sample has been analyzed by Rosenzweig and Evenson (1977).

The household-level sample used here is based on a panel survey of 4,200 rural households visited in 1969, 1970 and 1971 by the National Council of Applied Economic Research (NCAER, 1975). About one-quarter of the households were not used, because the village of residence fell in a district that did not report agricultural wage data. Only husband-wife intact primary families were considered, in which the wife was between the ages of 30 and 54. The household sample is divided into two subgroups for estimating the model, because of different labour market constraints confronting landless labourers and landowning cultivators (Rosenzweig, (1977). The major restriction on the sample is that the measure of sex difference in child mortality must be numerically defined. For this to be the case, the wife of the household head must have borne at least one boy and one girl. The primary effect of this restriction is to bias the sample towards older parents and those who had higher fertility and probably began child-bearing at an earlier age.[5] The final working sample includes 955 landed and 379 landless couples.[6] There are several reasons to anticipate differences in the estimates from the cross-section of aggregate district data and from the cross-section of household data, including the passage of a decade from 1961 to 1971. None the less, both samples provide roughly comparable variables spanning the cultural diversity of the Indian continent. Parallel tests of the basic hypotheses proposed in this chapter are reported with the Indian data at both levels of aggregation.

## *Empirical Specification*

The variables available to identify statistically equation (3) differ slightly at the district and at the household levels. Information on non-farm employment opportunities is used at both levels of aggregation — the number of factories in the district or village per household, the scale of those factories (i.e., percentage with more than ten employees), and (at the district level only) the modernity of the factory is represented by whether or not it uses fuel. These nonagricultural labour market conditions are thought to augment the demand for off-farm labour and, on balance, to enhance the employment prospects for women relative to men. These identifying labour market variables are assumed to directly affect the rate at which females and males participate in the labour force, and their effect, if any, on sex-specific child mortality patterns occurs only indirectly through their impact on labour force participation.

The proportion of Muslim women in the district is another factor affecting women's status,[7] primarily by restricting women's access to employment opportunities. Some aspects of Islamic culture may also directly influence the home environment of boys and girls differentially, exerting an independent impact on survival prospects even when labour market participation of men and women is held constant. The Muslim variable is thus retained in both the aggregate labour market and aggregate child mortality equations, although only its restrictive effect on female participation is widely documented.

From the household's viewpoint, certain variables that are endogenous at the aggregate level can be treated as exogenous to individual behaviour. Information from each district on daily wages for agricultural field labour (i.e., sowing, reaping, weeding and ploughing) for adult men and for adult women is reported monthly. These sex-specific agricultural wage rates are treated here as given for the household, while they are obviously endogenously determined at the district level by the aggregate supply of and demand for labour. The wage effects on household labour supply will embody both income and substitution effects, and thus have no prescribed sign. The age of the mother is included at the household level in the child mortality equation, but it could also have been rationalized in the labour supply equations;

neither proved statistically significant.

At the district level, variables are included for the average farm size and the proportion of landless households, whereas the comparable size-of-farm variable is included only in the regressions for the landed sub-sample. The extent of rainfall and irrigation indicate not only the wealth of the community and the value of a farm of given size, but may also dictate which crops are profitably grown, and where the opportunities are greatest for women to perform specialized functions, such as the planting of rice (Bardhan, 1974). The proportion of the district living in rural areas is intended to capture the widely noted rural/urban sex differential in mortality. It is not evident in the literature whether this sex mortality differential is accounted for by differences in the productive roles of rural and urban women. The comparable variables for the household sample are the 'village population size' and the 'distance from the village to the nearest town'. The household sample also provides information on nonearned or wealth income, which should reduce the incentive for women to work but should also exert a favourable wealth effect on the child mortality ratio. Whether the village is electrified is included, for access to electricity may facilitate irrigation and adopting other modern inputs. Finally, a set of four variables characterize two levels of educational achievement for men and for women, although they are measured in somewhat different ways at the household and district levels. It is not obvious whether a correlation between sex-specific education and sex differences in child mortality would indicate a causal effect or simply parallel investment decisions by parents from one generation to the next.

## Empirical Findings

### District Sample

Table 9.3 reports the characteristics of the district sample. The male-female child survival ratio is about 1.04 for India, whereas it tends to be about 0.95 for most industrially advanced countries. Women's labour market participation rate in the average district is 58 per cent, with a substantial standard deviation of 25 per cent. In contrast, men's participation rate is 94 per cent, with a standard deviation across districts of only 3 per cent. Table 9.4 reports the regressions, in which the male and female participation rates are treated as endogenous variables, identified by the excluded variables reported at the bottom of Table 9.3. The dependent variable for the first two regressions is

**Table 9.3: Variable Means and Standard Deviations, Indian Districts, Rural Population, 1961**

| Variable | Mean | Standard deviation |
|---|---|---|
| *Endogenous* | | |
| Male-female child survival differential | 0.0323 | 0.0445 |
| Male-female child survival ratio | 1.0366 | 0.0518 |
| Female labour force participation rate, 15-59 | 0.579 | 0.254 |
| Male labour force participation rate, 15-59 | 0.943 | 0.032 |
| *Exogenous included* | | |
| Average farm size (acres) | 12.01 | 10.19 |
| Percentage households with no land | 33.14 | 13.52 |
| Proportion of land irrigated | 0.125 | 0.189 |
| Normal rainfall (mm/year) | 298.6 | 601.4 |
| Proportion of district population rural | 0.840 | 0.114 |
| Proportion females with completed primary education, 15-59 | 0.031 | 0.039 |
| Proportion males with completed primary education, 15-59 | 0.123 | 0.084 |
| Proportion females matriculated, 15-59 | 0.00308 | 0.00722 |
| Proportion males matriculated, 15-59 | 0.0267 | 0.0251 |
| Proportion of females Muslim, 15-59 | 0.0364 | 0.0824 |
| *Exogenous excluded* | | |
| Number of factories per household | 0.150 | 0.163 |
| Percentage of factories with 10+ employees | 4.41 | 5.21 |
| Percentage of factories using fuel | 23.1 | 22.3 |

Number of districts: 230

Sources: 1961 population characteristics are from India, Office of the Registrar General, *Census of India, 1961*, parts IIb, IIc, IVb (New Delhi, 1965); agricultural data from India, Directorate of Economics and Statistics, *Agricultural wages in India, 1960-61* (New Delhi, 1964); and rainfall from India, Directorate of Economics and Statistics, *Indian agricultural statistics, 1961-62 and 1962-63*, vol. II (New Delhi, 1970).

the *difference* between the male survival rate (i.e., the number of males aged 5-9 to the number of males aged 0-4) and the comparable female survival rate. This approximates the dependent variable that is later used in the analysis of household data. The dependent variable in the third and fourth regressions is the *ratio* of the male survival rate to the female survival rate. (This ratio can also be replaced by its logarithm, as was suggested by the stable population model derivation on p. 212, without altering the estimates in any important respects.) Two specifications are reported with and without the set of education variables to determine the sensitivity of the results.

**Table 9.4: 2SLS Regression Coefficients: Male-Female Child Survival Differentials and Ratios; Rural Indian Districts, 1961 (t-values in parenthesis)**

| Variable | Male-female child survival rate[a] | | | |
|---|---|---|---|---|
| | Differential | | Ratio | |
| | (1) | (2) | (3) | (4) |
| Female participation[a] | −.119 | −.193 | −.120 | −.200 |
| | (2.24) | (2.68) | (2.03) | (2.45) |
| Male participation[a] | .274 | .793 | .362 | 1.023 |
| | (1.34) | (1.58) | (1.54) | (1.77) |
| Mean farm size ($\times 10^{-4}$) | −2.097 | −1.39 | −2.14 | −4.64 |
| | (0.65) | (1.07) | (0.58) | (1.10) |
| Percentage with no land ($\times 10^{-3}$) | .104 | .0744 | .0332 | .0395 |
| | (0.33) | (0.22) | (0.09) | (0.10) |
| Proportion irrigated land ($\times 10^{-3}$) | −.0489 | −.0671 | −.0449 | −.0680 |
| | (2.24) | (2.80) | (2.00) | (2.48) |
| Rainfall ($\times 10^{-4}$) | −.0817 | .0259 | −.0627 | .0369 |
| | (1.28) | (0.30) | (0.86) | (0.37) |
| Proportion district rural | .0639 | .0857 | .0569 | .0815 |
| | (2.36) | (2.73) | (1.80) | (2.27) |
| Proportion female primary education | − | −.263 | − | −.312 |
| | | (1.69) | | (1.73) |
| Proportion male primary education | − | .158 | − | .180 |
| | | (1.81) | | (1.83) |
| Proportion female matriculated | − | .350 | − | .920 |
| | | (0.31) | | (0.70) |
| Proportion male matriculated | − | .108 | − | .0823 |
| | | (0.69) | | (0.45) |
| Proportion females Muslim | .0696 | −.0167 | 1.11 | .0232 |
| | (0.84) | (0.17) | (1.13) | (0.20) |
| Constant | −.206 | −.680 | .727 | .117 |
| SEE | .039 | .038 | .044 | .044 |

Note: a. Endogenous.
Sources: 1961 population characteristics are from India, Office of the Registrar General, *Census of India, 1961*, parts IIb, IIc, IVb (New Delhi, 1965); agricultural data from India, Directorate of Economics and Statistics, *Agricultural wages in India, 1960-61* (New Delhi, 1964); and rainfall from India, Directorate of Economics and Statistics, *Indian agricultural statistics, 1961-62 and 1962-63*, vol. II (New Delhi, 1970).

Female participation in the labour force is associated with a decline in the male-to-female child survival difference or ratio at the 1 per cent level of statistical significance. Male participation is directly related to the differential between male and female child survival, but not to a statistically significant degree. The proportion landless or the size of farms among the landed is not notably associated with the sex differential in child mortality, when conditioned on the endogenous level of male and female participation rates. The greater the proportion of irrigated land, the lower the ratio of male-to-female survival, perhaps because irrigated areas are wealthier and labour productivity is generally greater, or because specifically female labour productivity is enhanced by the cultivation of crops that depend upon irrigation. Rural areas are found to exhibit higher male-to-female survival prospects than urban areas, even when conditioned on other measures of wealth and labour market variables. This may reflect the greater wealth of urban areas or a complex set of changes in women's welfare as households shift from rural to urban areas. The education variables, holding labour market behaviour constant, do not indicate strong patterns, but there is a tendency for female survival to be relatively greater in districts where more women obtain a primary education and relatively lower where male primary schooling is more extensive, although the absolute value of the female education coefficient exceeds that of male education. There is no association between child mortality and the proportion of Muslim women in the district, although Muslim areas do have lower female labour market participation (see Appendix, Table A-1 on p. 231).

In sum, at the district level, the labour market effects of women's participation are quite strong, incorporating in part the impact of off-farm employment opportunities and Muslim restrictions on women working. The wealth effects of land ownership and education are weak. The movement from rural to urban districts continues to be associated with improving survival prospects for girls relative to boys, and some linkage may exist between patterns of irrigation and the sex-specific survival prospects of children.

*Household Sample*

The summary statistics for the sample of landed and landless households are reported in Table 9.5. Women's labour force participation is 47 per cent in the landed and 52 per cent in the landless sub-samples, whereas for males the figures are 99 and 98 per cent, respectively. Table 9.6 reports household regressions, where the dependent variable is the ratio of the male child survival rate to the female child survival rate among own children. The two specifications are with and without the four education variables, within the sub-samples of landed and landless rural village residents.

**Table 9.5: Variable Means and Standard Deviations, Rural Indian Households, 1971, by Land Status**

| Variable | Landed | | Landless | |
|---|---|---|---|---|
| | Mean | SD | Mean | SD |
| *Endogenous* | | | | |
| Male-female child survival differential | .0088 | .267 | .043 | .315 |
| Female labour force participation rate | .468 | .222 | .520 | .270 |
| Male labour force participation rate | .990 | .022 | .976 | .061 |
| *Exogenous included* | | | | |
| Nonearnings income (rupees) | 130.9 | 556.1 | 88.24 | 375.2 |
| Gross cropped area (acres) | 11.05 | 11.75 | – | – |
| Irrigated land (dummy) | .533 | .499 | – | – |
| Village electrified (dummy) | .319 | .467 | .464 | .499 |
| Normal district rainfall (mm/year) | 413.2 | 847.1 | 573.9 | 1028 |
| Total village population | 2359 | 3716 | 2898 | 4210 |
| Distance of town from village (km) | 20.20 | 24.23 | 19.24 | 25.59 |
| Female with some formal education, but less than matriculate | .113 | .317 | .143 | .350 |
| Male with some formal education, but less than matriculate | .580 | .493 | .517 | .500 |
| Female matriculate or above (dummy) | .023 | .150 | .019 | .135 |
| Male matriculate or above (dummy) | .201 | .401 | .161 | .368 |
| *Exogenous excluded* | | | | |
| Factory in village (dummy) | .076 | .266 | .114 | .318 |
| Small-scale industry in village (dummy) | .084 | .277 | .129 | .336 |
| Age of female | 39.46 | 8.83 | 38.29 | 8.44 |
| District female agricultural wage | 1.89 | .874 | 2.05 | .937 |
| District male agricultural wage | 3.04 | 1.39 | 3.56 | 1.58 |
| No. of households | 955 | | 379 | |

Sources: NCAER's ARIS Survey described in NCAER, *Changes in rural income in India* (India, National Council of Applied Economic Research, 1975); district data and population data from India, *Agricultural wages, 1960-61* and *Census of India, 1961*; rainfall data from *Indian agricultural statistics, 1961-62 and 1962-63*.

**Table 9.6: 2SLS Regression Coefficients: Male-Female Child Survival Differentials, Rural Indian Households, 1971, by Land Status (t-values in Parenthesis)**

| Variable | Male-female child survival rate[a] | | | |
|---|---|---|---|---|
| | Landed | | Landless | |
| | (1) | (2) | (3) | (4) |
| Female participation rate[a] | −.093 | −.301 | −.140 | −.336 |
| | (1.27) | (2.83) | (1.87) | (2.66) |
| Male participation rate[a] | −.720 | −1.55 | −.021 | .116 |
| | (1.27) | (2.18) | (0.03) | (0.13) |
| Nonearnings income ($\times 10^{-4}$) | −.065 | −.271 | −.453 | −.600 |
| | (0.37) | (1.37) | (0.46) | (0.47) |
| Gross cropped area ($\times 10^{-4}$) | −10.0 | −19.1 | − | − |
| | (1.00) | (1.70) | | |
| Irrigation | −.022 | −.049 | − | − |
| | (1.01) | (2.03) | | |
| Electrification ($\times 10^{-2}$) | .694 | −.057 | −4.930 | −4.800 |
| | (0.32) | (0.03) | (1.16) | (1.04) |
| Rainfall ($\times 10^{-4}$) | −.367 | −.388 | −.124 | −.354 |
| | (2.09) | (2.16) | (0.47) | (1.20) |
| Village population ($\times 10^{-5}$) | .246 | .202 | −.830 | −.125 |
| | (0.62) | (0.49) | (1.21) | (1.71) |
| Distance town-village ($\times 10^{-3}$) | .266 | .563 | −.728 | −.472 |
| | (0.67) | (1.36) | (1.10) | (0.68) |
| Female primary education | − | −.076 | − | −.016 |
| | | (2.06) | | (0.29) |
| Male primary education | − | −.012 | − | −.075 |
| | | (0.46) | | (1.30) |
| Female matriculated | − | .148 | − | −.044 |
| | | (0.21) | | (0.34) |
| Male matriculated | − | −.075 | − | −.163 |
| | | (1.90) | | (2.03) |
| Constant | .790 | 1.763 | .194 | .224 |
| SEE | .268 | .267 | .315 | .314 |

Note: a. Endogenous.
Sources: NCAER's ARIS Survey described in NCAER, *Changes in rural income in India* (India, National Council of Applied Economic Research, 1975); district data and population data from India, *Agricultural wages, 1960-61* and *Census of India, 1961*; rainfall data from *Indian agricultural statistics, 1961-62 and 1962-63*.

Female labour market participation again has a negative effect, but reaches the 1 per cent significance level only when the education variables are included in the regression. The male participation rate of the household head exerts a negative effect on the male-to-female survival differences among the landowners, and it is unrelated to the child survival patterns among the landless. The size of landholding, the occurrence of irrigation on some portion of the household's land and the extent of rainfall all decrease the male-to-female child survival differential. This may be evidence of the hypothesized wealth effect; or it may be that with these inputs the cropping patterns are different and the productivity of women relative to men increases, but the wealth effects restrain any resulting increase in the overall rate of female participation. Nonearnings income has the anticipated negative sign, but never approaches statistical significance, and electrification of the village has no effect. The proxies for the rural/urban continuum find little support for the beneficial effect for female welfare of being close to a town or living in a larger village. As in the district level samples, there is some evidence that with increasing female primary education the welfare of girls increases among the landed, whereas male matriculates are associated, among both landed and landless, with improving female survival rates relative to males.

The evidence as a whole confirms the relationship between sex-specific child mortality and the extent of female labour force participation across households and across districts in India. Holding these productive roles constant, increases in income or wealth in terms of land or the productivity of the climate and the accessibility of inputs such as irrigation increases female survival prospects more than they do male. The evidence on this score, however, remains inconclusive and further exploration with other data sets is needed.

From the district-level regression (4), one obtains an estimate that the elasticity of the child survival ratio with respect to female participation is about 0.1. Increasing by one-third the level of female labour market participation in rural Indian districts from the sample mean of 58 per cent to 77 per cent is associated with the child survival ratio decreasing from 1.04 to 1.00 or parity. This would represent a rise in female participation of three-quarters of a standard deviation. If the *male* labour force participation rate fell by 2 percentage points, from 0.94 to 0.92, which is not an uncommon occurrence as development increases (Durand, 1975), the male-female survival ratio would decline from 1.04 to 1.02, or half of the way towards equality. It should be noted, however, that parity in child survival rates is not to be confused with parity in terms of the child's welfare or the household inputs to health.

It seems likely, given the observed sex-specific patterns of mortality in many other parts of the world, that equal inputs of resources at the family level to boys and girls would probably invert the Indian ratio, and the innate biological advantages of the female compared with the male child would yield a ratio closer to 0.95. Thus, despite the fact that increasing women's labour force participation can go a considerable way towards improving the welfare of women in a country such as India, other, equally fundamental, changes in the access of women to schooling and economic resources will be needed to achieve parity between the sexes. Urbanization may shroud other structural changes in women's status that may prove difficult to disentangle and manipulate separately.

## Conclusion

India began to experience a sustained decline in mortality in the late 1920s and 1930s, following the severe influenza epidemic of 1918-21. Male life expectation at birth, estimated as 27 years in 1921-30, had increased to 47 years by 1961-71. This gain for the male of a half a year of life per calendar year was not shared equally by women. India is one of the few countries in which male life expectancy has increased more rapidly than has the life expectancy for females. Indeed, since the 1940s, male life expectancy has exceeded that for females, a paradoxical reversal in the demographic pattern of mortality in most parts of the world — one that cannot be attributed to errors in measurement (Visaria, 1969). Death rates in India are greater for females than for males during childhood, during the years when women bear children, and in the later years of life.

The purpose of this study is to propose childhood mortality as one partial measure of the welfare of boys relative to girls when the allocation of consumption and investments inputs to offspring depend on parental decisions. The hypothesis is advanced that in this formative period children are accorded family resources that influence their health and survival prospects according to their relative expected productivity as adults. This relationship implies that child mortality is directly influenced by household resources, and that these resources are allocated by parents in accordance with the *returns to survival* for boys as opposed to girls.

The proposition is also advanced, although with less empirical support, that increased material wealth levels should encourage parents to weigh less heavily these production attributes of children according to sex and to weigh more heavily the consumption attributes of children that do not favour boys relative to girls. If these consumption benefits of children increase relative to the production benefits, as parental wealth increases, one might expect to find wealth associated with a convergence in the survival prospects of boys and girls, or indeed an advantage might be gained by girls, if their sex is genetically more fit.

The labour market evidence from India is clear. Muslim women and those living in rural villages far from non-farm employment opportunities have tended to participate less in the labour force. In these areas, girls fare less well than boys, at least in terms of my only objective measure of welfare: survival. The structure of agricultural production, the type of crops cultivated and the demands for specific types of field labour may also influence the vital balance of family resources allocated to boys and girls. But to clarify these issues requires richer data than those used here, and probably more theoretical structure to the model of family labour allocation and its interrelationship with the local market for wage labour.

On the basis of preliminary empirical results for rural India, obtained at two approximately parallel levels of aggregation, this study suggests that indirect measures of sex differentials in child mortality are linked to the extent of women's labour force participation. The results support the thesis that greater involvement of women in the labour market is probably an adequate surrogate for the productivity of women as viewed by the family. In a poor country, it is expected that the first claim on family resources must go to the current and future breadwinner. As women are more extensively engaged in the labour market, both in off-farm and on-farm productive activities, their health and survival prospects are of greater importance to the household. The relative health and survival prospects of women and girls may thus parallel their growing capacity as productive agents in the process of economic development.

## Appendix

### Table A-1: Reduced Form OLS Regression Coefficients: Labour Force Participation Variables; Rural Indian Districts, 1961 (standard errors in parentheses)

| Variable | Labour force participation (%) | |
|---|---|---|
| | Female | Male |
| Mean farm size | .125 | .033 |
| | (.171) | (.017) |
| Percentage no land | −.362 | −.021 |
| | (.154) | (.015) |
| Proportion irrigated land | −.225 | −.022 |
| | (.089) | (.009) |
| Rainfall (x10⁻²) | .689 | .015 |
| | (.370) | (.036) |
| Proportion district rural | 17.93 | −1.92 |
| | (13.38) | (1.32) |
| Proportion female primary education | −.293 | .095 |
| | (.794) | (.078) |
| Proportion male primary education | .256 | −.118 |
| | (.295) | (.029) |
| Proportion female matriculated | −7.85 | −2.26 |
| | (3.41) | (.336) |
| Proportion male matriculated | −.624 | −.151 |
| | (.739) | (.073) |
| Proportion females Muslim | −.138 | −.002 |
| | (.019) | (.002) |
| No. of factories per household | 22.26 | 1.46 |
| | (9.45) | (.931) |
| Percentage of factories with 10+ employees | .281 | −.097 |
| | (.333) | (.032) |
| Percentage of factories using fuel | −.118 | −.009 |
| | (.074) | (.007) |
| Constant | 59.10 | 98.92 |
| R² | .386 | .624 |
| SEE | 20.51 | 2.02 |

Sources: 1961 population characteristics are from India, Office of the Registrar General, *Census of India, 1961*, parts IIb, IIc, IVb (New Delhi, 1965); agricultural data from India, Directorate of Economics and Statistics, *Agricultural wages in India, 1960-61* (New Delhi, 1964); and rainfall from India, Directorate of Economics and Statistics, *Indian agricultural statistics, 1961-62 and 1962-63*, vol. II (New Delhi, 1970).

**Table A-2: Reduced Form OLS Regression Coefficients: Labour Force Participation Variables; Landless Rural Indian Households, 1971 (standard errors in parentheses)**

| Variable | Labour force participation rate | |
|---|---|---|
| | Female | Male |
| Nonearnings income (x10⁻⁴) | −1.191 | −1.421 |
| | (.600) | (.200) |
| Electrification | −.046 | −.030 |
| | (.050) | (.017) |
| Rainfall (x10⁻⁴) | −1.720 | −.047 |
| | (.400) | (1.00) |
| Village population (x10⁻⁵) | −1.295 | −.027 |
| | (1.000) | (.100) |
| Distance town-village (x10⁻³) | .809 | −.333 |
| | (.900) | (.300) |
| Female primary education | −.114 | .007 |
| | (.072) | (.024) |
| Male primary education | −.162 | .030 |
| | (.054) | (.018) |
| Female matriculated | −.066 | .039 |
| | (.170) | (.056) |
| Male matriculated | −.401 | −.008 |
| | (.076) | (.025) |
| Factory in village | −.052 | .033 |
| | (.077) | (.025) |
| Small-scale industry | .070 | −.024 |
| | (.073) | (.024) |
| Age of female | −.001 | .001 |
| | (.010) | (.010) |
| District female agricultural wage | −.030 | .017 |
| | (.028) | (.009) |
| District male agricultural wage | −.093 | −.005 |
| | (.015) | (.005) |
| Constant | 1.084 | .975 |
| R² | .291 | .162 |
| SEE | .429 | .142 |

Sources: NCAER's ARIS Survey described in NCAER, *Changes in rural income in India* (India National Council of Applied Economic Research, 1975); district wages and population data from India, *Agricultural wages, 1960-61* and *Census of India, 1961*; rainfall data from *Indian agricultural statistics, 1961-62 and 1962-63*.

**Table A-3: Reduced Form OLS Regression Coefficients: Labour Force Participation Variables; Landed Rural Indian Households, 1971 (standard errors in parentheses)**

| Variable | Labour force participation rate | |
|---|---|---|
| | Female | Male |
| Nonearnings income (x$10^{-4}$) | −.662 (.300) | −.060 (.100) |
| Gross cropped area (x$10^{-3}$) | −2.36 (1.36) | −.718 (.300) |
| Irrigation | −.134 (.032) | .004 (.007) |
| Electrification | −.033 (.037) | −.001 (.008) |
| Rainfall (x$10^{-4}$) | .151 (.300) | −.112 (.100) |
| Village population (x$10^{-5}$) | −1.46 (1.00) | .170 (.100) |
| Distance town-village (x$10^{-3}$) | 1.14 (.620) | .099 (.140) |
| Female primary education | −.059 (.054) | −.027 (.012) |
| Male primary education | −.118 (.038) | .028 (.009) |
| Female matriculated | .365 (.109) | −.046 (.024) |
| Male matriculated | −.311 (.052) | .038 (.012) |
| Factory in village | −.237 (.058) | .015 (.013) |
| Small-scale industry | .224 (.056) | −.035 (.013) |
| Age of female | .001 (.002) | −.001 (.001) |
| District female agricultural wage | −.006 (.019) | .003 (.004) |
| District male agricultural wage | −.057 (.012) | .004 (.003) |
| Constant | .892 | 1.014 |
| $R^2$ | .198 | .048 |
| SEE | .450 | .100 |

Sources: NCAER's ARIS Survey described in NCAER, *Changes in rural income in India* (India, National Council of Applied Economic Research, 1975); district wages and population data from India, *Agricultural wages, 1960-61* and *Census of India, 1961*; rainfall data from *Indian agricultural statistics, 1961-62 and 1962-63*.

## Notes

1. Two economic-demographic household surveys have been explicitly
designed around the time allocation framework and have been sufficiently
analyzed to suggest their value. The first was collected in 1975 and 1976 in
Laguna in the Philippines under the co-ordination of Binswanger, Evenson,
Florenico and White (1980) with support from the Agricultural Development
Council. The second was collected in 1976-7 in Malaysia under the co-ordination
of the Rank Corporation with support from US AID (Butz, DaVanzo, Fernandez,
Jones and Spoestra, 1978).

2. The 1961 census of India adopted a broad concept of 'worker' by
international standards. If the person put in an hour's work per day during the
major part of a working season, the person was treated as an economically
active worker. This may have inflated the participation rate in comparison with
the figures collected in the previous and following censuses of India, but for the
purpose here it usefully includes marginal female workers engaged within the
family in agriculture and household industry. For example, 'if a woman who was
basically engaged in attending to household duties, went to her husband's field
taking his lunch and for about an hour or so she tended the cattle, she was
straightaway treated as engaged in cultivation.' (India, 1972, p. 142.)

3. Pryor (1977, Appendix B) finds that the brideprice (or the negative value
of the dowry) is influenced by postmarital residence pattern (who has a claim on
the bride's time), the relative amount of work carried out by the spouses (as
emphasized here), whether herding is the major subsistence activity (reducing the
relative value of female labour) and the society's general level of development
(which raises the dowry level). Pryor bases his study on ethnographies from
some 60 tribes and ethnic populations worldwide, and reports a regression
analysis across these groups to support his economic theory of marriage and
exchange.

4. Hammoud (1977) suggests that the male-to-female mortality ratio peaks
after the fourth day, but most of the studies he cites are from high-income
countries; little evidence appears to be available on the age structure of sex
mortality differentials across a representative sample of low-income countries.
It is believed that the larger size and skull dimensions of the male increases male
mortality relative to female from obstetrical complications at birth.
Improvements in prenatal care and attendance at delivery, therefore, are thought
to increase the early survival of males relative to females for biological reasons.
Examination of US sex mortality differentials in utero suggests a very high ratio
of male-to-female mortality rates (about 3) in the third to fifth month of
gestation, which then declines to about 1.2 until the ninth month and birth
(McMillan, 1979). But these data for a contemporary high-income population
suggest that the sex mortality ratio in the last months of gestation declined
between the 1930s and the 1960s. Were this a general pattern with rising income,
it might help to explain the tendency for male-to-female ratios at birth to have
risen and be somewhat higher in industrially advanced countries today, on
average, than they are today in low-income countries. The improved prenatal
environment may contribute to the survival of a greater proportion of males,
increasing the male-female birth ratio with development. The working hypothesis
explored later in this chapter is that with rising wealth levels, male-to-female
mortality ratio after birth will decline, other things being equal. The two trends
could be largely offsetting, in so far as they affect the sex ratio of a cohort
reaching adulthood, and the average age at the first marriage.

5. In the full sample, the landed and landless groups by the age of 45 had, on
the average, five births with a standard deviation of two. About one-fifth of the

sample aged over 45, therefore, was excluded by the restriction of having at
least one boy and one girl birth. The proportion increased sharply at younger
cohorts that are much larger in the Indian population. Some observations were
also eliminated because of non-responses to the essential age, education,
agricultural and income questions. Since the starting and stopping of child-bearing
is to some degree an endogenous decision, I am considering here a choice-based
sample that yields somewhat biased estimates of the true population parameters
to the model, but the direction and severity of bias is not now clear.

6. The selection criteria of having at least one male and one female birth
restrict the working sample to less than half, since the age pyramid is much
larger at the younger ages when this condition is less frequently met. Some
attrition due to non-response is also unavoidable. Women over the age of 54 are
excluded because retrospective error in the recall of births and child deaths thirty
years prior to the survey is probably substantially greater than for younger
women.

7. This variable was collected in the household survey, but was apparently not
coded. Nor were any distinctions of caste.

## References

Acton, J.P. (1973) *Demand for health care among the urban poor, with special emphasis on the role of time*, R-1511, Santa Monica, Calif., The Rand Corporation

Arriaga, E.E. (1979) 'Infants and child mortality in selected Latin American countries', mimeo., US Bureau of the Census

Bardhan, P.K. (1974) 'On life and death questions', *Economic and Political Weekly* (New Delhi), 2, 32-4, special number (August), 1293-305

Ben-Porath, Y. and F. Welch (1972) *Chance, child traits and the choice of family size*, R-1117, Santa Monica, Calif., The Rand Corporation

Binswanger, H.P., Evanson, R.E., Florenico, C.A. and White, D.N. (1980) *Rural household studies in Asia*, Singapore, Singapore University Press

Boserup, E. (1970) *Women's role in economic development*, New York, St. Martin's Press

Butz, W., DaVanzo, J., Fernandez, D., Jones, R. and Spoestra, N. (1978) *The Malaysia family life survey: questionnaire and interview instructions*, Santa Monica, The Rand Corporation, WN-10147-AID

Chao, D.N.W. (1979) *Income, human capital and life expectancy*, International Program of Laboratories for Population Statistics, University of North Carolina

Coale, A.J. (1972) *The growth and structure of human populations*, Princeton, New Jersey, Princeton University Press

Durand, J.D. (1975) *The labor force in economic development*, Princeton, New Jersey, Princeton University Press

Dyson, J. (1977) 'Levels, trends, differentials and causes of child mortality', *World Health Statistics Report*, 30, 4

Engel, E. (1895) 'De levenskosten Belgischer arbeiter-familian fruher und jetzt', *ISI Bulletin*, 9, 1

Fuchs, V.R. (1974) *Who shall live?*, New York, Basic Books

Grossman, M. (1972) *The demand for health*, NBER occasional paper no. 119, New York, Columbia University Press

Hammoud, E.I. (1977) 'Sex differentials in mortality', *World Health Statistics Report*, 30, 174-206

India, Directorate of Economics and Statistics (1964) *Agricultural wages in India*,

*1960-61*, New Delhi
————, Office of the Registrar General (1965) *Census of India, 1961*, parts IIb, IIc, IVb, New Delhi
————, Directorate of Economics and Statistics (1970) *Indian agricultural statistics, 1961-62 and 1962-63, II*, New Delhi
————, Office of the Registrar General (1971) *Infant mortality in India, sample registration system (SRS) analytical series*, no. 1, New Delhi
————, Director of Census Operations (1972) *Census of India, 1971*, series 3, *ASSAM*, part II-A, *General population tables*, Assam
McMillan, M.M. (1979) 'Differential mortality by sex in fetal and neofetal deaths', *Science, 204*, 4388, 89-91
National Council of Applied Economic Research (1975) *Changes in rural income in India*, New Delhi, India, National Council of Applied Economic Research
Pollack, R.A. (1969) 'Conditional demand functions and consumption theory', *Quarterly Journal of Economics, 83*, 60-78
Pressat, R. (1972) *Demographic analysis*, Chicago, Aldine-Atherton
Preston, S.H. (1976a) *Mortality patterns in national populations*, New York, Academic Press
———— (1976b) 'Causes and consequences of mortality declines in less developed countries during the 20th Century' in R.A. Easterlin (ed.), *Population and economic change in less developed countries*, Chicago, University of Chicago Press
———— and J.A. Weed (1976) 'Causes of death responsible for international and intertemporal variation in sex mortality differentials', *World Health Statistics Report, 30*, 4, 144-88
Pryor, F.L. (1977) *The origins of the economy*, New York, Academic Press
Rosenzweig, M.R. (1977) 'Neoclassical theory and the optimizing peasant: an econometric analysis of market family labor supply in a developing country', *Economic Growth Center*, discussion paper no. 272, New Haven, Conn., Yale University
———— and R.E. Evenson. (1977) 'Fertility, schooling and the economic contribution of children in rural India', *Econometrica, 45*, 3, 1065-80
———— and T.P. Schultz. (1979) 'Sex specific child survival: labor market and wealth effects in rural India', mimeo., Yale University
Schultz, T.W. (1975) 'The value of the ability to deal with disequilibria', *Journal of Economic Literature, 13*, 3, 827-46
Stolnitz, G.J. (1955) 'A century of international mortality trends', *Population Studies, 9*, 1, 24-55
———— (1956) 'A century of international mortality trends, *Population Studies, 10*, 1, 17-43
———— (1965) 'Recent mortality trends in Latin America, Asia, and Africa', *Population Studies, 19*, 2, 117-38
———— (1975) 'International mortality trends', *The Population Debate*, New York, United Nations
Tax, S. (1953) *Penny capitalism: a Guatemalan Indian economy*, Institute of Social Anthropology, publication no. 16, Washington, DC, Smithsonian Institution
Teitlebaum, M.S. (1971) 'Male and female components of perinatal mortality: trends 1901-1963', *Demography, 9*, 4, 541-8
Visaria, P.M. (1969) *The sex ratio of the population of India, Census of India, 1961, I*, monograph 10, New Delhi, India, Office of the Registrar General
Welch, F. (1970) 'Education in production', *Journal of Political Economy, 78*, 1, 25-59
Wrigley, E.R. (1969) *Population and history*, New York, McGraw Hill

# PART FIVE: ECONOMIC DIMENSIONS INFLUENCING WOMEN'S ROLES

# 10 WOMEN AND THE URBAN LABOUR MARKET

Elizabeth Jelin

## Introduction

During the last decade, much of the discussion of women's position in society has been centred around the relationship between women and development. Since the publication of Esther Boserup's book (1970), which soon became a standard reference for studies about women, the attention of scholars and of the international community has been on the question of how development affects women. The answers have varied — from an early optimism about the beneficial effects of development in general, grounded in the terminology and the approach of 'modernization' theories, to pessimistic views about the 'evil' effects of the expansion of capitalism. Of course, no single answer, valid for the whole world and for all times, can be given.

This chapter marks out a specific area of concern within this general field — the type of economic activity women perform in urban areas of underdeveloped capitalist societies. It reviews the existing knowledge and approaches used to deal with the issue of female employment, attempting at the same time to raise some new questions and to offer suggestions for future research. Within that restricted focus, the relevant questions are: (i) how do the productive activities of women change with economic growth and the change in the overall economic structure of society? (ii) How do the positions women occupy compare to those of men; or what kind of sexual division of labour has evolved in the process of change? (iii) What are the relationships between these activities and the sexual division of labour, and some basic demographic phenomena, especially family structure, fertility and migration? Some of the dimensions relevant to analysis of such questions will be discussed in this chapter.

The urban population in underdeveloped countries is growing rapidly due both to natural population growth and to high in-migration rates. This implies a continuous change and reorganization of urban life. Within this context, the employment situation of women has to be considered as the result of at least three analytically separate dimensions: (i) the supply constraints, which are linked to the position of women within the household and, therefore, to the composition of the household, to the sexual division of labour, and to the relationship between domestic and market production; (ii) general labour market conditions prevalent in peripheral capitalist societies today, which imply in most cases a relatively abundant supply of labour, a relatively low absorptive capacity in the more dynamic and productive sectors of the economy, high rates of unemployment and low wages *for both men and women*, and the persistence of labour-intensive, low productivity jobs and of organizational productive forms that are not based on wage work; and (iii) specific explicit and implicit employment policies for women, including discriminatory practices and sex segregation of occupations.

With regard to the first dimension, 'employment' should be seen as part of a broader concept, that of 'economic activity', which also includes domestic tasks. The distinction between domestic tasks and outside work is solidly entrenched in everyday language, in official statistics, and in the social sciences. Usually 'work' refers to what adult persons do for a living, but it does not include unpaid domestic tasks. Yet, as recent discussions have pointed out (Harrison, 1973; Seccombe, 1974 and 1975; Coulson, Magas and Wainwright, 1975; Gardiner, 1975; Conference of Socialist Economics, 1976; Himmelweit and Mohun, 1977), domestic work constitutes an organic component of the capitalist organization of production; both the daily maintenance of the labour force and its generational reproduction are assured through domestic tasks within the household. Of course, theoretically, there could be alternative organizations in charge of these tasks, but, at present, the private household is the only sure source of a 'free' labour force.[1]

The subject of the relationship between domestic and outside work is relevant here because in most urban societies the division of labour has been such that adult men go out to work and adult women remain in charge of the privately performed domestic tasks. However, not all men work – the very young, the very old, the sick are excluded – and not all women are devoted exclusively and equally to domestic tasks. Domestic responsibility varies among women. Some very young, very old or sick women are totally dependent on the domestic work of others; others are in charge of a wide and complete variety of domestic chores. Furthermore, many women are also employed outside the home.

The explicit consideration of housework and reproduction within the framework of social production, a subject to which a section of this chapter will be addressed, does not preclude the consideration of women's participation in the labour force. Participation rates, their variations and the types of jobs women hold are obviously linked to their position within the household. Furthermore, the characteristics of the occupations women tend to perform are also shaped by their domestic roles. Thus, although increasing participation in the public sphere of social production may be a goal for women,[2] the goal cannot be any work at any price in jobs that are secondary to the domestic responsibilities. A guiding principle of this chapter is that an improvement in the position of urban women cannot come about only through changes in the labour market and in employment opportunities; it also has to involve a shift in their position in the household. Otherwise, women's opportunities for participation in the labour force will continue to be in jobs that are 'secondary', and labour force participation will continue to involve a double day of work.

On the other hand, development in itself is not a panacea that can assure participation and improvement, either for women or for men. High unemployment rates and poverty are widespread phenomena in many less developed countries, but overall economic growth does not assure that these conditions will change. Evidence from both peripheral and central capitalist countries, as well as from historical records, indicates that there are no 'automatic' social effects of economic growth. Improvement in the status of women will be the result of social movements and struggles carried out at specific historical conjunctures. Therefore, discussion of the participation of women in the labour force, or even of their contribution to growth and development, cannot be isolated from the issues of exploitation, poverty and unemployment. By focusing on women, however, analyses may show not only the specific condition of women, but also the patterns of domination or urban-subordinated sectors in peripheral capitalistic societies, where the structural heterogeneity of the labour force is very high and different types of wage work and other kinds of employment co-exist. Besides the 'typical' working-class household, based on the wage of the head and the domestic work of his wife, a variety of other household conditions may exist – some of them linked with the dissolution of precapitalist modes of production and the consequent 'liberation' of labour for various forms of production.[3]

Some of the issues raised and the conclusions reached in this chapter apply to other social formations, especially those in which the tasks of reproduction and daily maintenance of the labour force are largely performed in households. In addition to the degree to which labour is 'liberated' from precapitalist modes of production (as these are integrated with and subordinated to capitalism), an important dimension of intercountry variation is the degree to which some basic social

services are provided by the state. In socialist societies (and some
Western European societies), there are extensive welfare provisions
— health services, unemployment compensation, housing plans, and
retirement and educational facilities — that take some of the burden
away from the household. Such services are unavailable in most capitalist less developed countries, or access to them is very restricted;
thus alternative mechanisms based on informal, kinship and household
structures are extremely important.

## Domestic Production and Labour Force Participation

Labour force participation rates of women have been extensively
studied, and some patterns are well documented, having shown up in a
variety of countries in different areas of the world. Participation rates
vary with age, with family status, with education, with rural/urban
residence. The exact impact of each dimension may be different in
each country, and other societal aspects may be crucial in some specific
cases. For instance, low participation rates in Muslim countries were
traced to the cultural pattern of seclusion (Youssef, 1974). Several
structural aspects may also directly affect participation rates of women.
Thus, studies have shown that participation rates in rural areas vary
according to the type of landholding predominant in the area (Boserup,
1970; Durand, 1975; Standing and Sheehan, 1978). International
variations in participation rates by age have been summarized in four
basic curves, expressing different patterns of association between labour
force participation and stages in the domestic life cycle (Durand,
1975). Such international comparisons, although important at an
aggregate level and as a first approximation, are hindered by the usual
deficiencies in data comparability and especially by the differing social
definitions of what constitutes 'work' or 'economic activity'.[4]
    The effects of family status and education on female participation
are almost always in the same direction: there is a clear increase in
labour force participation with increasing education, except for a
relatively common downward bend between the women with no formal
education and those with some, indicating that at the lowest level —
no schooling — the need to work may be extremely high. And everywhere married women work in smaller proportions than single, divorced
or widowed women. Among the married women, those with children
participate less than those without small children at home (Youssef,
1974; Standing, 1978; Standing and Sheehan, 1978). From the supply

side of labour force analysis, then, it could be said that the availability of women for outside work is related to their responsibilities within the household (measured by their family status) and by their earning potential (measured by their education).

The first of these relationships — namely that between family status and participation rates — seems almost obvious: it is taken for granted in much of the literature and treated as if there were no need for further analysis or explanation. This attitude is based on the prevalence of the social definition of women's role as being primarily within the household and only secondarily in the public realm. The relationship should not be taken for granted, however, and its variations and patterns should be explored in depth.

In the first place, the role of women within the household requires further attention. At a theoretical level, there have been important developments not only in the discussion of domestic production in precapitalist formations (Meillassoux, 1977) but also in the discussion of the role of domestic work — including tasks related to both the daily maintenance of the labourers and the reproduction of labour — in relation to the capitalist modes of production. The debate is still going on,[5] although it is now widely recognized that, at present, domestic work plays a vital role in the maintenance and reproduction of the labour force and therefore has to be taken into consideration when analyzing the total picture of social production.[6]

The theoretical recognition of the importance of domestic work has some implications for empirical research and action plans, for it highlights the need to study questions related to domestic work:[7] what basis tasks are performed? Who performs them? What is the basis for the division of labour within the household? How are the tasks of daily maintenance of the labouring members related to reproductive tasks and the care of nonworking members of the household? Seen in this light, housework and reproductive activities become completely enmeshed in a net of social, economic and political phenomena. For instance, household composition is usually taken as a given which determines the requirements of domestic work. Instead, however, it should be seen as the *result* of the ways in which the tasks of maintenance and reproduction of the labour force are organized, and to whom they are assigned. Increased domestic labour requirements may be met by calling on older relatives (which sometimes involves migratory moves) or by extended family residential arrangements.[8] In addition, empirical research may show that in some cases the economic value of girls is related to their ability to help their mothers in household activities (a parallel to the theory that relates high fertility to the economic value of children in the labour market). Perhaps a measure of 'household dependency' could be devised (similar to the well-known 'dependency ratio' used in demographic research), which would show how many dependents there are in a household in relation to the number of members who perform domestic work. It would probably be an important predictor of the supply of female labour power to the market.

The scope of domestic tasks linked to reproduction (i.e., child-rearing) and to the maintenance of nonworking members (the old and the sick) is obviously also related to the type of social services available. Thus, the care of young children is different in cases where some collective-day-care facilities are available, and the presence of sick persons has a different weight if there are specific health services provided for them. (Variations in housework will also depend on the prevalent technology of domestic production — running water, electricity, domestic appliances, prepared meals and so on.) Historically, the struggle to enlarge the scope of social services has been a difficult one in most societies; it has been successful, for the most part, only when there have been changes in the labour demand that have led to the entry into the labour force of people (predominantly women) previously occupied in domestic work.

At a micro level, these subjects can be studied through the use of time-budget techniques, which analyze the division of labour within the household on the basis of the time spent by the various members in different types of activities. At this micro level, the inclusion of housework as a separate category in the economic models explaining the supply of female labour (Mincer, 1962; Becker, 1965) constitutes a significant step forward in the neoclassical economic tradition. Use of such models to describe and explain the inter- and intra-class variations, as well as historical change and cross-cultural comparisons, could help in our understanding of the problem. Analytically, however, there are several difficulties with such an approach: (i) it does not take into account the social relationships in which each of the tasks is performed; and (ii) it defines time only in a physical sense — as a linear, continuous and divisible dimension — and does not include social meanings and cultural elements in the definition.[9]

From a purely material point of view, the existence of household production and transformation of goods and services for consumption — such as preparing food, laundering, cleaning, taking care of children, old and sick persons, mending and repairing — implies a certain degree of substitution of domestic production for commercially obtainable commodities. Many goods and services produced in the household could be bought. Although in the long run, there may be a trend towards the substitution of market commodities for domestically produced goods, the trend is not linear, and there will not be total substitution unless there is a major change in social institutions. Furthermore, short-term reversals and shifts may take place, since domestic production is very flexible and can act as a buffer mechanism in times of crisis to protect a given standard of living. In the long run, also, the family may act as a mechanism to increase the standard of living of the working class (Humphries, 1977; Waerness, 1978).

At an aggregate macro level, these considerations imply that we need to revise our definitions of 'economically active', 'economically inactive' and 'gross domestic product'.[10] As it stands, there are great difficulties and ambiguities in the measurement of economic activity. For women who perform most domestic work, the distinction between economically active and economically inactive is very inaccurate, since domestic work is excluded from the 'active' side of the equation. What is the criterion for distinguishing between 'activity' and 'inactivity'? Why should housework be excluded from the social process of production? In terms of both the actual work and the end-product, it is no different from paid domestic work or from peasant production of use-values for self-consumption. In terms of the absence of monetary income, it is similar to the work of family helpers in any other activity. And, as seen above, it has a specific function within the general division of labour, for it is an intrinsic part of the global process of social production and reproduction. If a measure of productivity could be devised (based not on monetary units but on physical product or services rendered), it would probably show that domestic work is as productive as many other tasks performed for wages or in self-employed positions.[11]

Analysis of the human resource base (or potential labour force) existing in a society and measurement of its utilization should therefore include domestic production. The benefits of such a course would be twofold: (i) it would become clear that part of the 'inactive' population is not inactive at all, but is actually in charge of domestic production; and (ii) it would measure the extent to which part of the 'active' population is actually involved in a 'double' working day.

Although these comments do not — indeed are not meant to — provide an exhaustive analysis of domestic production, they do indicate that there is a need for a global model which would encompass all productive and reproductive activities within a given society, and provide a framework for analyzing the social division of labour and the differential assignment of tasks to categories of individuals within that society. Research efforts in this area would then be geared not to 'Who works?' but to 'Who does what?' — on the assumption that every-body (except the sick and the very young) has some socially deter-mined activity. There are many possible activities and combinations of activities: there may be students who work for a wage, housewives who are gainfully employed and (although they are the exception at present) male workers who also perform domestic tasks. A rough indication of the time devoted to each of the possible activities and of the changes in time allocation along the life cycle would give a much better picture of the social division of labour, and would bring out into the open the various forms of 'invisible' labour. It would go beyond the motivational or normative judgements involved in the usual definition of economic participation and allow a more objective approach to the study of labour supply (Singer, 1977).

By following this path, however, an important issue usually associ-ated with labour force discussions becomes more salient; namely that of the degree to which the existing human potential is socially utilized. Up to now, this issue has been discussed under the heading of labour productivity or of unemployment and disguised unemployment. Development of criteria for defining these concepts poses a difficult problem; in order to measure them there must also be some norm or standard of 'full employment', and it has proven impossible up to now to arrive at a widely agreed-upon definition of full employment (IPEA, 1975; Standing, 1978). The inclusion of domestic work would not increase such difficulties, I believe: indeed, by making explicit many of the unquestioned assumptions that pervade the problem, it might actually help. The difficulties in measuring productivity of housework, for example — as housewives know, 'there is no end to housework': one can always clean more, cook or wash better (Oakley, 1974a and b) — are to some extent parallel to those encountered in evaluating the productivity of other personal services and commerce.

One thing does become clear, however: it is likely that the solution to the problems of measuring social utilization of human potential will come from aggregate analyses of changes in social production and from comparative analyses of the relative well-being of populations rather than from endless attempts to devise different kinds of individual productivity measures.[12]

## Women in the Labour Market

In terms of their availability for participation in the labour market, women fall into four basic categories: (i) those who do not have important domestic responsibilities, either because they live by themselves or because there are other women in their households in charge of the domestic tasks; (ii) those who can hire substitute houseworkers and thus are freed from the daily routines and time-consuming household chores, although usually not from the responsibility of supervising and directing the work of domestic servants; (iii) those who are devoted solely to domestic chores; and (iv) those who are not able to hire domestic help but have to find gainful employment (usually because the income of other members is too low to support the household). In principle, only in the fourth case is the type of employment the woman looks for governed primarily by her domestic responsibilities.

Of course, women may be in different categories at different stages in their life cycles, according to changes in their marital status, in the number of preschool-age children they have at home, and in their socio-economic status. It should be noted that although the implicit hypothesis here is that there is a relationship between labour force participation and fertility, the link is not automatic or inevitable in either direction, and it is mediated by the type of household structure and by the availability of alternative workers for domestic chores.[13]

Various studies have shown that in most households — the 'nuclear family' being the typical case — the principal earner is a man: if the woman participates in the labour market, she does so as a 'secondary' worker, to supplement the income of the male principal earner (IPEA, 1975; Tokman, 1977). (This does not mean, however, that the income women generate is not at times crucial for the survival of their households.) Furthermore, a good proportion of households are not 'typical' — i.e., extended family arrangements, households headed by women, etc. — and in these cases the determinants of women's work are different.[14] When women who head households have to work, for instance, and do not have someone in their households to take care of domestic chores, the inevitable consequence is utmost poverty.

A thorough understanding of labour supply also requires that consideration be given to the way in which female employment is intrinsically tied into systems of interpersonal relations. For example, Arizpe's study of the *Marias* (Indian women selling goods in the streets of Mexico City) shows the intricate links between family, migration and women's jobs (Arizpe, 1975). Studies of domestic servants in Latin American cities also show that although they seem to be alone (they migrated to the city by themselves and live in their employer's households), they are actually enmeshed in a complex system of kinship ties and social relations, both in the city and in their communities of origin (Smith, 1973; Leff, 1974; Jelin, 1977; for Africa, see Little, 1976).

Besides the constraints on the quantitative aspects of the supply, there are constraints as to the *type* of employment some women (those with heavy domestic responsibilities) can take on. How do we classify 'types of employment' in this respect? Studies of working women in industrialized countries show that women with domestic responsibilities look most often for part-time employment; they are most often employed in jobs that have flexible hours, that allow them to regulate the amount and rhythm of work for themselves, and that are relatively easy to get and just as easy to leave when the need for cash diminishes or when a household crisis requires full-time attention (Morse, 1969).[15] Although there are fewer studies of women in urban centres of developing countries, the same probably holds true for them.

If there were a strong relationship between domestic responsibilities and flexibility in employment conditions at any given time, women would show higher rates of absenteeism and turnover, and higher percentages of part-time employment than men. In the long run, the work history of women would show entries and exits from the labour force according to the changes in their family life. If this were the case, women with domestic responsibilities could not have a long-term job commitment. However, the actual picture of employment conditions of women is not only the result of these supply constraints. It has been shown that at times of labour shortages (such as war) and rising wages, women with domestic responsibilities are 'flexible' enough to overcome their double tasks, and they participate more fully in the labour force (Hauser, 1964). Under such conditions of increased demand, they may change the composition of their households (by calling in older relatives to take care of domestic tasks while they go out to work), find alternative paid houseworkers, or increase their own workloads (by adding outside work to their domestic responsibilities). However, in most developing countries this demand for labour does not exist. In most cases, labour is abundant and unemployment rates are high, especially among 'secondary' workers (Tokman, 1977). Furthermore, in both developed and less developed countries, there seems to be greater differences in the relative employment conditions of men and women than would be warranted by the differences in household responsibilities of men and women.

Unfortunately, there is almost no evidence regarding the effect of all these factors on the labour force participation of women — what types of jobs they hold, the conditions of employment, and what changes they make as their domestic positions and responsibilities change. The information that is available is based on census reports and deals primarily with the determinants of participation rates (Durand, 1975; Standing, 1978). Only very rarely is information regarding the occupational distribution of the female labour force included (Youssef, 1974; CEPAL, 1975). The situation in various Latin American countries has been reviewed by Kirsch (1975), who shows that women in urban areas are concentrated in low-status service jobs, including domestic service. As can be seen in Table 10.1, about one-third of the economically active women in each country are employed in such jobs (Table 10.1 excludes agricultural employment from the total).[16] About 10 per cent are employed in industrial wage work, and a small percentage are involved in traditional crafts, either as self-employed workers or as family helpers. Except in Paraguay, the proportion of women in traditional crafts is rather limited and is lower than that among males. About 15 per cent of the women, and a somewhat lower percentage of males, work as sales personnel — a mixed category, which includes sales work in stores as well as street vending.

As Table 10.1 shows, women often hold white-collar jobs, and the proportion of women in such employment seems to be on the increase. But this increase does not indicate necessarily a change in opportunities for women:

the upward shift in female employment status constitutes an improvement in their situation vis-à-vis males. But this does not mean an unrestricted improvement. Besides the increase in female administrative personnel in Argentina, a great part of the change is found in categories such as dependent professionals, small commercial entrepeneurs, clerical workers . . . And this casts doubts as to the significance of the apparent greater 'equality' of the women participating in the labor force. On the contrary, it seems to indicate that opportunities increase in the intermediate categories, where there is no male competition; that there is a general increase in unnecessary positions in the public bureaucracies; that women are in a disadvantaged position in professions such as medicine, architecture and engineering professions which can be carried out independently

Table 10.1: Occupational Distribution of the Nonagricultural Labour Force in Six Latin American Countries, by Sex, 1970

| | Argentina M | Argentina F | Chile M | Chile F | Mexico M | Mexico F | Nicaragua M | Nicaragua F | Panama M | Panama F | Paraguay M | Paraguay F |
|---|---|---|---|---|---|---|---|---|---|---|---|---|
| *Upper and middle strata* | *21.4* | *26.2* | *15.6* | *22.8* | *21.4* | *18.0* | *15.5* | *22.1* | *16.1* | *17.5* | *15.3* | *19.4* |
| Clerical workers | 6.4 | 1.7 | 3.4 | 2.0. | 7.7 | 5.1 | 2.3 | 1.2 | 2.1 | .8 | 3.5 | 1.5 |
| Administrative personnel | 5.1 | 4.1 | 1.7 | .9 | 2.6 | 1.3 | 2.1 | .4 | 5.4 | 1.2 | 1.0 | 2.2 |
| Independent professionals and semi-professionals | 1.3 | 1.6 | .8 | .8 | 1.4 | .7 | 1.1 | .6 | .6 | .4 | 1.5 | .9 |
| Dependent professionals | 3.1 | 14.6 | 4.9 | 14.1 | 4.9 | 7.0 | 4.3 | 9.1 | 5.7 | 13.0 | 3.2 | 11.1 |
| Self-employed and employers commercial establishments | 5.5 | 4.1 | 4.6 | 4.9 | 4.7 | 3.9 | 5.5 | 10.7 | 2.1 | 2.1 | 6.4 | 5.6 |
| *Sales personnel, street vendors* | *13.2* | *18.8* | *14.4* | *16.3* | *13.4* | *16.3* | *10.3* | *11.1* | *14.1* | *24.4* | *11.9* | *8.0* |
| *Lower strata, manufacturing* | *48.9* | *17.1* | *50.3* | *18.7* | *43.0* | *11.6* | *49.8* | *17.0* | *52.5* | *13.6* | *51.7* | *37.7* |
| wage workers | 40.1 | 12.2 | 40.8 | 11.0 | 35.0 | 8.3 | 37.7 | 6.7 | 42.0 | 8.6 | 35.9 | 9.0 |
| self-employed and family helpers | 8.8 | 5.0 | 9.5 | 7.7 | 8.1 | 3.1 | 11.9 | 10.3 | 10.5 | 5.0 | 15.8 | 28.7 |
| *Lower strata, service sector* | *4.9* | *28.2* | *5.5* | *34.2* | *5.3* | *19.8* | *7.1* | *39.9* | *10.7* | *35.7* | *5.7* | *31.8* |
| wage workers | 4.4 | 25.9 | 5.0 | 31.0 | 4.4 | 15.7 | 5.7 | 36.0 | 8.8 | 30.8 | 4.7 | 28.4 |
| self-employed and family helpers | .5 | 2.3 | .4 | 3.1 | .9 | 4.2 | 1.4 | 3.9 | 1.9 | 5.4 | 1.0 | 3.4 |
| *Others nonspecified* | *11.6* | *9.7* | *14.2* | *8.1* | *16.9* | *34.3* | *17.6* | *9.9* | *6.7* | *8.8* | *15.3* | *3.0* |
| Total | 100.0 | 100.0 | 100.0 | 99.9 | 100.0 | 100.0 | 100.0 | 100.0 | 100.0 | 100.0 | 100.0 | 100.0 |

Source: Recalculated from H. Kirsch, 'La participación de la mujer en los mercados laborales latinoamericanos' in CEPAL, *Mujeres en América Latina: aportes para una discusión* (Mexico, Fondo de Cultura Económica, 1975), pp. 192-3.

and that were traditionally reserved for males . . . (Kirsch, 1975).

A thorough study of female employment in Brazil since 1920 concludes, with a slight change of emphasis, that the new opportunities in industry and services are in more productive, more integrated, positions. Although the increase in the number of positions is not very high, qualitatively the change is important, since it implies a shift in female employment away from agriculture and towards wage work. The authors conclude, however:

> The real fact is that meanwhile, the number of new opportunities for female employment generated by economic development seems to be much smaller than the number of urban women. Therefore, there is, on the one hand, an increase in domestic servants, which for many women reconciles the need to work with the performance of typically female tasks . . . On the other hand, there is a growth of unemployment, especially disguised unemployment, among urban women. Participation rates in non-agricultural activities declined from 1940 to 1950, and have remained low since. Although many of these women seem to be devoted to individual tasks (housework), it seems likely that a good many of them would rather enter the socially productive activities if opportunities were available (Madeira and Singer, 1973).[17]

For some Latin American cities, more specific occupational information exists, and this provides the basis for more detailed analysis of the type of jobs women hold.[18] Merrick (1976 and 1977) reports that while 19.3 per cent of males in Belo Horizonte, Brazil, worked in the 'informal sector', 53.9 per cent of the women were employed in that sector (which included domestic service). These statistics are similar to those for Salvador, Bahia, in Northeastern Brazil, where 21.1 per cent of males and 56.4 per cent of females work in petty production or domestic service (Jelin, 1974). For Mexico City, Arizpe (1977) reports that while 18.1 per cent of active males earn less than the legal minimum wage, the corresponding figure for women is 35.6 per cent. In terms of specific occupational categories, she reports that women were 72 per cent of the unskilled service workers (including domestic service) and 40 per cent of all street vendors. For Peru, Webb reports that women make up 46 per cent of those employed in the 'urban traditional sector' but only 18 per cent of those in the modern sector. Within the traditional sector, women constitute 61 per cent of the self-employed category (Webb, 1974, p. 32). And a study of Cordoba,

**Table 10.2: Household Positions and Type of Employment, by Sex, Belo Horizonte, Brazil, 1972**

|  | % employed | % employed in the informal sector | No. |
|---|---|---|---|
| Males |  |  |  |
| Heads | 85.0 | 14.9 | 1,972 |
| Others | 46.5 | 27.1 | 1,723 |
| Females |  |  |  |
| Heads | 64.0 | 47.3 | 439 |
| Spouses | 15.4 | 36.2 | 1,348 |
| Others | 22.5 | 24.5 | 2,102 |
| Domestic servants | 100.0 | 100.0 | 425 |

Source: T.W. Merrick, 'Employment in the urban informal sector in Latin America', paper presented at the Seminar on Urbanization, Unemployment and Environmental Quality, Johns Hopkins University, 7 March 1977, p. 19.

Argentina, shows that women constitute 63 per cent of 'informal sector' workers (Sanchez, Palmieri and Ferrero, 1976).

Beyond this information about the proportion of women in specific occupations little is known about the conditions of employment or the characteristics of the women involved. Several detailed studies of the informal sector have been carried out that deal both with the productive units and with the workers (Sanchez *et al.,* 1976; Marulanda, 1976); however, very seldom is the information broken down by sex.[19]

Regarding the general relationship between the type of labour force participation and the domestic position of women, the Belo Horizonte study (Merrick, 1977) does give some information (see Table 10.2). For example, it shows that while most male heads of household are employed, fewer of them work in the informal sector than do men who are not heads of households. Among women, the heads of households are also more likely to work, but more of them are in the informal sector than are women who are not household heads. Spouses are less likely to work than 'other' females and, when they do, they tend to work more often in the informal sector than do those in the 'other' category — a result perhaps of the spouses' greater domestic responsibility.

The information just presented gives an idea of the situation of women in the labour market, as well as clear indication of the scarcity of relevant studies.[20] It is likely that the pattern in Latin America of a predominance of women in informal sector jobs and in services and commerce is also widespread in non-Muslim Africa and Asia. It is also likely that in other areas of the world, too, women are entering routine white-collar positions. Unfortunately the data needed to support or refute such suppositions are not available.

## Discrimination and Sex Segregation of Occupations

The conditions of female employment described above cannot be blamed only on the conditions dictated by the role of women in their households. Besides general labour market conditions that affect both men and women, there are specific aspects of the market's operation that bear on the position of women.

Empirical evidence of discrimination against women in the labour market comes from (i) studies showing wage discrimination; (ii) studies showing occupational segregation — that is, certain occupations are closed to women, while others are socially defined as 'women's jobs'; and (iii) discrimination in recruitment criteria — for instance, higher educational levels are required for females in each occupational category than for males. In general, the prevalence of occupational segregation precludes a thorough investigation of the other two dimensions of the problem, since it is very difficult to standardize the male and female populations so as to control for the different occupational structures.[21]

For Third World countries, perhaps the most visible aspect of discrimination is occupational segregation, that is, the definition of some jobs as 'appropriate' or 'inappropriate' for women. Women usually perform tasks that can be seen as extensions of their domestic role. This applies not only to domestic service jobs and those in the informal sector (Jelin, 1974 and 1977) but also to wage work:

In general, tasks reserved for women in the wage labor market are very often analogous to women's responsibilities in the household; they continue performing tasks related to the reproduction of the labor force as teachers, nurses and service workers, while when working in clerical positions they have to satisfy the menial daily needs of industrial and financial enterprise. Thus, while their work is not directly linked to the productive process, it is crucial for the functioning of the capitalist system . . . (Schmink, 1977, p. 1216).

How can such discriminatory practices be explained and conceptualized? Economic theories of discrimination have to rely on 'non-economic' dimensions — or, as economists like to say, on 'labour market imperfections' — to account for the various types of discrimination.[22] Diverse perspectives on the processes of segmentation of labour markets have been developed that apply to developed capitalist economies (Doeringer and Piore, 1971; Gordon, 1972). Up to now, the outcome of such efforts has been the recognition of the need for historical and institutional analyses of the functioning of the labour market (Piore, 1973; Reich, Gordon and Edwards, 1973).

The situation in developing capitalist economies is different, and perhaps more complex, since the historical roots of segmentation have to be traced back to the partial dissolution of precapitalist organizations, as well as to diverse institutional arrangements that are not always well known. These have produced during the last several decades a rapid population growth and rapid urbanization, leading to a large supply of labour that cannot be incorporated into the capital-intensive new industries (tied usually to transnational capital). The results — which would have to be specified for each historical context — have been the development of a highly heterogeneous labour force and the systematic exclusion of large groups of the population from certain occupational opportunities.[23]

In this, women have had to suffer a double burden. On the one hand, both men and women share the consequences of the limited demand for labour. On the other, women are not hired because it is thought that their domestic responsibilities will prevent them from being effective workers. This sexual dualism has been traced to the different sex-related income opportunities, and these, in turn, to the 'peculiar constraints facing women workers, in terms of their actual or probable need to combine employment with child-care responsibilities' (Standing, 1978).

Resorting to 'sexual dualism' as an explanation of discrimination towards women begs the question, however. Such an argument takes for granted the 'natural' role of women in domestic work, and treats all women as if they were equally burdened with or responsible for domestic production. Yet the sexual division of labour within the household is as much the result of historical processes as the segmentation of the labour market itself. Employers and even the women themselves have come to define the supply of labour in this way, but the actual situation — as opposed to the theories about it — may be different, or at least changing.

At a global level, discrimination against women results from a strategy of development and economic growth that excludes large parts of the population from participating in its benefits. Explicit policies to control labour relations and to adapt the ample supply of labour to a limited demand are part of such strategies. At that level, women are one more category of potential workers to be exploited and oppressed through discrimination.

## A Special Case: Female Heads of Households[24]

The discussion presented in this chapter is based on the premiss that the type of economic activities women perform is linked to their domestic responsibilities. Much of the discussion in previous sections assumes that the households in which women live include other adults who work and earn an income, and that women's decisions about labour force participation are therefore related only to their domestic roles. As was mentioned above, however, there are exceptions to the 'normal' household composition, and in such cases the reasons for female participation in the labour market and the nature of that participation will be different from the norm. In this section, the special case of the household headed by a woman will be analyzed, since it presents a test case for several commonly held ideas about employment and domestic responsibilities.

The empirical importance of female-headed households is unquestionable. They are numerically significant in a variety of countries and settings. In rural areas, where men migrate more than women, or where the pattern of temporary migration of males is prevalent (Borawoy, 1976), households may have a woman as head for long periods of time. In these cases, however, there may be some cash remittances from the men that help in the survival efforts of the household, and the woman head and the remaining members are mostly involved in subsistence farming combined with domestic work (Palmer, 1977).

A different situation is that of urban areas, where the large number of households headed by females result from high rates of separation and divorce, widowhood, and the serial monogamous pattern.[25] Furthermore, several authors agree that the percentage of urban households in this category is increasing, although longitudinal data taking into consideration socio-demographic profiles of the households involved are unavailable.[26] There is probably a higher incidence of female-headed households at certain stages of the life cycle (widowhood, for instance, is more likely at older ages), although changes in patterns of divorce and separation will have direct effects on their prevalence at other stages.[27] It is also true, as Ross and Sawhill (1975) point out, that the female-headed household is 'transitional' in a double sense: (i) it is a transitional stage in the life cycle of the woman, since it is preceded and followed by other types of household composition; and (ii) it is a transitional stage in the larger sense in that society's models for marriage and family are changing.

Besides their increasing numerical importance, female-headed households also deserve attention because they are among the poorest households. In their study of Belo Horizonte, Merrick and Schmink (1978) report that while 27.4 per cent of the male-headed households fall below a 100 cruzeiro per person per month poverty line, 44.9 per cent of the female-headed households are in that category. When single heads are excluded, the poverty group accounts for 49 per cent of households with female heads and for 60 per cent of households with widowed heads. Evidence from other studies is consistent with such findings (Durbin, 1975; Sawhill, 1976; Blumberg, 1976).

It is in attempting to explain poverty among female-headed households that the effect of constraints on women's employment becomes most obvious. This is a female population which must earn an income. Work is not of a 'complementary' nature. Female heads are not secondary workers, so that the usual interpretation stressing the lack of labour commitment of secondary workers does not apply. Yet they face a labour market governed by discriminatory norms, especially regarding women with domestic responsibilities. And in this case the domestic responsibilities are likely to be especially heavy, since there is probably a smaller number of other adult females with no outside employment, and at times the household includes an adult male who is unable to work.

Regarding the working status of the female heads, the study of Belo Horizonte shows that 84 per cent of the poor married heads and 70 per cent of the widowed and separated heads work. Among those working, 85 per cent have informal sector jobs. Unfortunately, the study does not report the time devoted to work. It is very likely that their domestic responsibilities do not allow them to work full-time — so that their low income and, probably, high job instability are due to both their informal sector participation and the part-time nature of their employment (Merrick and Schmink, 1978). The authors conclude that:

For poor households headed by women, the economic situation is more difficult and the option of relying on additional workers is less feasible. First, because they are females, heads of these households are more likely to be unemployed, or if employed to have occupations in the informal sector, with correspondingly lower wages than those for male heads. Second, other household members are more likely to be outside the prime working age, and to be female rather than male, therefore facing the same job and earnings constraints as the head. As a result, female-headed households have fewer secondary workers to help bring up family income, and thus the major survival strategy utilized as a whole is less viable to this sub-group (Merrick and Schmink, 1978, p. 25).

The contrast between the employment pattern of the women heads of household in Belo Horizonte and in New York, as reported by Durbin (1975), is striking. The poverty of the former is the result of their difficulties in obtaining stable and well-paid jobs, and therefore of having to take informal sector jobs that can hardly cover the income needs of 'primary' workers. In New York, on the contrary, a good number of women heads of households survive without gainful employ-ment, since they are eligible for welfare payments that discourage their labour force participation. Work in one case, and discouragement in the other, result in poverty. Neither condition — low paying and unstable jobs or welfare payments — is satisfactory, but there seems to be no alternative in societies where the whole institutional structure is based on the expectation that people live in 'nuclear' households, with men as principal earners and women as dependents.

The results of this Belo Horizonte study have been reported in some detail in order to point out the contradictory pressures on women in urban environments who must balance domestic responsibilities and the need to bring in an income. Further studies of female heads of house-hold may show even more clearly the patterns of discrimination and segregation in the labour market, since these are the women who suffer most from discrimination. Studies of households that are not nuclear in structure also call into question the conclusions about women and the labour market that take for granted that the 'normal' and 'natural' condition of women is that of 'spouse' in a nuclear family household.

## Conclusions

This chapter has attempted to discuss the position of women in the urban labour market of developing capitalist societies, placing the subject in its broader context. Within it, special attention has been paid, on the one hand, to the general conditions of the urban labour market in such societies and, on the other, to the specific conditions affecting women, namely the relationship between their domestic work and their availability for outside work, and the discriminatory effects of social norms governing female employment.

Specific studies on the subject to be carried out in the future will have to deal with these issues from a historical perspective, so as to detect interrelated processes of change. Thus, since economic activities are performed both inside the private domestic realm of the household and in socially recognized and specialized units of production, the processes of change in each of them — including the tasks performed, the social relations of production, the technology and the sexual division of labour — have to be analyzed in order to detect the changes in the relative status of men and women (and of different categories of women). Furthermore, since the process of capitalist expansion occurs through the formation and transformation of social classes, the historical change in their patterns of relationships has to constitute the framework for such studies. There are no abstract, universal women, but women immersed in systems of social class relations. Thus, the study of women's activities, as determined by their position in the household, requires a characterization of the variety of households according to their position in the class structure and their change over time.

The former are general orientations which may guide future research. Concrete research suggestions have been included throughout the chapter, when reference was made to the lack of data about various issues. I believe future research projects should start with two theoretical and methodological tasks: (i) the disaggregation of the concept of economic activity, and (ii) the explicit consideration of the household as a mediating structure in women's position in the labour market.

(i) *Disaggregation of the concept of economic activity.* Presently, 'labour force participation' is the dimension most often studied. What is now required is a reconceptualization of 'work' and 'nonwork', a new characterization of various economic activities, be they domestic tasks or 'employment'. Relevant dimensions have to be specified in each type of activity, and historical analysis has to show the transformation diverse tasks go through in specific processes of social change.

(a) Characterization of domestic tasks. Dimensions to be studied include the kind of activities, the technological base and the network of social relations in which the tasks are performed (including the extension of the household into kin and neighbourhood networks), the time required for each task, and the alternative mechanisms for

satisfaction of needs (such as public services).
(b) Characterization of 'employment'. Besides the usual dimensions of type of occupation, type of industry and position, and employment characteristics, other aspects relevant to low-income women include the place of work, job stability, short- or long-term prospects for advancement, time devoted to the job and to connected tasks (transportation, for instance), flexibility of schedules, rhythms of work, and so on.

(ii) *The household as a mediating structure.* Studies of the position of women in economic activity have to include the consideration of household structures and the varying position of women in them, including the study of their historical changes.

(a) Characterization of household structures. Studies of household composition, including other, 'non-nuclear' patterns; and analyses of the division of labour within the various types, in relation to both domestic production and outside employment.

(b) The internal transformation of the household along its domestic cycle and the life cycle of its members. The intra-household division of labour becomes a central point, as it changes over time with the addition of new members, the transformation of domestic tasks, and the employment situation of its members. Basic population-related processes — fertility, mortality, migration — can then be placed in perspective and linked to the daily activities of household members.

Demographic phenomena — fertility, mortality, migration — are intrinsic aspects of the dynamics of the position of women. It is difficult at this point to establish unequivocal causal links or methodologically to separate 'independent' and 'dependent' variables. The methodological path implied in this chapter calls instead for looking for interrelations or chains of events along time, which involves an explicit consideration of the time dimension — both historical and biographical time (Jelin, 1976).

In this dynamic perspective, what becomes significant at the micro level is how an event at one moment in time — completing a certain degree of education, migrating, entering the labour force in a given position, marrying, having a child (or, for that matter, significant changes in the household where the woman lives, such as the death of a close relative, migration of siblings, and so on) — closes or opens up new options for future development by having direct and indirect effects on changes in other relevant dimensions.

At that micro level, then, a basic framework for describing and interpreting processes and events is that of the *life cycle*, the technique for gathering information being the life history.[28] In the context of the issues raised in this chapter, only through systematic study of life histories could the links between domestic responsibilities of women at various stages of the family life cycle and their availability for outside work be investigated. Furthermore, such methods allow the study of the type and stability of employment, of the objective links between other events and labour commitment, and of the existence or absence of occupational career patterns of women. For certain subgroups of the population, the sequential link may not be fertility-participation, but the reverse: changes in career-job attainment may influence the timing of child-bearing.

When relating the individual needs to the larger social context, cohort analysis is a useful instrument (Ryder, 1971).[29] Once the disaggregation of the time dimension is introduced, the interpretation of 'age' as a variable in survey and census analysis gains a new importance, because the dimension 'age' combines the life cycle and the cohort. Successive cohorts were born and raised in different circumstances, having different educational opportunities, different patterns of rural and urban residence, different family- and fertility-related patterns of behaviour. Given the types and rates of change in most societies during the present century, it is impossible to assume that each new cohort will follow the life cycle of the previous one. Lower participation rates of older women at a given moment, or higher proportions in informal sector jobs, do not warrant inferences regarding the future of the younger women, or the past of the older ones: there may be a tendency to leave the labour force with advancing age, or to shift to informal sector jobs. But it is more likely that the differences reflect a process of change that is taking place through intercohort shifts (Jelin, 1970).[30]

Finally, the explicit introduction of the time dimension brings up the issue of the relationship between individual biographies and historical time (Jelin, 1976). How can the historical time of social development be combined with the biographical time of the life cycles of people who, as individuals, adapt themselves to the historical time they live in and, as part of society, also 'make history'? The collection of life histories can tell much, especially in qualitative terms, about day-to-day functioning of a given society, and about the processes of change. But it requires the supplement of macro-historical data to complete the picture of change.

## Notes

1. The complete socialisation of domestic labor requires the socialization of the reproduction of living individuals, and, at the same time, capital requires the 'freedom' of these individuals in the labor market. Suppose capital incorporates under its own relations of production the reproduction of living individuals. If they are commodities, then they are themselves private property, and cannot function as the 'free' wage-laborers necessary for capitalist production. If they are not commodities, then capital is not capital, for the rationale of capitalist production – the extension of value – has disappeared. Thus, in either case, for capital to produce the living laborer is to subvert its own relations of production (Himmelweit and Mohun, 1977, p. 25).

An analogous but more complex counter-factual argument could be developed in relation to the state taking over domestic labour within a capitalist mode of production.
   2. Aside from mention of the social isolation in the performance of domestic tasks, the dimension of participation in the 'private' and the 'public' spheres as related to the position of women in different societies has not been explored in depth, either from a theoretical or from a comparative perspective (Rosaldo and Lamphere, 1974; Larguía and Dumouilin, 1975; Jelin, 1977).
   3. On the distinction between *production* of a labour force for capitalism and *reproduction* of the labour force within capitalism, see Singer (1977).
   4. A recent study carried out in Kenya, for instance, shows that 'greatly different labor force participation rates resulted from questions based on words such as "jobs" and "work" . . . In the present survey, for example, use of the word "job" caused an underestimate of female participation, because unpaid family work was frequently not considered as a "job". Using only the word "work", on the other hand, caused an overestimate of female participation, because housework was frequently considered as "work".' (Anker and Knowles, 1978, p. 159).
   5. Issues under discussion include whether domestic labour produces the commodity 'labour power'; whether it can be considered a mode of production (although a subordinated one); whether it should be considered as 'productive labour' or 'unproductive labour'; whether it is indispensable within capitalism or alternative organizations could exist. In most of these discussions the family and the domestic realm are approached from the perspective of their 'functionality' within capitalism. An alternative approach, in which the family is seen as a working-class asset in its struggle against capital, is presented by Humphries (1977). A further issue opened up to future analysis is the need for an explicit distinct consideration of the maintenance role of the household and its reproductive role. The structural conditions of performance of both tasks may not be the same, thus posing different challenges to the expansion of capitalism (see Deere, Humphries and Leon de Leal, in Chapter 4 of this volume).
   6. 'Domestic labor is therefore a twofold process: it is both the means of maintenance and reproduction of the worker, and it is the means whereby, via 'the annihilation of the necessities of life' (Marx), the worker is continually 'free' to reappear in the labor market. Not only are the participants in the domestic and capitalist labor process thereby reproduced; so are the respective relations of production' (Himmelweit and Mohun, 1977, pp. 28-9).
   7. Recent historical studies have shown that in the West the clearcut separation between women in the private home and men in the public sphere is to some extent a product of industrialization (Oakley, 1974a). For descriptions

and interpretations of other, non-Western cultures, see Boserup (1970), Reiter (1976) and Meillassoux (1977). Extreme cases of spatial segregation between work and residence, which involve seasonal migrations, are discussed by Borawoy (1976) and Meillassoux (1977).

8. As a first approximation, in this chapter it is assumed that in urban areas of underdeveloped capitalist societies, households are the basic social units for the set of activities required for the daily maintenance of the labour force, for the reproduction of the population and the socialization of the new members, and for the care of other nonworking members of the family. No assumption is made as to the prevalent household composition, or kin or family structure, which may be extremely variable and require in-depth study as they are affected by — and affect — the position of women. However, there may be different networks of social relations, not necessarily co-residing in households, in charge of the various tasks, involving at times long-distance moves and residential shifts at various stages in the lifecycle (see Oppong in Chapter 6 of this volume).

9. The following is one example of many such criticisms:

the absence of markets for domestic labor has not deterred some bourgeois economists [Mincer, 1962; Becker, 1965; Gramm, 1974 and 1975] from applying their commodity fetishisms to non-commodities. This proceeds by such methods as considering the allocation of a wife's time between house-work, wage-labor and leisure to be part of the constrained utility maximisation problem for a household. Like all 'analysis' set in such a framework, this approach is superficial because it does not penetrate the actual relations of *production* involved; it considers only the products, and there only as providers of utility. (Himmelweit and Mohun, 1977, p. 19)

The problem of the reduction of domestic work and wage labour is commensurate of time is present in other authors as well (Harrison, 1973).

10. The exclusion from the GNP of goods and services that are produced and consumed in the home creates artificial changes when goods or services that had been marketed are consumed in the home or vice versa. The paradox of a man marrying his maid and thereby decreasing the GNP is by now a classic example. Estimates of the monetary value of housework vary and are increasingly attracting the attention of social scientists (Glazer-Malbin, 1976; see also Kahne and Kohen, 1975).

11. Historically, the productivity of domestic work has not increased as rapidly as that of other economic activities. Although there have been some technological innovations, domestic production has not experienced changes in its social organization.

12. It could be interesting to approach the different social activities from the point of view of their contribution to the standard of living or well-being of a population. Household production and the family gain a new light when seen in this perspective (Humphries, 1977).

13. The relationship between female participation in the labour force and fertility is extensively discussed by Youssef in Chapter 8 of this volume.

14. Little is known about variations in household structures cross-culturally, and about their change over time and as families go through the process of migration and urbanization. Undoubtedly, a better understanding of the supply of female labour calls for a more thorough knowledge — both theoretical and empirical — of this subject. For an important step in this direction, see Garcia and Oliveira (1978a and b); Garcia, Munoz and Oliveira (1978).

15. The location of the job is also a crucial consideration. Women with small children can work in their own homes and therefore disrupt their domestic

chores less than they would if they went out to work.

16. The case of Mexico seems to be deviant, but it probably is not so, given the very high proportion in the 'other nonspecified' category. It is very likely that most of the women in the latter category are actually employed in the lower status jobs in the service sectors. This would be congruent with the other countries and with the information regarding Mexico in 1960 (Kirsch, 1975, p. 194).

17. Data for Venezuela (Schmink, 1977) also lead to the same general conclusions.

18. Several definitions and characterizations of types of jobs have been proposed in the literature, but they cannot be discussed in detail here. For the conceptualization of the 'informal' sector, see Mazumdar (1976); Sethuraman (1976); Souza and Tokman (1976); Merrick (1977); Senghass-Knoblich (1977). For other relevant characterizations of employment structures in urban peripheral capitalist areas, see Singer (1977), and the discussions on marginality in Nun (1969), Cardoso (1971), and Germani (1973).

19. The study by Webb does provide data about income differentials in Peru. In comparing the incomes of men and women in the largest categories in the traditional and the modern sectors, namely the self-employed in the former and the factory workers in the latter, Webb found that: 'Though the mean income of factory workers is 50 percent higher, it is clear that this can be entirely attributed to the much larger proportion of women in the self-employed group. In fact, self-employed men enjoy a slightly higher income tham male "factory workers" ' (1974, p. 36). The data are the following:

|  | Self-employed | Factory worker |
| --- | --- | --- |
| Mean income (1,000 soles) | 2.0 | 3.0 |
| Male | 3.3 | 3.0 |
| Female | 1.1 | 2.1 |

20. Although an effort was made to cover studies in other Third World areas, I was unable to locate any except for one by Youssef (1974), which shows the limited participation of women in Arab countries and their relative concentration in professional jobs, and several others that dealt with participation rates rather than employment conditions and occupational distribution (Durand, 1975; Standing and Sheehan, 1978). An effort to collect the existing local studies, and to reanalyze them from a comparative perspective, is urgently needed.

21. These issues are discussed, and the relevant literature is reviewed, in Kahne and Kohen (1975). The various articles included in Lloyd (1975) cover the situation in the United States. In general, the studies available were done in developed, rather than developing countries. They show that although a great part of the income differential can be explained by the different occupational distribution, there are still some important differences left once that factor is controlled for.

22. The various approaches and issues raised here regarding occupational segregation of women are discussed in the articles included in Blaxall and Reagan (1976). Economic theories of discrimination regarding women are reviewed in Kahne and Kohen (1975).

23. The relevant literature for Latin America includes the widely discussed issues of 'marginality' and 'dependent development'; see Cardoso and Faletto (1969); Nun (1969); and Cardoso (1971). For a theoretical discussion directly linked to the political economy of work, see Singer (1977).

24. A thorough discussion of the subject would require a critical investigation of the social and census definitions of 'household head'. Undoubtedly, there are

social and cultural constraints in defining a woman as household head when there are adult males in the house. In the following pages, the notion of head is taken at face value, recognizing that research is needed as to the content of the definition.

25. Information from diverse places and sources indicate the importance of this situation. In New York City in 1970, 30% of all households were headed by women (40% of nonwhite households) (Durbin, 1975); 13% of all households in Brazil in 1970 and 16.6% in Belo Horizonte (Merrick and Schmink, 1978); 14% in Guayaquil, Ecuador, and 20% in Santiago, Chile (Wolfe, 1975). It can be assumed that these figures are lower than the actual number of cases, given the prevailing cultural norms valuing the 'complete' family. Underreporting may be serious at times.

26. Thus, Merrick and Schmink (1978) report that the percentage of female-headed households increased from 10.7% to 13% in Brazil between 1960 and 1970; and Sawhill (1976) indicates that the growth of female-headed households in the United States is nearly ten times higher than that of two-parent households. See also Tinker (1976).

27. Barroso (1978), analyzing the situation in Brazil, shows that the incidence of female-headed households increases with the age of the head. She includes among the explanatory factors the fact that younger women with children, when they separate, tend to go back to the parent's home, while older women tend to remain in their own households, probably because they do not have homes to go to.

28. An example of the type of analysis feasible with life histories dealing with education, migration, family formation and occupations in a sample of ten men is found in Balan, Browning and Jelin (1973). Recent developments in life history analysis have shown it to be a means for drawing social inferences that go beyond the micro-level cases (Bertaux, 1978).

29. An example of cohort analysis of female participation rates is found in Recchini de Lattes (1978).

30. Thus, the construction of 'synthetic cohorts' at times of rapid social change is unwarranted. A similar technique, used in anthropological studies to construct domestic development cycles, is evidently more reliable the less social change is taking place (Goody, 1958; Arizpe, 1973).

# References

Anker, R. and J.C. Knowles (1978) 'A micro-analysis of female labor force participation in Africa' in Standing and Sheehan

Arizpe, L. (1973) *Parentesco y economía en una sociedad nalma: Nican Pehua Zacatipan*, Mexico, Instituto Nacional Indigenista

―――― (1975) *Indígenas en la ciudad de México: el caso de las 'Marias'*, Mexico, Sepsetentas

―――― (1977) 'Women in the informal labor sector: the case of Mexico City', *Signs*, 3, 1

Balan, J., H.L. Browning and E. Jelin (1973) *Men in a developing society: geographic and social mobility in Monterrey, Mexico*, Austin, University of Texas Press

Barroso, C. (1978) 'As mulheres chefas de familia no Brazil', mimeo., paper presented a the meeting of the Associacao Brasileira de Estudos de Populacao, Sao Paulo, October

Becker, G. (1965) 'A theory of the allocation of time', *Economic Journal, 75*

Bertaux, D. (1978) 'Une image toute differente. De l'approache biographique à la transformation de la pratique sociologique', mimeo., paper presented at the 9th World Congress of Sociology, Uppsala, 14-19 August

Blaxall, M. and B.B. Reagan (eds.) (1976) *Women and the workplace: the implications of occupational segregation*, supplement to *Signs, 1,* 3, part 2

Blumberg, R.L. (1976) 'Fairy tales and facts: economy, family, fertility, and the female' in Tinker and Bramsen

Borawoy, M. (1976) 'The functions and reproduction of migrant labor: comparative material from Southern Africa and the United States', *American Journal of Sociology, 81,* 5

Boserup, E. (1970) *Woman's role in economic development,* London, George Allen and Unwin

Cardoso, F.H. (1971) 'Comentarios sobre los conceptos de sobrepoblación relativa y marginalidad', *Revista Latinoamericana de Ciencias Sociales, 1-2*

—— and E. Faletto (1969) *Desarrollo y dependencia en America Latina,* Mexico, Siglo XXI

CEPAL (Comisión Económica para América Latina) (1975) *Mujeres en América Latina: aportes para una discusión,* Mexico, Fondo de Cultura Económica

Conference of Socialist Economics (1976) *On the political economy of women,* CSE Pamphlet no. 2, London, Stage One

Coulson, M., B. Magas and H. Wainwright (1975) 'The housewife and her labor under capitalism', *New Left Review, 89*

Doeringer, P. and M. Piore (1972) *Internal labor markets and manpower analysis,* Lexington, Mass., Heath Lexington Books

Durand, J. (1975) *The labor force in economic development,* Princeton, Princeton University Press

Durbin, E. (1975) 'The vicious cycle of welfare: problems of female-headed households in New York City', in Lloyd

Garcia, B. and O. de Oliveira (1978a) 'Hacia una caracterización sociodemográfica de las unidades domésticas en la ciudad de México', mimeo., Mexico, El Colegio de Mexico

—— —— (1978b) 'La división del trabajo en unidades domésticas de diferentes grupos sociales', mimeo., Mexico, El Colegio de Mexico

——, H. Muñoz and O. de Oliveira (1978) 'Migración, familia y fuerza de trabajo en la ciudad de Mexico', paper presented at the Symposium on Internal Migrations and Development, UNESCO-CLACSO, Mexico, September

Gardiner, J. (1975) 'Women's domestic labor', *New Left Review, 89*

Germani, G. (1973) *El concepto de marginalidad,* Buenos Aires, Nueva Vision

Glazer-Malbin, N. (1976) 'Housework', *Signs, 1,* 4

Goody, J. (ed.) (1958) *The developmental cycle of domestic groups,* Cambridge, Cambridge University Press

Gordon, D. (1972) *Theories of poverty and underemployment,* Lexington, Mass., Heath Lexington Books

Gramm, W.L. (1974) 'The demand for the wife's non-market time', *Southern Economic Journal, 41*

—— (1975) 'Household utility maximisation and the working wife', *American Economic Review, 65*

Harrison, J. (1973) 'Political economy of housework', *Bulletin of the CSE, 3,* 1

Hauser, P. (1964) 'Labor force' in R. Faris (ed.), *Handbook of modern sociology,* Chicago, Rand McNally

Himmelweit, S. and S. Mohun (1977) 'Domestic labour and capital', *Cambridge Journal of Economics, 1,* 1

Humphries, J. (1977) 'Class struggle and the persistence of the working-class family', *Cambridge Journal of Economics, 1,* 3

IPEA (1975) *Sistemas de informacão para politicas de emprego*, Brasilia, IPEA

Jelin, E. (1970) 'Estructura occupacional, cohortes y ciclo vital', *Conferencia Regional Latinoamericana de Población*, Mexico, Actas 2

—— (1974) 'La bahiana en la fuerza de trabajo: actividad doméstica, producción simple y trabajo asalariado en Salvador, Brasil', *Demografía y Economía, 8*, 3

—— (1976) 'El tiempo biográfico y el cambio histórico: reflexiones sobre el uso de historias de vida a partir de la experiencia de Monterrey', *Estudios Sociales No. 1*, Buenos Aires, CEDES

—— (1977) 'Migraton and labor force participation of Latin American women: the domestic servants in the cities', *Signs, 3*, 1

Kahne, H. and A.I. Kohen (1975) 'Economic perspectives on the roles of women in the American economy', *Journal of Economic Literature, 13*, 4

Kirsch, H. (1975) 'La participación de la mujer en los mercados laborales latinoamericanos', in CEPAL

Larguía, I. and J. Dumouilin (1975) 'Aspects of the conditions of women's labor', *NACLA's Latin America and Empire Report, IX*

Leff, G. (1974) 'Algunas características de las empleadas domésticas y su publicación en el mercado de trabajo de la ciudad de México', thesis, Mexico, UNAM

Little, K. (1976) 'Women in African towns south of the Sahara: the urbanization dilemma', in Tinker and Bramsen

Lloyd, C.B. (ed.) (1975) *Sex, discrimination and the division of labor*, New York, Columbia University Press

Madeira, F.R. and P. Singer (1973) *Estrutura do emprego e trabalho feminino no Brasil: 1920-1970*, Sao Paulo, CEBRAP, Caderno 13

Marulanda, O. (1976) *El sector informal en la economía urbana de Bogotá*, Bogota, OFISEL

Mazumdar, D. (1976) 'The urban informal sector', *World Development, 4*, 8

Meillassoux, C. (1977) *Mujeres, graneros y capitales*, Mexico, Siglo XXI

Merrick, T.W. (1976) 'Employment and earnings in the informal sector in Brazil: the case of Belo Horizonte', *The Journal of Developing Areas, 10*

—— (1977) 'Employment in the urban informal sector in Latin America', paper presented at the Seminar on Urbanization, Unemployment and Environmental Quality, Johns Hopkins University, 7-9 March

—— and M. Schmink (1978) 'Female-headed households and urban poverty in Brazil', mimeo., paper prepared for workshop on 'Women in Poverty: What Do We Know?', Belmont, Maryland, 30 April-2 May

Mincer, J. (1962) 'Labor force participation of married women: a study of labor supply' in National Bureau Committee for Economic Research, *Aspects of Labor Economics*, Princeton, Princeton University Press

Morse, D. (1969) *The peripheral worker*, New York, Columbia University Press

Nun, J. (1969) 'Superpoblacion relativa, ejército industrial de reserva y masa marginal', *Revista Latinoamericana de Sociología, 5*, 2

Oakley, A. (1974a) *Housewife*, London, Penguin

—— (1974b) *The sociology of housework*, London, Martin Robertson

Oppong, C. (1978) 'Family structure and women's productive and reproductive roles; some conceptual and methodological issues', Chapter 6

Palmer, I. (1977) 'Rural women and the basic needs approach to development', *International Labor Review, 115*, 1

Peek, P. (1978) 'Family composition and married female employment: the case of Chile' in Standing and Sheehan

Piore, M.J. (1973) 'Fragments of a "Sociological" theory of wages', *Papers and Proceedings, American Economic Review, 63*

Recchini de Lattes, Z. (1978) 'Las mujeres en la actividad económica en Argentina, Bolivia y Paraguay', mimeo., Buenos Aires, CENEP

Reich, M., D.M. Gordon and R.C. Edwards (1973) 'A theory of labor market segmentation', *Papers and Proceedings, American Economic Review, 63*

Reiter, R. (1976) *Toward an anthropology of women*, New York, Monthly Review Press

Rosaldo, M.Z. and L. Lamphere (1974) 'Women, culture and society: a theoretical overview' in M.Z. Rosaldo and L. Lamphere (eds.), *Women, culture and society*, Stanford, Stanford University Press

Ross, H.L. and I. Sawhill (1975) *Time of transition: the growth of families headed by women*, Washington, The Urban Institute

Ryder, N. (1971) 'The cohort as a concept in the study of social change', *American Sociological Review, 30, 2*

Sanchez, C.E., H. Palmieri and F. Ferrero (1976) *Desarrollo urbano y sector informal en la ciudad de Córdoba (Argentina)*, Geneva, ILO mimeo., World Employment Programme research paper, restricted

Sawhill, I. (1976) 'Discrimination and poverty among women who head families' in Blaxall and Reagan

Schmink, M. (1977) 'El desarrollo dependiente y la division del trabajo por sexo: Venezuela', *Revista Mexicana de Sociología, 39, 4*

Seccombe, W. (1974) 'The housewife and her labor under capitalism', *New Left Review, 83*

—— (1975) 'Domestic labor − reply to critics', *New Left Review, 94*

Senghass-Knoblich, E. (1977) 'Informal sector and peripheral capitalism: a critique of a prevailing concept of development', *Manpower and Unemployment Research, 10, 2*

Sethuraman, S.V. (1976) 'The urban informal sector: concept, measurement and policy', *International Labor Review, 114, 1*

Singer, P. (1977) *Economia politica do trabalho*, Sao Paulo, Editora HUCITEC

Smith, M.L. (1973) 'Domestic service as a channel of upward mobility for the lower class woman: the Lima case', in A. Pescatello (ed.), *Female and male in Latin America*, Pittsburgh, University of Pittsburgh Press

Souza, P.R. and V.E. Tokman (1976) 'The informal urban sector in Latin America', *International Labor Review, 114, 3*

Standing, G. (1978) *Labor force participation and development*, Geneva, ILO

—— and G. Sheehan (eds.) (1978) *Labor force participation in low-income countries*, Geneva, ILO

Tinker, I. (1976) 'Introduction: the seminar on women in development' in Tinker and Bramsen

—— and M. Bramsen (eds.) (1976) *Women and world development*, Washington, DC, Overseas Development Council

Tokman, V. (1977) *Dinámica del mercado de trabajo urbano: el sector informal urbano en América Latina*, Santiago, PREALC

Waerness, K. (1978) 'The invisible state: women's work at home', *Acta Sociologica*, supplement

Webb, R. (1974) 'Income and employment in the urban modern and traditional sector of Peru', mimeo.

Wolfe, M. (1975) 'La participación de la mujer en el desarrollo de America Latina', in CEPAL

Youssef, N. (1974) *Women and work in developing countries*, Population Monograph Series, no. 15, Berkeley, University of California

# 11 SEX DISCRIMINATION IN THE URBAN LABOUR MARKETS: SOME PROPOSITIONS BASED ON INDIAN EVIDENCE

T.S. Papola

## Urbanization and Women

Urbanization, a natural corollary of development, is accompanied by an increase in production per worker and in levels of income generally, and a shift from subsistence and precapitalist production to commercialized, surplus-producing production. The effects of these changes, however, are not felt uniformly by different groups in the population and work force. The opportunities that result from urbanization are rather unequally shared between the urban-born and better-educated and -trained residents, on the one hand, and the illiterate and unskilled rural migrants, on the other. One of the most serious inequities generated by urbanization in developing countries is in the difference of its impact on men and women. In India, at least, the first effect that can be seen is a change in the sex ratio in urban areas; the number of females relative to males declines as male migrants swell the ranks of the urban population and women are left behind in the villages. Because the urban labour market discriminates against women much more than the rural labour market, the participation of women in economic activity declines. Finally, the limited opportunities available to women are mostly in low-paid, low-status jobs in the unorganized sector, jobs that do not offer any opportunity for advancement or for the training that could give them a chance to enter the organized sector at a later stage.

These demographic and economic consequences of urbanization for women in general, and for women workers in particular, have not yet been studied in sufficient detail to provide definite conclusions for analytical and policy purposes. This chapter explores the question of women workers in the urban labour market in developing countries on the basis of evidence available from studies of two of the largest urban centres in India.[1] It focuses particularly on the women workers in the informal sector. Because of its exploratory character, it raises more questions than it answers; its main objective is to highlight the types of questions that need to be examined in further research.

268

## Urban Labour Market Segmentation

In order to study the condition of women workers in an urban situation and to identify sex discrimination in employment opportunities and earnings, a number of variables other than sex must be controlled for, as sex discrimination can also entail discrimination based on social class, domicile (resident/migrant) status, etc. It is not easy to analyze the effect of each of these multiple sources of discrimination separately; one possible method, however, is to consider population groups that have somewhat homogenous attributes.

The formal-informal sector dichotomy has been adopted here as a frame of reference, although it is recognized that the distinction does not have any great scientific or analytical validity. Certainly, the dichotomous framework is not adequate for most analytical purposes in the study of the structure of urban economies. Even in the informal sector, differences in modes of work – regular wage labour, labour in small organizations, casual wage labour and self-employment – are glaring enough to suggest a multitude of situations and to imply a probable continuum of modes and organizations of production through the entire urban economy. The dichotomy is used here only because it can highlight certain important features of women's employment, if it is defined in a way that broadly distinguishes between regularity/ irregularity and security/insecurity of employment, and that shows sharp differences in levels of earnings.

The labour market in the informal sector is characterized by ease of entry and informality of hiring procedure, and that of the formal sector by severe restrictions on entry (because of the standardization of hiring norms) and formalization of hiring procedures. This difference is a major source of segmentation of the labour market; analysis relying on this dichotomous classification of an urban economy is likely to be particularly useful for studying women workers' issues, because it has been observed that women find it difficult to break the norms and procedures barrier, and to enter the more structured organizations of the formal sector. Their failure to enter this segment of the urban labour market is clearly a result of discrimination by employers, although the reasons for this discrimination are not yet clear.

The fact that certain highly structured and socially conscious organizations like public services do have a significant proportion of women among their work force suggests that discrimination may be based on prejudice rather than on any inherent differences in capability, productivity or efficiency between the sexes. Pre-entry discrimination is found to be most rampant in middle-level organizations: small enterprises that use hired labour but are relatively unstructured and unregulated. The highly organized sector does allow women to enter – even if only in small numbers. The unorganized sector, of course, has no bars to entry and, therefore, a sizeable proportion of women workers work in this sector.[2] Post-entry discrimination in the placement of women workers is practised even by the organized sector, where it is rationalized on the basis of occupational suitability. Wage discrimination is difficult to practice in organizations in this sector, but it is likely to be fairly widespread in the semi-organized and unorganized sectors.

## Women Workers in the Urban Informal Sector

The proposition that the discrimination in employment of women is, to a certain extent, a function of the structure and degree of formalization of production organization can very well be extended beyond the formal-informal sectors to include different modes and patterns of production.

As was pointed out in the preceding section, even in the informal sector (which, in the definition we have adopted, includes employees of small establishments, casual workers and self-employed workers), there are significant variations in employment patterns, working conditions and wages of women workers. For example, among the casual workers (i.e., wage earners not regularly attached to any employer or establishment but employed on a day-to-day basis), women constitute around 15 per cent of the workers, but they form only 6 per cent of the regular work force of the small establishments (those employing less than 10 workers in any activity) and 4 per cent of the 'independent' workers (self-employed workers operating with negligible amounts of capital, whose earnings could mostly be considered as 'wages'). Although in all three categories the women workers in the samples from Bombay and Ahmedabad worked for almost all the days in a month, the casual workers earned an average of Rs.105 per month, those working for small establishments earned Rs.217 per month, and independent workers earned Rs.250 per month. The relative differences among the three categories are similar for men, although – as will be shown below – men earn more than women in all categories. What is significant is that the subsectors with the highest proportion of women workers (i.e., those with the least bars to entry) also generally pay the lowest wages. On this basis, we can distinguish not only between the formal sector (in which about 6 per cent of the workers are women in the cities I have studied) and informal sector (10 per cent are women) but also among the various segments of the informal sector itself.

Age is one characteristic that indicates differences in treatment of women workers and male workers in the formal and informal sectors in India. The average woman worker in the formal sector is 30 years old, her male counterpart is 36 years old; in the informal sector, the average female worker is 34 years old, the average male worker 32 years old. Women have a higher average age than male workers in the casual and independent categories, but women workers in small establishments are much younger than not only their male counterparts but also female workers in other segments of the informal sector. Since employment in small establishments is somewhat the same as employment in the formal sector, it can be said that women who work in the informal sector are significantly older than women in the formal sector as well as men in the informal sector.

Several hypotheses can be suggested to explain this finding, all of which need further investigation. It may be that female workers take up employment only after an increase in family size and other factors drive the family to economic distress, and therefore they enter the informal sector because they either have no work experience or have not worked for some time. Another explanation is that women in the informal sector stay there, while men do get a chance to graduate to the formal sector.[3] An additional factor is education: jobs in the formal sector are available mostly to the educated and, since education of women is a relatively recent phenomenon, the women who are educated and can qualify for jobs in the formal sector tend to be younger. Still another hypothesis is that these women are mostly migrants and may have been engaged in economic activity in their villages before they migrated to the city.

In the case of women workers of the informal sectors of Bombay and Ahmedabad, it is plausible to argue that most of them entered the labour market rather late and only when compelled by the economic circumstances of their households; they did not intend to become part of the labour force from the outset. This is particularly true of the majority of women migrant workers (who constitute one-half of the informal sector women workers and only 25 per cent of the formal sector women workers). Although the migrant women who are currently working in the informal sector migrated at an average age of 17, they did not start work immediately. While the migrants on the whole waited for an average period of six months before starting work, the average woman migrant did not start to work until about five years after migration. It seems a natural consequence of the pattern of motivations of the women migrants: 85 per cent of women migrants came to the city to join the family; only 15 per cent migrated specifically with a view to finding employment in the city. Yet all these migrant women are now working in the informal sector. It seems that rising prices and increasing family size compelled them to work in order to supplement family income. If we look at the entire sample of informal sector workers (men and women), we find that 35 per cent of the women in these households are working or looking for work, as compared to only 10 per cent of women in the entire population. Within the group of informal sector workers, women's participation rate bears a consistently negative relationship with the income levels of the households. For example, among the casual workers' families with very low income (less than Rs.100 per month) over 60 per cent of the women members work, while in the families with incomes of Rs.100-200 and RS.200-300 per month, the proportion of women working out of the home are as low as 8 and 1 per cent, respectively.

The force of economic hardship caused to the household of these workers seems to have overriden the need for mothers to stay at home to look after their young children. In fact, the common hypothesis that the women withdraw from the labour force temporarily during the child-bearing and child-rearing years does not seem to hold in the case of casual and independent women workers of the urban informal sector. The participation rate among women belonging to households headed by male or female informal sector workers is found to be lower among women with no children than among those with one or two children below the age of five. Among the casual workers' families, 30 per cent of the women with no children participate in economic activity, but their participation rate shoots up to 70 per cent as soon as they have one or two children below the age of five. The young children may need the care of their mothers, but supplementing family incomes seems to be of greater importance. Among a number of categories of casual and independent workers (e.g., vegetable vendors with fixed locations and construction workers), children are taken along to the place of work by their mothers, a 'convenience' which is not available to the women workers of the formal sector.

Economic necessity does not permit the casual women workers to withdraw from the labour force to look after their children; it seems that having children in fact compels them to participate in work outside the home. The participation rate among the women of these households is found to be high in all age groups: 37 per cent in the group aged 15-25, 35 per cent in the group aged 25-30, 37 per cent in the groups aged 30-40 and 40-50, and 26 per cent in the group aged 50-60. There is a slight decline in the participation rate in the 25-30 age group, as compared to the earlier age group, but it is not substantial enough to validate the 'withdrawal-due-to-children' hypothesis, particularly in view of the evidence cited earlier regarding the relationship between participation rate and children. In fact, the hypothesis implies that women are free to choose to work or not to work away from home. But in the case of women in the very low-income groups, such as the informal sector workers, such a choice does not seem to be available.

## Sex Discrimination in the Urban Informal Sector

The need to supplement meagre household income leads to significant work participation among women belonging to the households of informal sector workers, but such participation does not seem to improve their economic status *vis-à-vis* either the men in the household[4] or those in the labour market. In 75 per cent of the families in the urban samples in India, one or more of the women members work, but women are principal earners in only 15 per cent of the households. This is not because these women work for shorter periods than men – women and men in these families both work for about 25 days per month – but because women earn much less than men. A male casual worker earns an average of Rs.200 per month, but a female casual worker earns only Rs.105. A male independent worker earns Rs.392 per month, while a female independent worker earns Rs.250. In small establishments, a male employee earns Rs.240 and female employee Rs.217. The degree of discrimination, measured as the ratio of male wage to female wage, is thus highly significant in the informal sector of the urban labour market.

How much of this discrimination is due to restriction on entry to certain types of occupations and how much to post-entry discrimination in the form of payment of different wages to male and female workers? In the urban informal sector, the highest wages are found in manufacturing, followed by selling, vending and hawking of goods, construction and transport work, and, at the lowest end of the scale, personal services, laundering, sanitary services and domestic work.

Women workers are distributed among these various activities more or less exactly in the reverse order of earnings. The largest proportion (one-quarter) is in domestic work, another 15 per cent in sanitary services, 12 per cent in construction, 8 per cent in hawking and peddling of goods, 7 per cent in transport and 10 per cent in other occupations.[5] Approximately 15 per cent of working women are employed in manufacturing, but usually in such peripheral activities as packing and labelling, rather than in the central processing activities that carry relatively higher wages. Such skilled jobs are mainly occupied by men. Therefore, the relatively low levels of earnings of women workers in the informal sector reflect, to a large extent, the pattern of occupations in which they are engaged.

The difference in men's and women's wages for the same jobs is a better indicator of discrimination, however. As Table 11.1 shows, in some cases, men earn two or three times more than women in the same occupations. It should also be noted that the earnings of women who are self-employed are quite comparable to — sometimes even higher than — the earnings of their male counterparts, as can be seen from Table 11.2.

The different patterns of male-female earnings in the two categories of workers suggest that the discrimination against women in the payment of wages has no real economic basis. If they work independently, women's earnings are quite comparable to men's, but once they work for others, their wages are significantly lower than men's. The discrimination is the result of a system of production based on wage labour; it is not based on differences in men's and women's productivity and performance, but rather is a result of employers taking advantage of certain characteristics of the labour supply that are unfavourable to women.

What are these unfavourable characteristics? Employers, who are interested in minimizing costs, will not hesitate to pay low wages to their workers — or to as many of them as possible. Therefore, whether and to what extent a group of workers is discriminated against would depend on the power that they can wield with the employers. Generally, workers' power is directly proportional to the extent to which they are organized. In the informal sector, workers — male or female — are generally unorganized, and that may be one reason why they get lower wages than those working in the formal sector. But lack of organization is a common disadvantage and does not explain special discrimination against women in the informal sector.

The source of wage discrimination is, therefore, to be sought in the

## Table 11.1: Average Monthly Earnngs of Male and Female Casual Workers in Ahmedabad, India, 1976

| Occupation | Average monthly earnings (Rs.) | |
| --- | --- | --- |
| | Male | Female |
| Sales assistant | 197.25 | 75.00 |
| Hawkers, peddlers and street vendors | 194.75 | 102.25 |
| Tailors, dressmakers and garment-makers | 246.00 | 101.75 |
| Tool-makers, machinists, welders and metal-engravers | 201.25 | 90.25 |
| Bricklayers, plasterers and other construction workers | 135.00 | 93.25 |
| Checkers, testers, sorters and related workers | 177.25 | 165.50 |
| Compositors, printers, engravers, book binders and related workers | 160.00 | 135.00 |
| Weavers | 166.25 | 79.50 |
| Cleaners, sweepers and watermen | 150.00 | 160.24 |
| Cooks and domestic servants | 125.00 | 40.00 |

Source: T.S. Papola, 'Informal sector in an urban economy: a study in Ahmedabad', mimeo., Giri Institute of Development Studies, Lucknow, 1978.

## Table 11.2: Average Monthly Earnings of Self-Employed Men and Women, Ahmedabad, India, 1976

| Activity | Average monthly earnings (Rs.) | |
| --- | --- | --- |
| | Male | Female |
| Hawking, peddling and street vending | 369.16 | 316.64 |
| Spinning, weaving, knitting, dyeing, etc. | 230.00 | 500.00 |
| Shoemaking and shoe repairing | 271.06 | 270.00 |
| Pottery and other clay formations | 482.50 | 300.00 |
| Laundering and washing of clothes | 350.00 | 383.33 |
| Basket-weaving | 350.00 | 370.00 |

Source: Papola, 'Informal sector in an urban economy'.

nature of the supply of and demand for labour. The labour market as a whole is found to discriminate against women in terms of job opportunities. The occupations and organizations in which women could find work are limited in comparison to openings for men. The relative lack of demand for female labour seems to be a result primarily of socio-historical factors, rather than of differences in the real economic value of the labour of men and women. In a situation of relative scarcity of job opportunities, tradition and social values stress the importance on men having employment rather than women. Further, the mobility of women workers in general is limited, which also restricts their job opportunities. Among the informal sector women workers in the Indian cities studied, only 27 per cent expressed willingness to move to other places for work, while among male workers it was as high as 80 per cent. In some cases, women are available for work only in their homes: either they undertake work they can do at home, or they do not engage in economic activity at all. In other words, the opportunity cost of their time is low, and employers take advantage of this situation to pay them incredibly low wages. In a town in Northern India, women artisans were found to be earning only Rs.1.00 per day (about 4 hours) for specialized embroidery work. They did not seem to object to the low wages, however, probably because the community to which they belong observes restrictions on women's movement outside the home, and no other work opportunities are available. In any case, even low wages would be some supplement to meagre household incomes.[6] The fact that, in many cases, women workers are considered to be secondary earners and are not regarded as the family's primary source of income seems to create an atmosphere in which they will settle for much lower wages than men. This phenomenon is a result of the same social attitudes towards the role of women that lead to discrimination against women in hiring.

## Conclusion: Questions for Further Study

The crucial task of labour market analysis consists in analyzing the nature of supply, demand, marketing and allocation of labour, and level of wages. Far too few studies focus on sex differentials in an effort to provide an explanatory framework for discrimination in the labour market.

The Indian data cited here would seem to indicate that the disadvantaged position of women in the labour market is a result of certain deep-rooted social and economic factors that restrict both the supply of and demand for women workers. A set of social, historical, biological and religious restraints have kept women out of the labour market; at the same time, such restraints have been used to justify discrimination against women in allocation of job opportunities and setting of wages.

Discrimination against women in the labour market is to a certain extent akin to a social system's discrimination against those not endowed with the ownership of means of production. But all sex discrimination is not class-based. Women of a class or socio-economic group are also discriminated against in favour of men of the same class. It is found that women working in low-status, low-paid jobs in the informal sector belong to families whose menfolk work in similar jobs, primarily because they are not endowed with material resources that provide access to the high-status, better-paid jobs. But it also seems to be true that a woman is more likely than a man to be able to find job opportunities only in the informal sector; and she will probably be paid less than he for the same work. The proponents of the class hypothesis would like to equate sex discrimination with the exploitation of the propertyless (the women) by the propertied (the men). This framework requires superimposition of sex differences on the differences between classes irrespective of sex. The validity of this approach will depend on the extent to which discrimination is found to be significant even after accounting for differences in the class background of women workers *vis-à-vis* that of the men workers. It is, therefore, important to investigate how much of the discrimination against women workers is due to the fact that they belong to certain socio-economic groups and how much is due to their being women.

On the other hand, there is the approach of the traditional economists which attempts to explain low demand as a function of low productivity and low supply as a function of low wages and high opportunity cost of working out of the home. But these explanations are not adequate, for it seems to be an overall lack of employment opportunities *combined* with social attitudes towards the role of women in productive work that has depressed both the demand for and supply of labour. In addition, the belief that their work and earnings are only of a supplementary nature has kept women's earnings low.

One theory holds that an expansion in job opportunities, in general, would lead to a larger demand for female labour, which would induce a larger supply and would also lead to greater integration of the labour markets for men and women. But even if this proposition holds – and it should be studied – women may continue to be the marginal workers and to be discriminated against in situations where job opportunities cannot be expanded rapidly enough to provide jobs to all men and women who want to work. And that is the situation in a large part of the underdeveloped world.

An analysis of labour market participation of women, then, must look at several sets of questions. One set relates to the low level of participation of women in economic activities: What are the real constraints on women's participation — social inhibitions and attitudes, or lack of work opportunities? The other set of questions has to do with the functioning of the labour market in relation to women workers: why is it that women are relegated to the peripheral jobs? How is it possible to have lower wages and more unfavourable conditions for women than for men even when they are in the same occupations? Does the degree of discrimination vary in different modes and organizations of production? Factors like education, training, socio-economic background, lack of organization or low opportunity cost may be the basis for sex discrimination in employment and earnings; if so, the issue goes beyond conditions in the labour market to conditions in society as a whole and the reasons why women are at a disadvantage in attaining the attributes essential to obtaining a better job and higher earnings.

A study of sex discrimination in the labour market would need to tackle the above issues at two broad levels: (i) analysis of factors that tend to restrict the supply of and demand for female labour; and (ii) analysis of the factors that lead to unfavourable treatment of women workers in the payment of wages and conditions of work. The two issues are interrelated, as has been argued earlier, but they may have to be separated for analytical convenience. The pattern of activities and occupations in which women generally work, as compared to the occupational distribution of men workers, is found to be one factor that gives rise to the differences in the levels of earnings between men and women. The probe can be extended in two directions from this premiss: (i) to the reasons for women's concentration in low-wage activities, in terms of their own and the employers' preferences; and (ii) to the issue of wage discrimination between sexes in the same job. Women may be employed in certain activities rather than others because their physical abilities, natural aptitude and innate skills suit some activities better, or at least they and the employers think so; or, because employers prefer women in these jobs because women workers make less fuss about being exploited. Women may also be more willing than men to accept low-paying jobs. In such a segmented labour market, the demand and supply conditions and degree of organization and protest in one segment of the labour market does not affect the other segment. It is important to probe the extent and manner in which the labour markets for men and women are compartmentalized.

'Pure' discrimination, in terms of unequal wage rates for men and women in the same jobs, can be practised only in an extremely fragmented labour market — one that is fragmented not only in terms of activities and production units but also in terms of individual workers: that is, where the employer deals with a worker individually and the worker has no information on the wages being paid to his colleagues. Often efficiency is put forward by employers as a basis of inequality of wages between men and women in the same job. Whether such a difference would prevail if payment were based on a piece rate rather than a time wage should be investigated. The finding outlined above about the earnings of independent women workers contradicts the efficiency hypothesis of wage inequality. Assuming that the employer would prefer to pay lower wages to any worker who is willing to accept them, the issue that needs to be investigated is what makes women workers accept a lower wage — lack of information or a belief that they are not as efficient as men, or that they ought to be paid less than men.

An analysis of the functioning of labour markets could identify the factors that tend to exert differential influence in the demand, supply and wages of the men and women workers. The scope of analysis could be widened to include not only the actual market conditions but also the socio-economic background of the workers. It would also be possible to examine the extent to which the employers' and the workers' beliefs regarding the differential suitability and capabilities of men and women are valid or are the result of the employers' prejudices about the women workers (or women workers' beliefs about themselves). An analysis based on labour market behaviour of demand, supply and wages, however, would be inadequate for analyzing the reasons why women are not given education and training, and why prejudices prevail regarding the role and capabilities of women; studies based on wider socio-historical analysis are required for this purpose.

## Notes

1. The evidence cited in this chapter is derived mainly from the author's unpublished studies of labour markets in Bombay and Ahmedabad. The studies were based on sample surveys of about 400 women workers — 200 in each centre. In this chapter, the two samples have been combined.

2. In India, 94% of women workers are in the unorganized sector (of which, of course, 80% are in agriculture). See ICSSR (1975). Of the total women workers in Ahmedabad, 72% were in the unorganized sector and only 28% in the organized sector, according to an estimate prepared by K.R. Picholiya of the Indian Institute of Management (IIM), Ahmedabad in connection with his study

of urban poverty in Ahmedabad.

3. Occupational and interemployer mobility so as to enable workers to move into better-paid and more stable jobs in the organized sectors is found to be more limited for women than for men of the same occupation and background: a study of scavenger women in Delhi revealed that while the men of their families have moved up to better jobs out of the traditional scavenging occupation, women have generally remained in scavenging. See Karlekar (1978).

4. That a working-class woman's economic independence or status in the family does not improve by virtue of employment is well brought out in Karlekar's study of Balmiki women in Delhi (1978).

5. In Delhi, one out of four scavengers were women, but only one out of thirty of those employed in trade and commerce and manufacturing. Karlekar (1978).

6. See Singh, Shrimali and Mathur (1976).

# References

Indian Council of Social Science Research (1975) *Status of women in India: a synopsis of the report of the national committee on status of women,* New Delhi

Karlekar, M. (1978) 'Balmiki women in the development process', paper presented at the International Congress of Anthropological and Ethnological Science, New Delhi, December

Singh, V.B., Shrimali, P.D. and R.S. Mathur (1976) *Survey of urban handicrafts in Uttar Pradesh* (chikan work at Lucknow), Giri Institute of Development Studies, Lucknow   .

# CONTRIBUTORS

*Richard Anker* International Labour Office, Geneva.

*Mayra Buvinic* Director, International Center for Research on Women, Washington, DC.

*Carmen Diana Deere* Economics Department, University of Massachusetts.

*T. Scarlett Epstein* School of African and Asian Studies, University of Sussex.

*Jane Humphries* Faculty of Economics and Politics, University of Cambridge.

*Elizabeth Jelin* Centro de Estudios de Estado y Sociedad (CEDES), Buenos Aires.

*Magdalena León de Leal* Colombian Association of Population Studies, Bogotá.

*Eva Mueller* Population Studies Center and Department of Economics, University of Michigan.

*Christine Oppong* International Labour Office, Geneva.

*T.S. Papola* Giri Institute of Development Studies, Lucknow, India.

*Constantina Safilios-Rothschild* Pennsylvania State University.

*T. Paul Schultz* Economics Department, Yale University.

*Nadia H. Youssef* Research Director, International Center for Research on Women, Washington, DC.

# INDEX

206-20; sex differentials 20-1, 41,
202, 206-30
Moses, Y.T. 122, 187
mothers-in-law 31, 34, 39, 162
Mueller, Eva 12, 19-20, 21, 23, 24,
55-86, 185, 281
Mukherjee, R. 140, 195

Nag, M. 174
Namboodiri, K. 175
Nash, J. 134
Nath, K. 160, 163
NCAER 220
Nelson, C. 125
Nepal 68, 69, 78
Nerlove, M. 177
New Guinea 165
Nigeria 163
Nsarkoh, J. 127

Oakley, A. 136, 246
Okonjo, K. 120, 121, 123, 125
Olsen, D.H. 117
Oppong, Christine 14, 16, 20, 22,
26, 121, 124, 126, 127, 133-50,
195, 281
Otterbein, C.S. 140; K.F. 140

Palmer, I. 255
Palmieri, H. 252
Papola, T.S. 17, 18, 25, 268-80, 281
Paraguay 249
Paxon, L.M. 142
Peru 13, 63, 69, 178, 251
Philippines 66, 177, 194 *see also*
Laguna
Phillips, C.E. 117
Piepmeier, K.P. 173, 193, 194
Pinchbeck, I. 95
Pinelli, A. 180, 181
Piore, M. 254
Poland 66, 67
polygamy 161, 162, 187, 188
power: female 13, 15, 19, 22, 25, 27,
117-32, 186-7, 193; from men
119-24, 126, 127
Preston, S.H. 207, 217
Price, J. 97
Puerto Rico 177, 178

Quizon, E.K. 73, 74, 80, 81

Rath, R. 177
Reich, M. 254

religion 46, 61, 68, 161; *see also*
Islam
reproduction 12, 13, 21, 61, 87,
92-4, 96, 97, 99-106, 117,
119-21, 126-7, 129, 138, 139,
146, 147, 156-7, 162, 240-4
*passim*
Requeña, M. 177
residence patterns 134, 135, 137-45
Ridker, R. 176
Robinson, J.P. 74, 77
Rosen, B.C. 194
Rosenzweig, M.R. 220
Ross, H.L. 256
Rowbotham, S. 97
rural: area 90, 97, 100, 174, 180,
182, 194-5, 225; women 18, 23,
24, 29, 34, 39-40, 103-10, 157-66,
173, 179, 182, 185-91, 222
Ryder, N. 260

Safa, H. 100
Safilios-Rothschild, Constantina 13,
19, 22, 25, 117-32, 181, 194, 281
Salaff, J. 195
Sanchez, C.E. 252
Sanday, P. 188
Sanjek, L. 141; R. 141
Sawhill, J. 256
Schmink, M. 253, 256, 257
Schultz, T. Paul 15-16, 21, 22, 177,
202-36, 281; T.W. 135, 136, 137,
216
Seccombe, W. 97, 240
self-employed 17, 274, 275
sex discrimination, segregation *see*
employment
sexuality 123, 124, 125, 139
Sheehan, G. 242
Shields, N. 18
siblings 18, 20, 31, 39, 72, 73, 76,
78, 80, 120, 135, 138, 139, 143,
144
Sierra Leone 140
Simmons, E.B. 124, 125, 194
Singer, P. 246, 251
Singh, K.M. 137
Smith, M.G. 139; M.L. 248
socialization 12, 14, 21, 134, 139,
142-5, 160-1, 164, 166, 167
Solien, N.L. 140
Soviet Union 30, 144, 180
Srinivas, M.N. 160
Stack, C.E. 139